MOMENTS OF UNCERTAINTY

in Therapeutic Practice

Robert Waska

MOMENTS OF UNCERTAINTY

in Therapeutic Practice

Interpreting Within the Matrix
of Projective Identification,
Countertransference, and Enactment

COLUMBIA UNIVERSITY PRESS   *NEW YORK*

COLUMBIA UNIVERSITY PRESS
Publishers Since 1893
New York   Chichester, West Sussex

Copyright © 2011 Columbia University Press
All rights reserved

Library of Congress Cataloging-in-Publication Data

Waska, Robert T.
Moments of uncertainty in therapeutic practice : interpreting within the matrix
of projective identification, countertransference, and enactment / Robert Waska.
p. ; cm.
Includes bibliographical references and index.
ISBN 978-0-231-15152-8 (cloth : alk. paper)—ISBN 978-0-231-15153-5
(pbk. : alk. paper)—ISBN 978-0-231-52523-7 (e-book)
1. Countertransference (Psychology)   2. Acting out (Psychology)
3. Projection (Psychology)   4. Psychoanalysis.   I. Title.
[DNLM: 1. Countertransference (Psychology)—Case Reports.
2. Acting Out—Case Reports.   3. Projection—Case Reports.
4. Psychoanalytic Therapy—method—Case Reports.   WM 62]
RC489.C68W37   2011
616.89'14—dc23   2011011805

Columbia University Press books are printed on permanent and
durable acid-free paper.

This book is printed on paper with recycled content.
Printed in the United States of America

c 10 9 8 7 6 5 4 3 2 1
p 10 9 8 7 6 5 4 3 2 1

References to Internet Web sites (URLs) were accurate at the time of writing.
Neither the author nor Columbia University Press is responsible for
URLs that may have expired or changed since the manuscript was prepared.

CONTENTS

PREFACE

THIS BOOK INVITES the reader to accompany a Kleinian psychoanalyst as he shares the intimate, day-to-day, moment-to-moment clinical experience that unfolds when treating a wide variety of patients in private practice. The author creates a genuine, user-friendly, experience-near atmosphere in which the reader has the chance to see how a modern psychoanalytic practitioner actually conducts Kleinian treatment. The nuts-and-bolts approach of the "he said/she said" dialogue opens a wide window into the actual clinical exchange.

The general public—not to mention students currently studying in the field of psychology—can sometimes have the false impression that Freud is "old hat," ancient, outdated, or even silly and useless. However, when helping patients maneuver through their complex and painful problems, many of Freud's discoveries and basic theoretical tenets remain powerful.

Likewise, Melanie Klein's original thinking in her work with children and adults is sometimes seen as outdated or out of pace with the modern therapeutic climate. Again, when working intensely with neurotic, borderline, narcissistic, and psychotic patients, Klein's highly original elaboration of Freud's work still proves vital in the analytic setting. This volume provides a wealth of clinical material to illustrate this point.

Some of the most popular or prevalent perspectives in psychoanalysis today owe a great deal to Klein's discoveries, have compatible aspects of theory and technique, or dovetail in important clinical constructs. The American relational school has embraced such Kleinian concepts as projective identification and, in its own way of conceptualizing and utilizing this idea, has come to make regular clinical use of it. While operating from viewpoints sometimes quite in opposition to the Kleinian approach, relational analysts such as Seligmann, Cooper, Altman, and Aron nevertheless include the Kleinian cornerstone of projective identification in their theoretical and technical methods.

Mitchell (1995) has written extensively about the common ground and contemporary importance of both the interpersonal/relational schools and the Kleinian tradition. He notes that while emerging from quite different starting points, they arrive at perspectives on the concept of analytic interaction that complement each other. He outlines how Klein took Freud's ideas of the life and death instincts seriously, seeing the infant as struggling with biologically rooted, instinctually driven unconscious forces. However, Klein's followers, especially in the last few decades, have emphasized the value of the environment alongside that of the biological, unconscious aspects of the patient's psychology.

Here, Kleinian theory and technique also dovetail with the current interest in attachment theory. Fonagy and Target both espouse a more attachment-based version of Klein's discoveries. Modern Kleinian thinkers value the significance of the internal phantasy interaction between self and object as well as the external environmental interaction between infant and caretaker. This is echoed in the sharp focus that Kleinians place on the interpersonal interaction between analyst and patient.

Melanie Klein focused on both the environment and on the internal landscape of the self and object, but she emphasized the importance of relationships in the mind of the infant and the patient. Fairbairn, Winnicott, and others put the emphasis on actual external interactions with real people in real time, while the Kleinian school considers the unconscious relationship between self and object—as colored by the paranoid-schizoid position and the depressive position—to be the bulk of the individual's subjective experience in life. In looking at these unconscious processes, Klein discovered the dynamics of projective identification, in which aspects of the self are communicated or expelled into the object for a variety of motives. One mind puts its contents into the mind of another, in the form of a profoundly intense, intimate interaction. For Melanie Klein, this was purely an unconscious phantasy process.

However, my own contemporary Kleinian approach as well as the more modern stance currently held by most Kleinian analysts has been to expand this internal view of projective identification to the more inclusive view of its being both an intrapsychic and an interpersonal, interactional process. This interpersonal expansion of Klein's landmark discoveries began with the work of Bion, evolved from there to my own work, and is now foremost in the current views of Betty Joseph. This more inside/outside, unconscious/interaction view of projective identification has spread from its birth in the Kleinian tradition to become one of the main aspects of many relational, interpersonal, and even modern Freudian approaches.

In fact, Klein's powerful concept of projective identification is now being integrated into most of contemporary psychoanalytic culture. At a 2009 scientific meeting at a psychoanalytic institute, a paper entitled "A Neuropsychoanalytic Perspective on Unconscious Communication" was delivered. This presentation included a discussion of how projective identification, from a more Kleinian perspective, is part of an intricate mix of factors colored by elements of neuroscience and attachment theory. Interestingly, a major proponent of the relational school spoke of the "sensational contribution" of the paper—as well as its substantial difference from his own point of view. Betty Joseph's modern Kleinian work was brought up in the audience discussion as pivotal for the argument. The close connection between projective identification and the mirror-neuron system was noted as well.

Enid Young is one of several contemporary Kleinians writing about and lecturing on the elements in neuroscience and brain function that complement original and current Kleinian theory. Studies in infant development are also beginning to confirm Melanie Klein's own work with infants and young children. Klein's ideas about the infant's capacity for strong object-relational connections at an early age have now been proven by observational studies and developmental research.

Other aspects of Kleinian theory and technique that stand the test of time and now fortify many other contemporary psychoanalytic schools are the concepts of countertransference, enactment, and interpretation.

Joseph (1989) is among many of the contemporary Kleinians (Schafer 1997) to have shown the value of the countertransference as a specialized tool in locating and understanding the nature of the patient's anxiety and the immediate transference situation. In addition, much of the current thinking regarding enactments in the relational, interpersonal, self psychology, and modern Freudian schools is an outgrowth of the pioneering work of the contemporary Kleinian school.

My own work is grounded in the classic Kleinian school but is certainly deeply influenced by the contemporary movement of such modern Kleinian thinkers as Betty Joseph, John Steiner, Hanna Segal, Ron Britton, Elizabeth Spillius, and others. I place pivotal clinical importance in the ongoing interplay between transference, countertransference, projective identification, and the interpretive process. The foundation of Melanie Klein's work and that of her followers is the view that the moment-to-moment, here-and-now interpretation of both positive and negative transference and the unconscious phantasy state are essential to the steady work of building and maintaining a psychoanalytic process. In turn, this process gradually assists the patient to work through his or her core conflicts, resulting in a more stable emotional foundation and a higher degree of psychological integration. This Kleinian emphasis on the importance and value of the consistent interpretation of the transference in the context of the object-relational realm has been proven clinically effective by current research. Probably the most robust of this emerging research are the recent AMA findings. In a 2008 *JAMA* article (Leichsenring and Rabung 2008), the researchers demonstrated the successful outcome of psychodynamic therapy lasting longer than a year, noting it to be superior to other forms of therapy and clinically more effective than treatments of shorter duration. The researchers defined this mode of therapy to be as the same as Gunderson and Babbards's (1999) findings of "a therapy that involves careful attention to the therapist-patient interaction, with thoughtfully timed interpretations of transference and resistance embedded in a sophisticated appreciation of the therapist's contribution to the two-person field." This definition certainly describes the essence of all Kleinian treatments as well as my own Kleinian approach to what I have termed "analytic contact."

In psychoanalytic treatment, we strive to identify, understand, and work with the core unconscious phantasies that shape, distort, or constrict patients' experience of themselves, others, and their day-to-day existence. We seek to analyze the phantasies that create imbalance or anxiety in the patient's internal and external world. In order to do this work, we strive to create the best conditions to learn about and then transform these psychological conflicts. When successful, this clinical situation is best described as the establishment of analytic contact (Waska 2007).

This is a therapeutic process that holds transference as the primary vehicle of change, but it also considers the elements of containment, projective identification, countertransference, and interpretation to be critical to therapeutic success. Dreamwork, genetic reconstruction, analysis of conflict and defense, and extratransference work are all seen as valuable and essential. The concept of analytic contact is tied not so much to external factors, such as the use of a couch or the frequency of visits, as it is to building a clinical forum for the understanding and modification of the patient's deepest phantasies. Analytic contact is about finding a foothold into transference and into the core phantasy states that have the greatest effect on the patient's feelings, thoughts, and actions.

In working to establish analytic contact, I employ a combination of classical and contemporary Kleinian approaches to reach the patient at his current internal experience of self and object. Again, this involves the consistent exploration and interpretation of all conflictual self↔object relational states and the struggle between love and hate within them. Countertransference is vital to untangling the jumbled threads of transference and to understanding the nature of the projective-identification communications or attacks that are so frequent in most treatments.

Just as Joseph (1985) spoke of the total transference situation, I think we also need to be clinically aware of the complete countertransference situation. By this, I mean an awareness of not just the basic "I feel x, so patient must be projecting that feeling into me" method of understanding countertransference. Instead, we must be alert to the overall atmosphere of mood, action, thought, sensation, urge, and emotional climate that exists within the treatment setting. The complete countertransference situation is elusive and fleeting in most treatments and is not something easily formulated. But if the analyst is paying equal attention to the countertransference and transference and the dynamics of projective

identification, analytic contact is possible. With this therapeutic contact, a clinical process in which the patient's core phantasies will be revealed, understood, interpreted, and worked through is possible.

When attempting to establish analytic contact, I am, of course, still
examining and addressing the patient's current external problems and
symptoms, but within a wider, deeper, and more comprehensive context. In this sense, I offer the patient two ways of achieving growth,
change, and conflict resolution. The patient may accept, because of his
or her transference, phantasy, and defense response, only the external
problem-solving potential of psychoanalytic treatment. We would still
have had the opportunity for more, but the patient may resist accepting
or creating more. If nothing else, the attempt to establish analytic contact may give the patient a lingering taste of what he or she might want
to try later on in his or her life. Sometimes, I think that because of trans-
ference↔countertransference issues many analysts give up too soon on
offering, establishing, and maintaining an atmosphere of analytic contact with patients. The recommendation of supportive counseling over
psychoanalytic work is therefore often a collusion with unexplored
transference climates in which analytic contact is avoided, attacked,
and devalued by both parties.

In the moment-to-moment transference, the patient either is actively
engaged or actively disengaged with the psychoanalyst on many levels.
This aliveness or deadness of the total transference situation (Joseph
1985) and the interpretation or noninterpretation of it is what can define
a treatment as either analytic or nonanalytic. The interpretation of the
current state of the transference and the patient's phantasy experience
of the object world (rather than interpretation of the past or external
matters) is critical in general (Joseph 1989) but even more so when the
patient's phantasies, transference stance, and defenses have begun to
shift the treatment into something less than analytic. Certainly, the analyst's own countertransference enactment of projective-identification
dynamics or personal conflict can escalate this problem. Overall, the
resulting loss of analytic contact often occurs within the more interpersonal realm of the analytic relationship. Feldman (1997) has stressed
the idea of how a patient's projective-identification process can organize or disorganize the analyst by pushing him into a pathological reenactment of certain object-relational patterns. I would add that these

projective-identification attacks include attempts to disable, distort, or destroy the analytic contact between patient and analyst, shifting the treatment into more of a supportive counseling situation. This often has multiple motives, including control of the object, hiding out in the non-exploratory pseudoparenting mode of supportive friendship, manipulation of who in phantasy is the authority or parent and who is the child, and, finally, the wish to merely evacuate conflict rather than own and process it. Mourning is avoided and growth or change is aborted. The psychoanalyst must contain, translate, and interpret these psychological maneuvers in order to restore the analytic contact. Otherwise, pathological, collusive enactments will create a perversion of healing rather than a genuine opportunity for psychic change.

Melanie Klein's pioneering work with children and adults expanded Freud's clinical work and is now the leading worldwide influence in current psychoanalytic practice. The key Kleinian concepts include the total transference, projective identification, the importance of countertransference, psychic retreats, the container/contained function, enactment, splitting, the paranoid-schizoid and depressive positions, unconscious phantasy, and the value of interpreting both anxiety and defense. The components of the Kleinian approach have become so commonplace in the literature and adopted by so many other schools of practice that it is easy to forget that object-relations theory and technique was Melanie Klein's discovery.

In broadening Klein's work to match today's clinical climate, my approach of analytic contact makes use of Kleinian technique in all aspects of clinical practice, with all patients, in all settings. In this contemporary therapeutic modality, the analyst is always attempting to engage the patient in an exploration of his or her unconscious phantasies, transference patterns, defenses, and internal experience of the world. Regardless of frequency, the use of the couch, length of treatment, and style of termination, the goal of psychoanalytic treatment is always the same: the understanding of unconscious phantasy, the resolution of intrapsychic conflict, and the integration of self↔object relations, both internally and externally. Psychoanalysts use interpretation as their principal tool, and transference, countertransference, and projective identification are the three clinical guideposts for those interpretive efforts. Viewed from the Kleinian perspective, most patients use projective identification as a psychic cornerstone for defense, communication, attachment, learning, loving, and aggression. Therefore, projective identification constantly shapes and colors both the transference and countertransference.

By attending to the interpersonal, transactional, and intrapsychic levels of transference and phantasy with consistent here-and-now and in-the-moment interpretation, the Kleinian method can be therapeutically successful with neurotic, borderline, narcissistic, or psychotic patients, whether seen as individuals, couples, or families and at varied frequencies and duration.

The Kleinian method of analytic contact strives to illuminate the patient's unconscious object-relational world, gradually providing the patient with a way to understand, express, translate, and master his or her previously unbearable thoughts and feelings. We make analytic contact with patients' deepest experiences so they can make personal and lasting contact with their full potential.

Successful analytic contact involves not only psychic change but also a corresponding sense of loss and mourning. At every moment, analytic contact is an experience of hope and transformation as well as dread and despair, as the patient struggles with change and a new way of being with him- or herself and others. Successful analytic work always involves a cycle of fearful risk taking, hasty retreats, retaliatory attacks, anxious detours, and attempts to shift the treatment into something less than analytic, something less painful. The analyst interprets these reactions to the precarious journey of growth as a way of steering the treatment back to something more analytic, something that contains more meaningful contact with self and other. The support that we give our patients includes the implicit vow that we will help them survive this painful contact and walk with them into the unknown.

ACKNOWLEDGMENTS

THIS BOOK IS about my work with a wide variety of patients, in various states of distress and growth, and about my own struggles in finding the best way to assist them interpretively. The practice of psychoanalysis is about this delicate and complex journey, a therapeutic focus specific to each case. Once truly engaged with a patient and earnestly exploring his or her private internal world, it is easy for any analyst to see why Sigmund Freud, Melanie Klein, and many others viewed psychoanalysis as first and foremost a clinical venture. Psychoanalytic theory provides the base for understanding the human condition, but it is the moment-to-moment work with patients that brings the theory to life. In this regard, I wish to thank my patients for helping me see the true clinical value of psychoanalysis and its place in the healing arts.

Theoretical, political, academic, and organizational debates are sometimes necessary or helpful. However, I believe psychoanalysis should always be defined by what goes on in the therapeutic setting. I am grateful to have had the chance to establish a meaningful therapeutic process—an analytic contact—with individuals, couples, and families who are working to better their lives. It is a privilege to be a part of their desire for change and evolution. All case material has been disguised, altered, or censored in a manner that maintains confidentiality.

My wife, Elizabeth, continues to help me in innumerable ways, providing the support, encouragement, and gentle criticism that bring focus to my writing.

I am grateful to the various journals that allowed me to reproduce previously published material. I acknowledge the *Scandinavian Psychoanalytic Review* for allowing material used in chapter 1 (Waska 2009b), *The Bulletin of the Menninger Clinic* for material used in chapter 2 (Waska 2009d), the *International Forum of Psychoanalysis* for material used in chapter 3 (Waska 2009c), *Issues in Psychoanalytic Psychology* for material used in chapters 6 and 8 (Waska 2005b, 2009e), and *Psychoanalytic Social Work* for material used in chapter 7 (Waska 2009).

MOMENTS OF UNCERTAINTY

in Therapeutic Practice

INTRODUCTION

EACH CHAPTER IN this book follows a wide spectrum of cases and clinical situations where patients are provided the best opportunity for health and healing through the establishment of analytic contact. Interpretation is the primary tool that clinicians use to make meaningful contact with the phantasy states and dynamic conflicts each patient suffers with. However, during the course of any treatment, what we say, do, think, and feel can become taxed, distorted, or contaminated by the influences of the patient's projections and the analyst's resulting countertransference struggles. This can lead to various forms of enactment, most often in the form of interpretive acting out.

The case material in each of the following chapters closely tracks how a patient's phantasies and transference mechanisms work to increase, oppose, embrace, or neutralize analytic contact and, in the process, create difficulties in the interpretive process.

Section 1 examines how the analyst is drawn inevitably into playing out various aspects of the patient's phantasies. Chapter 1 considers how during the course of an analytic treatment patients will project unwanted, unfinished, and unspoken aspects of their internal self↔object world. The analyst has to find a helpful way to understand, transform, and communicate those expelled, orphaned, and unbearable phantasies without the patient feeling assaulted, accused, seduced, or persecuted.

However, even when we do our best at interpreting these inner conflicts, the patient may experience the internalization, ownership, and acceptance of our interpretive message as us forcing them to give up a secret, lifelong hope for a particular connection with their object. For them, change can signal grief, loss, and mourning.

As a result, the patient will resist, hide, or fight our efforts to assist them. This combative communication often occurs through the dynamics of projective identification. Projective mechanisms frequently aim at enlisting the analyst to be a part of some repetitious object-relational cycle that serves to gratify, punish, protect, empower, or enrich the patient as a part of their unconscious phantasies.

Caught up in these projective-identification patterns, the analyst may end up interpretively enacting some of these phantasies by becoming the object rather than translating its presence in the transference, by overemphasizing one side of the patient's conflict over another, or by interpreting accurately but prematurely. We can become seductive, persecutory, guilt inducing, or withdrawing by noting one aspect of the patient's internal issues in our interpretations but not another. When interpretively acting out, the analyst may end up participating actively or passively within these pathological cycles. All these types of acting out are inevitable and must be constantly monitored and worked through with the aid of the countertransference. Extensive case material is utilized to further define these moments of interpretive imbalance or enactment.

Chapter 2 looks at the many factors that need consideration when pursuing a line of psychoanalytic interpretation. Interpretation is always a provisional exercise, in which we propose something to the patient to consider and then wait to see his or her reaction. Whether or not our interpretation is correct is not as important as the patient's reaction to it. Does it cultivate insight, does it spur defensive reactions, does it feel helpful, does it leave the patient hurt or misunderstood, or does it aid the patient in facing their anxieties and exploring them in a way that might facilitate change? These are just some of the possibilities when we voice our opinion about what might be happening at an unconscious level in the patient's immediate experience. Interpretations may be correct and address the patient's phantasies and transference state, but they can also, at the same time, be part of a pathological projective-identification system. In other words, the interpretation itself can be a collusive acting out that both helps the patient to grow but also serves their defensive structure—thus helping them to retreat at the same time.

This chapter uses case examples to explore clinical moments in which interpretive enactment or interpretive acting out occur. The constantly shifting emotional states produced by transference, countertransference, and the dynamics of projective identification make the interpretive process prone to instability, fallibility, and uncertainty. The unavoidable pros and cons of interpretive acting out are examined with material from several psychoanalytic treatments.

Chapter 3 uses one extensive case presentation to examine the clinical difficulty of making accurate and helpful interpretations that do not become part of the patient's defensive system. This chapter focuses on how interpretive acting out is inevitable in the psychoanalytic process. However, if properly monitored, understood, and contained, these interpretive enactments can sometimes actually benefit the overall treatment. Issues of projective identification, countertransference, and the importance of realizing our transference role in the patient's changing phantasies are discussed throughout the case material.

A patient's reliance on projective identification is a significant complication in establishing analytic contact. In fact, projective identification is often the primary defense in patients who have an intense reaction to the establishment of analytic contact. In addition, projective identification is common in most treatment situations and often snares the analyst into partaking in the patient's phantasy states. Chapter 4 starts with the theoretical assumption and clinical observation that projective identification is a natural, constant element in human psychology. Then, clinical material is used to illustrate how projective identification–centered transference states create situations where the acting out of the patient's phantasies and conflicts by both parties is common and unavoidable. Some forms of projective identification encountered in clinical practice are easier for the analyst to notice and interpret, because they are more obvious. Other forms are more subtle and difficult to interpret. Finally, some forms, whether subtle or obvious, seem to create a stronger pull on the analyst to act out blindly. If analytic contact is experienced by the patient as dangerous or harmful to himself or to the analyst, the projective-identification reaction can be severe.

In these circumstances, some patients attempt to discharge permanently their projective anxiety, phantasy, or conflict into the analyst,
with a marked resistance to reown, examine, or recognize this projection. Some of these patients are narcissistic in functioning, others are
borderline, and many attempt to find refuge behind a psychic barri-
cade or retreat (Steiner 1993). In other forms of projective identification, the patient enlists the analyst to master their internal struggles
for him or her. This occurs through the combination of interpersonal
and intrapsychic object-relational dynamics. This "do my dirty work
for me" approach within the transference can evoke various degrees of
countertransference enactments and transference/countertransference
acting out.

Yet another level of projective identification involves patients who
want to expand their way of relating internally but who are convinced
that they need the analyst to validate or coach them along. They are
willing to participate in analytic contact but become anxious or uncertain, so they stimulate transference/countertransference tests and conduct "practice runs" of new object-relational phantasies within the therapeutic relationship. The patient may gently but repeatedly engage the
analyst in a test, to see if it is ok to change his or her core view of reality
while continuing to engage in analytic contact. Depending on how the
analyst reacts or interprets, the patient may feel encouraged or discour-
aged to continue in his or her new method of relating to self and object.
Of course, the patient's view of the analyst's reactions is distorted by
transference phantasies, so the analyst must be careful to investigate
the patient's reasoning and feelings about the so-called encouragement
or discouragement of the analyst. This does not negate the possible
countertransference acting out by the analyst, in which he may indeed
be seduced into becoming a discouraging or encouraging parental figure
who actually voices suggestion and judgment.

All these levels of projective identification surface with patients
across the diagnostic spectrum, whether in higher-functioning depres-
sives or in more disturbed paranoid-schizoid cases. However, the emergence of analytic contact seems to bring out a greater reliance on this
mental mechanism. Whether immediately obvious or more submerged
in the therapeutic relationship, the analyst almost always takes part in
some degree of acting out. Therefore, the analyst's countertransference

is critical to monitor and utilize as a map toward understanding the patient's phantasies and conflicts that push him or her to engage in a particular form of projective identification.

Chapter 4 continues the theme of the previous chapters by examining the variety of interactions and enactments that take place in psychoanalytic treatment, often stemming from the patient's reaction to analytic contact. During the course of every psychoanalytic treatment, there are moments within the transference↔countertransference relationship in which the analyst becomes overly involved in the landscape of the patient's phantasies. This leads to the analyst acting out certain aspects of those phantasies, sometimes in isolation but usually in tandem with the patient's acting out of corresponding aspects of his or her phantasies. This situation is all the more predictable when projective identification is the primary dynamic shaping the transference. Case material is used to illustrate the inevitable pull of the patient on the analyst, creating a psychological invitation to play out pieces of the patient's internal life. There seems to be certain places within an analytic treatment in which it is either easier or harder for the analyst to regain therapeutic balance and begin interpreting the unfolding process rather than living it out in repetition with the patient.

These projective-identification systems are internal situations that encompass the patient's many and varied phantasy conflicts. These include unconscious desires to learn, be taught, or to not know. Other common elements include conflicting needs for control or autonomy, connection or independence, and power or loyalty, all of which shape the transference and trigger different degrees of acting out. Following the main branch of Kleinian thinking on the subject, this chapter illustrates how projective identification always includes an external object, but the object is not always conscious of being affected by the patient's interpersonal manifestation of their intrapsychic struggles. Therefore, the analyst constantly struggles to find a therapeutic foothold within these omnipresent wishes, fears, guilt, and hostility. The presence of these transference↔countertransference struggles often means that analytic contact has been established but is in a delicate state of balance. If these enactments and projective-identification cycles are not interpreted and worked through, there is a danger that the analytic contact may deteriorate.

The shifts and growth of patients' internal world is usually reflected in how they utilize projective identification and how their projective mechanisms shape, restrict, or enrich the transference process and their ability to take in new knowledge about self and object. Projective identification is often the primary vehicle in which persecutory and primitive depressive phantasies play out in the interpersonal and intrapsychic realm of the transference. With the more regressed and defensive patient, there can be chaotic and confusing moments in which acting out by both patient and analyst is common. The analyst can easily stumble within the countertransference, falling into a mutual object-relational enactment. More than any other time, the tool of analytic interpretation is most crucial with these difficult patients. Interpretation of projective identification, the defensive manifestations of the death instinct, and the fears and anxieties concerning analytic contact are all needed in the resolution of core transference conflicts. With these hard-to-reach cases, the analyst must try to work on his or her feet and consistently interpret the in-the-moment relational situation regarding analytic contact, since the flow of interaction tends to be rapid and unpredictable.

In Section 2, chapters 5 and 6 use extensive case material to illustrate several points. Chapter 5 gives the reader a close view of how Kleinian couples' treatment unfolds and the specific theoretical and clinical nuances that emerge. In addition, this chapter is an illustration of how we are practicing an imperfect art that often produces a mixed bag of therapeutic results. Sometimes we can really help a patient or a couple to find a greater degree of psychological integration and personal clarity. Other times, both progress and failure results from the therapeutic endeavor. Finally, some treatments simply never get off the ground because the patient, analyst, or the combined forces of both are acting against change.

Chapter 6 highlights this difficulty of private practice and demonstrates the real-world, on-the-ground truth of psychoanalytic work with hard-to-reach patients. The confusing and trying climate of countertransference and projective-identification dilemmas bring the analyst face to face with the frequent dead ends and escalating acting out that so commonly occurs with the more disturbed patient in most practice settings. Again, this chapter shows the reader a situation with more troubled patients, in which the treatment quickly stalls, becomes a stage for various enactments between patient and analyst, or simply ends in a quick and messy fashion. While not ideal by any means, it is important to realize the very fragile and humbling nature of our capacities as analysts and the precarious ability we have to establish analytic contact with the more disturbed and conflicted patient. These types of cases make it that much more vital that we are always examining our countertransference and trying to regain our balance as soon as possible when we realize we are in some type of enactment or interpretive acting out. As pointed out throughout this book, the vehicle of projective identification is often the culprit, and therefore the better understanding the analyst has of how, why, when, and where this psychological dynamic is occurring in the treatment process, the better chance he or she has of rebalancing a wayward clinical moment.

In Section 3, the focus shifts to patients who are constantly trying to manage and control their objects. In working psychoanalytically, it is common to encounter patients who need to control their immediate objects for a variety of internal fears and desires. This is evident in their stories about external life at home, at work, and with friends as well as in how it emerges within the transference. However, when this level of control becomes too intense, it confines the patient's life to a chronic struggle to master depressive and persecutory anxieties. This intense defensive, reparative, and aggressive effort can create a multitude of countertransference difficulties and episodes of acting out by the analyst.

In chapters 7 through 10, case material is used to examine this phenomenon of control as it occurs in psychic retreats, paranoid phantasies, and within depressive anxieties. While there are major differences between these three clinical categories, certain commonalities regarding gaining control over the object will be highlighted. These include the desire for idealized objects, the drive to resurrect fallen objects, and the need to avoid cruel and attacking objects that have taken over and replaced the sought-out ideal.

Throughout section 3, clinical material is used to explore patients who seem to live in an emotional foxhole, where they try desperately to avoid the full wrath of both their paranoid and depressive anxieties. Unlike a pathological organization, in which they might feel like they have successfully thwarted the hateful or harmed object, these patients live within a fragile psychic retreat. While constantly trying to control the object to restore it or avoid its revenge, they experience life as a place where they are never quite able to find respite from or establish contact with the object. Their emotional lives are reminiscent of a desperate infantryman trapped in a foxhole in the middle of a battlefield. To emerge seems like assured death, but to remain means to live in the crosshairs of the enemy. Again, the analyst may become partially paralyzed or go temporarily off course during the more intense moments of establishing analytic contact with these patients. Countertransference balance must be regained, and the dual nature of the patient's unconscious plight must be consistently interpreted to best assist him or her in bringing hope and possibility to this otherwise bleak set of fantasies.

SECTION 1

Interpretive Acting Out

1
—

CONTAINING, TRANSLATING, AND INTERPRETIVE ACTING OUT

The Quest for Therapeutic Balance

WHEN DEALING WITH the task of correctly interpreting the patient's anxiety and core phantasy at the point of greatest urgency, the analyst is often on slippery ground. Despite our best efforts, when interpreting, we are often both colluding with certain defensive or projective mechanisms *and* helping the patient toward internal growth, integration, and change. Rather than it being a dichotomy—either making correct, timely, and purely therapeutic interpretations or falling into pathological enactments and countertransference boundary violations—the actual clinical reality of interpretive work is more messy and layered.

This chapter uses extensive material from several psychoanalytic cases to illustrate the often flawed nature of our interpretive efforts. When we attempt to filter, contain, translate, and interpret a patient's phantasies and feelings, we will always leave something out or overemphasize one aspect over another. Any given interpretation is hopefully more right than wrong, more on target than not, embracing most of the patient's phantasy conflict that is active at that given moment. However, it is inevitable that we miss certain aspects, act out others, and prioritize one over another. This clinical climate is made all the more uncertain when the dynamics of projective identification are used in intensive ways by the patient to ward off, hide, or play out certain phantasies that in turn create overwhelming anxieties for the patient and sometimes for

the analyst. Under the constant influence of splitting and projective defenses, the analyst is prone to fall into certain moments of interpretive
imbalance or deviation. Acting out can make its presence known in the
types of interpretations made or the general pattern or approach that
emerges when interpreting (Steiner 2006).

Clinically, we are constantly deciding what side of the coin to move
toward at a given moment, what aspect of the patient's conflict or projection to grapple with, and what chapter of their transference struggle
to untangle. The patient's most immediate state of anxiety certainly provides a useful map, just as our countertransference does. But, in many
clinical situations, the moment of urgency is not singular. We may think
it is, but other equal or more urgent aspects of the patient's struggle
may be hidden, expelled, or isolated through projective-identification
mechanisms. Even though it may seem that we are focused accurately
on what is really causing the patient distress in the moment, we will always be slightly ahead, behind, or out of touch with other aspects of his
or her current internal battle. Moment-to-moment clinical psychoanalysis is always a game of catch-up, revisiting, reassessing, and regrouping.
Our job is to be the emotional translator, but, like when dealing with a
complex foreign text, there is never just one interpretation, never just
one translation that encompasses all of the threads of the inner drama
unfolding before us.

Sandler (1976, 46) mirrored many contemporary Kleinians in his
ideas about projection, countertransference, and acting out. He took up
the value of understanding the nature of the patient's unconscious in-
tent when he or she tries to shape us into various objects from his or her
phantasy world. He notes,

> In the transference, in many subtle ways, the patient attempts
> to prod the analyst into behaving in a particular way and un-
> consciously scans and adapts to his perception of the analyst's
> reaction. The analyst may be able to "hold" his response to this
> "prodding" in his consciousness as a reaction of his own which
> he perceives, and I would make the link between certain counter-
> transference responses and transference via the behavioral (verbal
> and non-verbal) interaction between the patient and the analyst.
> Paula Heimann went as far as to point out that the analyst's re-

sponse to the patient can be used as a basis for understanding the patient's material, often by something which he catches and holds in himself. I should like to try to take this a little further.

This chapter uses extensive case material to show how the patient can coerce the analyst to act out, via interpretation, various roles in the patient's unconscious phantasy life. This interpretive acting out may be subtle and passive or more aggressive and active. If not monitored, contained, and understood, it can be destructive to the therapeutic situation. However, if properly handled, it can shed important light on otherwise hidden aspects of the patient's internal struggles and conflicts that, up to that moment, could only arise through a projective-identification process. While these moments of interpretive acting out can coincide with uncorrupted interpretive work, the overall analytic contact (Waska 2007) can suffer. While such acting out is probably unavoidable, the quicker the analyst can notice, contain, and understand such deviations, the better the chance that analytic contact can be reestablished and maintained.

CASE MATERIAL

Sarah and her two sisters were raised by very strict and critical parents. Sarah's father was particularly demanding: he constantly told Sarah what she should be doing with her life and noted how she was failing him. She loved her father and felt they had some degree of resolution in their relationship before he died five years ago, but she still views her parents as "never really understanding her and quick to find fault. It was hard for them to ever imagine what I might be going through, whether it is positive or negative."

During her career as a hospital manager, Sarah was frequently told she was too slow and disorganized. Part of this was the result of her emotional struggle with authority, in particular with men, and her feeling the need to take on everything so she could please the authority she also resented. But taking everything on meant that she was always overwhelmed, and she did a sloppy job as a result, displeasing her supervisors. At the same time, she always felt very fatigued. During a routine physical examination, her doctor discovered she had a disease that would only get worse over time. She went on disability about the same time she began her psychoanalysis.

Now in her fourth year of analytic treatment, Sarah is doing much better in many ways. She is not as severely depressed or anxious, and she has reduced her self-sabotaging patterns. Her difficulty relating to men remains. She has not had a boyfriend or had sex for almost ten years.

One theme within Sarah's transference was prominent from the beginning and remains a central thread. Sarah sees me as an intimidating male authority from whom she wants to receive fatherly guidance, but she imagines that this will always be given alongside of judgment, sternness, and anger. She relates to me in a way that pulls me into that role. I will make various interpretations that are fairly on the mark, regarding a wide variety of topics. Soon thereafter, she will start to tell me about something she did that makes her seem naïve, lazy, or forgetful. I will ask for details. Sarah will offer clarification that reinforces this impression of her as clueless, stupid, or immature. At that point, I will sometimes end up making a comment about how it seems obvious that she should have done it this way or that way instead of how she did it.

Sarah will respond by telling me that she didn't think of it or that she forgot. This makes me feel hopeless about her intelligence and frustrated about her motivations. Indeed, sometimes she tells me she "just didn't feel like it" or "I don't care if it was my fault. I guess I'm just lazy." Depending on how she says it, I might feel empathetic, want to hear more about it, and help her find the solution to whatever the problem was. Or I might feel like she is being a lazy little brat and want to lecture her on the correct way of proceeding. I am caught up in either being an attentive, gentle, guiding father or an irritated, lecturing one.

When we both began to understand better this complicated climate of acting out by discussing our mutual ways of relating in that moment, certain things came to light. It often turns out that she in fact knew exactly what to do in the situation she was describing or that she had *already* taken care of whatever it was—but had failed to include that detail in her story. We can then see how she successfully provoked or invited me to be like a nice teacher who is ready to help but is also easily turned into a scolding, impatient teacher. We have explored how this pattern is a repetition of her childhood experience and memory of her father, combined with her wish for a different experience or memory. In analyzing this, we have come to see that it is now she who can be judgmental, impatient, and disappointed with either herself or others and that in the transference she puts me in that role as well. At the same time, she wants to be with a new, more loving man, but she feels that she must be a helpless, naïve little girl to do so, which then shifts the object back to being a critical and scolding father, leaving her feeling like a disappointing daughter.

Over time, by consistently examining and monitoring my counter-transference and my occasional lapses into interpretive acting out, I have been better able to reduce my enactments. And, as we work to learn, understand, and change her father↔child phantasies, there is much less provocative and teasing transference from her to draw me in. In fact, she now exhibits much more maturity, confidence, and pride. Her stories about her week are much more likely to be about her successes and how she figured out how to solve various problems. This demonstrates her ability to see herself as a more independent and vibrant woman relating to me as more of a proud, understanding father who respects his daughter's autonomy and personal choice. When I bring this up, I also have interpreted that she seems not yet ready to see us as equal adults, because in so doing she would have to give up some of the nice father/happy daughter gratification she has with me now. She responded by saying, "I am getting there, but even if I can see myself as stronger and more able, the fact is that I still need your help. Sometimes, that feels like a good thing, and I like depending on you. Other times, I resent it and feel bad, because it reminds me of how much I am still struggling with my life." We are having more of these genuine, important exchanges, and there is less acting out on both sides of the equation.

CASE MATERIAL

Nancy came to see me for her first visit looking rushed and anxious. She had never been in any type of therapy before, but she told me she had been thinking about seeking help for many years and "now it was time."

She was feeling more and more depressed and "found herself sleeping a lot and crying a lot." She said her drinking was "out of control" and that she had known that for a long time but now was "taking a hard look at it." I asked for details. Nancy had been drinking four to eight drinks almost every day for "the past ten years, or maybe more." She described blackouts and a high tolerance. She was "really ready to try and get the drinking under control" and wanted help so she could "finally lick that problem." She said, in a desperate and demanding tone, "I'm willing to do anything to get your help. I'm ready to change. Just tell me what to do!"

Nancy was an attractive woman, so besides the demand for immediate and instant change, which I took as a transference stance and a diagnostic clue, I felt that she was setting up an erotic transference in which she was "willing to do anything" and in which I could "just tell her what to do." My reply was an analysis of the transference and an attempt to gather more diagnostic information. I said, "The way you said that shows you are really motivated to make some important changes in your life. The way you say it also seems to be a way of giving yourself over to me, putting me in charge. Is that familiar in any way?" Nancy responded by associating to deeper material, replying, "Wow. That's exactly how I would describe most of my relationships with guys. I throw myself on them and let them call the shots. I see them as kings who are the perfect fit with me, and I'm sure we'll live happily ever after. And this is after meeting them for five minutes at a party. It usually doesn't work out too well, but I keep trying and run after them until they sort of dump me, and then I'm depressed for a long time." I suspected that I might end up being another "king" and that our "perfect fit" might end in some type of tragedy.

The striking aspect of her drinking problem was that "without it I don't think I will be a part of my friends. Without drinking, who am I, and why would they care?" I took this as also being a transference remark and said, "You probably worry that if you stop drinking, we will not have that to focus on anymore, and then maybe more difficult matters will surface." Here, I think I could have fallen into making interpretations and asking questions about her drinking. On the one hand, this might seem appropriate, given the severity of her problem. On the other, I think I would have been colluding with her, interpretively, by helping her avoid issues of greater difficulty. I chose to adopt a wait-and-see attitude.

I was glad I did, because Nancy then looked anxious and became silent. She gathered herself and said, "There are other things I need to talk about. I know they have affected me, and I have known for years I should do something to understand it, but I have put it off." After more silence, she said, "I was raised by two very nice parents. They were good to me and my older brother. They did their best, and I don't really have any bad childhood memories of them. But when I was nine years old, my brother told me it would be fun to 'fool around.' We started to have sex whenever we could. I would sneak into his room after my parents went to bed. Or if we were visiting someone and had to share a bed, we would have sex. It wasn't every night or even every week, but it was pretty consistent from when I was about nine 'til I was twelve. He is four years older. After about a year or so, I didn't want to do it anymore. But I never said anything. So I would just lie there pretending I was asleep. He would go ahead and do it anyway." I said, "It sounds like you were uncomfortable asking him to stop. So you hoped he would notice your being passive and acting asleep and understand that you didn't want to anymore." She agreed. "I think that has impacted my life in ways I don't know. It probably affects my relationships with men. I think it's time to find out about it."

Finally, Nancy repeated, with the same frantic wish for immediate results and gratification, some of what she had said earlier about wanting to stop drinking and start "a new life." She also repeated her fear about what life could be like without drinking and "how empty and alone she would feel if no one wanted to be with her anymore."

From a psychoanalytic perspective, Nancy displayed a transference that combined borderline pathology with an erotic, manic way of relating. I saw her as having to rely on drinking to prevent an inner collapse, abandonment anxiety, and primitive loss (Waska 2002). She had high hopes for the object, but these hopes rapidly caved into disappointment, which she internalized as rejection. The history of sexual relations with her brother seemed to have a great effect on her psychological well-being and shaped her current view of self and object, leading to a passive yearning and a helpless fear. It was still unclear what other early events or experiences in her life might also have left their mark. I noticed a pull to pigeonhole everything into her sexual-trauma theory, so I instead tried to maintain my analytic balance and kept that counter-transference pull as a piece of data to refer to later if needed.

Toward the end of the session, I told her that I thought she didn't see herself as having much value or identity unless it was defined by me or others. I said that if she gave herself over to me and did whatever I wanted her to, she might end up different, but it would be a change I had chosen instead of one she had. I added that we would have to see if being herself with me presented a danger. If so, we would need to learn about that.

Several themes unfolded over the next few months. At about the six-month mark of her psychoanalytic treatment, on the couch, Nancy was doing much better. However, her progress has been part of a manic goal of pleasing me and "doing whatever I should or that you tell me so I can finally get my life together." Even though she had reduced her drinking, stopped sleeping around with men to "capture their love and attention," and begun to see her pattern of idealizing and devaluing, which went back to early childhood, she was now engaging in a particular type of transference with me. This was a seductive, manipulative method of relating in which, to keep me attentive and interested, she provided me with what she thought I wanted.

Nancy thought I wanted her to work hard and fast to achieve insight and change. She was actually doing quite well in her treatment and was achieving genuine progress and insight. But the work she was doing in treatment was also part of this attempt to guarantee my approval. By making interpretations about her internal struggles, I was both helping her to change and grow and enabling her and colluding with her in this pseudotransformation and instant victory.

With Nancy, there is a delicate balance between interpreting her material and enacting her projective-identification process. One way this emerged in the treatment was in how I noticed obvious parallels in her material to her sexual experience with her brother. I saw these parallels in the transference and in her stories about her work and friends. I began making these types of interpretations but quickly noticed that I kept bringing them up in a way that felt perverse, voyeuristic, provocative, and rapid. These countertransference alarms made me realize that

Nancy was subtly drawing me into making rather fast links to her brother in a slightly erotic, invasive, or authoritarian manner. This became a perverse acting out within the transference/countertransference. Therefore, I tried to refrain from this interpretive acting out and instead attempted a contain-and-interpret approach (Rosenfeld 1987; LaFarge 2000), in which I waited to gather and understand the various countertransference reactions I experienced before formulating an interpretation that put together the different aspects of her object-relational conflict.

In one particular session, I said, "I think you are trying to pull us along very quickly, so we don't have to linger on anything too painful. It would be nice to come up with a one-two-three formula to solve everything, linking everything to your brother. But I think that would be a reaction to something else we don't understand yet." Nancy replied, "I tend to jump around and want things to happen right away. I want it simple and fast." I said, "It sounds like that can lead to results you actually don't want." She said, "Well, that's a big part of how I screw it up with boyfriends. I always speed it up and try to create a perfect instant relationship with them. I get so excited and happy in the beginning. Then, I think things are going great, but the guy doesn't like me or doesn't call or something. Then I feel completely rejected and depressed."

Sometimes, it was appropriate to make interpretations that linked her experience with her brother to current issues. After telling me how she had ignored her parents' drinking during their recent visit but then felt mysteriously angry and sad the next morning, I said, "I think you are aware of your parents' drinking, but you put it out of your mind to avoid any conflict or rejection. You tolerate their behavior and suffer the embarrassment to keep the bond safe. But you can't keep it out of your mind too long, because you are angry and hurt. So, the next morning, like an emotional hangover, you are upset and angry, but you don't let yourself really know why. It looks like you're sick and tired of seeing your parents drunk, but that may be the only bond you have with them, so it is also frightening to look at it too closely. You said you don't have much in common with them. It looks like you are angry and hurt that drinking is the one thing you do have in common." Nancy replied, "Jesus Christ! I never saw it like that before. You're right. That does seem to be the only thing we ever do together: get drunk. In the morning, I'm angry, but I never put two and two together to realize it's about the night before."

I also interpreted, "I think that may be the same pattern of hiding your feelings that you used with your brother. Perhaps you tried to ignore your feelings about having sex with him, but the next day those feelings were still there, and you did your best to keep them separate in your mind from everything else. By keeping your feelings about your brother or your parents separate from everything else, you don't have to face the perverted relationship you have with them and the pain that goes with that. That way you don't have to tell me about your feelings either, and then you don't have to feel ashamed or embarrassed with me." Nancy said, "No wonder I drink so much!" I replied, "up to now, that has been your best way of coping. Maybe we can come up with a better approach." She said, "I'm all for that!"

During another session, we were discussing how Nancy doesn't ever think about our work together between visits and that "our connection doesn't really exist outside of this room." I asked her if she thinks I remember her. Nancy told me she "fears being forgotten." She told me, "I feel like I only last for a day or a night in people's minds, so I have to find the one thing they want or that we have in common to please them and win them over, so they might keep me in their mind and not forget me." Here, I again noticed the pull to bring up her brother's sexual acts and her feeling that she had to please him. But I decided that this was again part of our constant projective-identification dynamic, in which I was invited to bring up her brother again and again, directly after very obvious references to him in her material. Rather than waiting for her to elaborate on her material, I was being invited to quickly pounce on the genetic link and almost re-molest her with it.

I managed to contain my urge to act out interpretively, and instead said, "I think you are sometimes scared to think for yourself. You want me and others to think for you, and then if you let us be the leaders in the relationship, we won't forget you. But that also means you have to feel surrounded by people who just want to dominate you, and then you are only loved for what you can sacrifice. You end up feeling like an empty vessel needing to be filled up by others." This last comment felt like I had dropped back into a moment of interpretive enactment, using a sexualized phrase in my comments. Nancy replied, "I have done that my whole life, waiting to be filled up by someone. And you're right. I end up feeling empty and worthless, just waiting around to see what others want and hoping they will like me."

Reviewing the first year of Nancy's analysis, I noted several interesting points regarding technique. Overall, I felt caught between two types of interpretive work. On the one hand, I made consistent and focused interpretations of the transference, her phantasies and conflicts regarding wanting my love, her fear of "turning me off," her doing what she could to keep me "turned on," and the empty, hollow victory she ended up with that led her into a pathological cycle of idealizing and devaluing both self and object.

While all these interpretations were accurate, helpful, and healing, I also became aware of another aspect of interpretive work that I was neglecting. Even though we were making progress and she was working well to integrate her dramatically split-off personality, I was often caught up in her manic patterns of getting us both to feel a mutual bliss, constant progress, and immediate gratification. All was well. We were skipping along the merry road of analytic success.

On the one hand, we were analyzing her manic defense of pleasing me and being the perfect patient, creating analytic bliss without conflict or question. At the same time, we were acting this out, feeling good, successful, and complete about noticing and exploring everything and figuring it all out. It just seemed too good to be true: a well-motivated, insightful, hardworking patient and my concise, well-placed interpretations.

By monitoring the complete countertransference climate and steadily assessing the total transference situation, I began to get a better grip on these dual clinical portraits. At that point, I started to interpret the manic manipulation and control. Gradually, this new line of interpretation reduced Nancy's flight into magical transformation and helped her come down from her phantasies of bliss, mutual love, acceptance, and control of my mind.

Without the safety, control, and magical bliss of her idealizing phantasies, Nancy was left with her own humanity and day-to-day experience of herself. Now, she told me, "I am not in crisis anymore, so I don't think I need to keep coming. If I'm not able to feel like there is a dramatic victory or like we are putting out a terrible fire, there is nothing left. Nothing exists between these two places." Here, Nancy was facing a primitive state of loss, in which depressive abandonment loomed heavily without any hope of rebirth or reunion. For her, this internal void was endless and forever.

I interpreted that Nancy felt she didn't exist if we were not magically joined by success all the time or mired together in a constant crisis. Simply to be with me and be with herself was unfamiliar and even unbearable. Nancy responded, "What's the point? If I don't exist, why bother? I want to matter to somebody." I interpreted that she never cared about mattering to herself, and that dismissive attack on herself left her worried that others would ignore her the same way she ignored herself. She told me, "I know I do that to myself, but if I can get someone to care about me, I am fine throwing myself overboard." I interpreted that this was the attack and rejection she feared so much from me and others. She agreed but added that she "didn't really feel motivated to learn about herself or just hang out and talk." I replied, "You don't value yourself unless it is through the eyes of another. If I said coming here would help you catch a man who would stick around and love you—" Nancy interrupted and yelled, "I would be here twice a day every day of the week!"

For the last few months, we have struggled with Nancy's indifference to herself and to me. We are in the empty void away from crisis or bliss. In her mind, we have no value to each other or to others. She says all she really wants "is the highs and the lows." Nancy dreads coming to her analytic sessions some of the time. She sees me bored with "just silly old me," but she is also slowly managing to risk seeing herself as valuable without having to sacrifice her identity to others or be a victim who needs to be rescued. While this state is much less comfortable for both of us, she is more often in the realm of her core conflicts. Phantasy integration is possible rather than the prior manic defense that kept her helpless. Also, my interpretations are more often in touch with her current anxieties and less in collusion with her defensive posturing.

Several months later, some things have changed, and others remain to be worked on. During a recent session, several transference events highlighted how Nancy still tries to control me, please me, and enlist me in her fan club to avoid my rejection. In doing this, she draws me into being a part of her phantasy of loss and manipulation.

We were discussing her fears of rejection and her need to have all her relationships be "super passionate," because otherwise it "feels like it is dead and gone." I made a transference interpretation about this, saying she is putting great pressure on us to deal with these frightening expectations. If her gamble pays off, we are in a wonderful state of passionate bliss. But if we can't reach or maintain that state, we die, and one or both of us is rejected. I pointed out that while she usually fears being the one who looks dead and useless and therefore rejected, she is describing how she does that very thing to the object as well. I was therefore interpreting her projective-identification phantasy. She told me she "wants us to always be having a 'eureka' moment; otherwise it feels like we are doing nothing and that she is failing."

Nancy mentioned her fear of the other person losing interest in her and how much she worries about that. I thought of how much she must have to work at keeping a link between herself and her object and how desperate and pressured that must feel. I wondered how she might feel about our link when I told her of my upcoming vacation. When I told her that I would be away the following week, Nancy said, "and you'll let me know if there are extra times I can see you when you get back, right?" I had told her we might be able to meet an additional time, which I often do if I have an opening. In this case, I interpreted that her needing my reassurance about the extra session, even though I was the one that had brought it up, was her way to make sure I hadn't forgotten or lost interest in her. I added, "You're watching very closely to see what kind of condition we're in, how close we are, and if we're ok or not ok."

Nancy said, "Everything you just said hits home. I am always on the watch to find out if you are paying attention or if you have lost interest. I do that with everyone. If I don't, it feels too out of control." She added, "There is something else about what I said about the extra times in the schedule. You had said it originally, so I thought I should say it too. I mimic you because I think you want me to be like you."

I asked her what she meant. Nancy explained that she had noticed me opening my appointment book at the beginning of many sessions and confirming our upcoming times. She said she thought I would like it if she developed the same habit. When she said this, I realized I had noticed her pattern of doing this for several months and had always felt a strange sensation about it, as if something was off. During those moments, it felt like there was an awkward tension in the air and something ajar. Interestingly, I never investigated this countertransference feeling. Instead, I went along with something I didn't understand and didn't really feel good about. Looking at it this way, in a sense I was now going along with the brother's sexual abuse without saying anything, just feeling wrong and hoping something would change or get better.

Once I let myself think about this and tried to understand it, I became aware of a similar situation. Whenever Nancy comes into a session, she takes out her payment and hands it over to me in a very official manner. When I brought this up, Nancy said she "does it like that because she wants to always separate *that stuff* from our time together." I said it sounded like "*that stuff* was somehow repulsive or bad," so she "had to keep it away from the other stuff that felt good or comforting." Here, I was interpreting a splitting process and possibly a projective-identification situation in which she was depositing something unwanted or repulsive into the money.

"I don't want it to be something that feels dirty," she said. I made an interpretation based on my thoughts about her experience with her brother, using her words of "dirty" and "wanting to keep things separate." I said, "The way you talk about it makes it sound like prostitution. Maybe you feel like a dirty prostitute with me?" Here, I was thinking of her as the prostitute and me being the one using her. This was a mistake, an interpretive acting out, which was caused by my sense of her feeling as awkward and helpless and me then, in my mind, stepping into the role of the one making her feel awkward and helpless. In other words, I ignored that I was the one feeling helpless and used. Fortunately, Nancy corrected me. "No. It's actually the other way around. I feel like the loser, the one going to a prostitute, paying you for something I should be able to get on my own." Once I heard this, I felt more on track and was able to pursue a more helpful line of interpretation.

I brought up that it is difficult for her to depend on me without feeling like she is weak or pathetic and that it is something that feels almost dirty and repulsive. She agreed immediately and told me that she needs to confide in me and looks forward to seeing me but that she also struggles with feeling that this is wrong and weak. Here, I pictured her feeling guilty about wanting to be with her brother and needing him but also feeling that what she was doing was wrong. I chose not to bring this up, because even though I thought it was accurate, to bring it up at that moment felt might have been an interpretive enactment that would simply sexualize our relationship instead of assisting her to find her own way to these very complicated and difficult feelings.

Finally, Nancy told me how her effort to please me by mimicking my behavior was an attempt "to truly know you. I am trying really hard, but almost in a panic, to know who you are and what you want." I interpreted that this desperate attempt to please me and know me was really more about being able to control my love, so as to guarantee that I would be there for her instead of rejecting her.

I added that in trying so hard to "be me," she actually was missing opportunities to learn about me and what I want. By controlling me, she lost touch with me. I illustrated that point by bringing us back to the example of her mimicking my scheduling. I told her that I was taking out my appointment book almost every session to verify our schedule not because I wanted to but because during that period she was often canceling or rescheduling many of her sessions. So, rather than it being a choice, habit, or something I wanted to do, I felt forced to check constantly when we were meeting next. (Looking back on that, I was acting out my countertransference instead of finding a helpful way to interpret it.)

Now, when we were more settled into our schedule, I had no need or desire to check our schedule constantly, but Nancy didn't realize that, because she was still busy mimicking my prior behavior. In her current mimicking to please me and know me, she was actually creating an awkward distance, because she was out of touch with the current me. This left her feeling alone and even more desperate, which made her try to control me even more.

Now, as a result of our examination of this object-relational struggle, we were beginning to work on this vicious cycle within the transference.

CASE MATERIAL

Todd was a computer engineer who came to treatment some three years ago for help with his marriage. I actually attempted to conduct couple's therapy at first, but his wife displayed such classic borderline acting out that each session became exclusively about how she was feeling rejected, offended, or misunderstood by me. She would pout and become enraged until she finally stopped attending, saying that I "didn't treat her fairly." I continued to see Todd. Since that time, they have seen two other couple's therapists with the same results.

Todd comes from a family where "everyone does everything they can to help others and to make sure everyone is happy. That's the theme throughout the house. If someone is not happy, find a way to help out and make them happy. It was a 'look out for the other person' creed that we lived by. Giving was the centerpiece of my upbringing." Early in his analysis, I interpreted that with such an emphasis, any needs he had of his own might feel taking or demanding and, consequently, hurtful. Todd agreed and said he never really thought of his own needs, only those of others. I interpreted that he might experience his own needs with me, his wife, and others as selfish, especially if he thought that they were in conflict with our needs. Todd said, "Growing up, we never really talked to each other. We communicated about what needed to happen around the house but never about feelings or anything like that."

Just as these historical threads were a part of his marital problems, they quickly colored the treatment setting and became part of the transference. Todd wanted no conflict with me or anyone else. He said, "I do not want any conflict, ever!" Over time, I interpreted that he wanted me to hold and hide his forbidden feelings of need, anger, disagreement, desire, and difference, just as he tried to hide and deny them. I added that he also wished I would translate and reveal these secrets for him, like he wished he could do for himself. Todd agreed and told me that he "understands it better when I point out what he feels, because then he is able to consider it more without retreating from it immediately."

I would interpret that he was telling me a story, usually about his wife, and that he wanted me to know how angry he was and how he wanted to say or do something on his own behalf, but that made him very anxious. So, instead, he told me the story in a way that made me fill in the blanks and provide the emotional side of his story for him, I interpreted that he wanted me to show him it was ok to have such feelings and, in a way, he got me to give him permission to have those types of feelings by making me the one who said it first. He agreed. Over the course of two years, he began to claim more of these feelings, and he would often voice them before I did or was quicker to agree with me when I pointed out how he must be feeling.

In one way, I was doing very traditional and successful psychoanalytic work, making interpretations that simply revealed his anxiety and his transference stance. However, at the same time, I was interpretively acting out by being his spokesperson. I was holding his anxieties, by being the one that went first in voicing these forbidden feelings and wishes. In this way, I was dominating and preventing him from gaining his independence and ability to explore and experiment with new ways of being. He had successfully projected his anxieties and forbidden wishes into me.

It was a very difficult and agonizing process for Todd to have these types of feelings or phantasies himself, as it meant something very bad and destructive. He said, "if I take what we are talking about out into the world, it would mean I was a selfish and angry person! I would be angry and violent!" Sometimes, I found myself pulled into putting his wife down, wanting to tell Todd, "This is not your fault. Of course you're angry. Your wife is crazy!" I also noticed myself wanting to urge him to take command of the marriage and stand up to her like a man. I interpreted that he, in a roundabout way, was getting me to fill in the blanks of his stories with feelings and ideas he was frightened of, thereby depositing the worst and most frightening aspects of his internal conflict into me. Again, Todd said he felt "bad to have me sit with that stuff, but I still feel so guilty and uncomfortable about all of it. I know it's mine, but I don't want it! It makes me feel like a bad person doing bad things." He could acknowledge the feelings he was projecting but did not want to reclaim them.

Hearing this helped me be very patient and willing to put up with Todd's seemingly slow pace of change, instead of becoming pushy or impatient with him. But I was also becoming aware of two directions in which I could possibly act out in my interpretations. I could tell him to hurry up and speak his mind at home and therefore act out his sense of frustration and resentment, or I could tell him I was unhappy with him and that he had better hurry up and change, thus acting out his guilt and self-punishment for being angry in the first place. Fortunately, I was able to stay more on course and help him slowly face his own anxiety and guilt without colluding with his desire to escape those troubling phantasies.

At one point, he told me of a recent incident: Todd was five minutes late in picking up his wife, and she yelled at him for making her feel abandoned, rejected, and attacked. He was only able to pick her up at all after asking his boss for special permission to get off early. After telling me about it, Todd said he didn't think we had made any progress. I interpreted that to make progress means to him to be angry and violent. Todd thought about it for a minute and said, "You know, we have made a lot of progress. In fact, I am amazed sometimes at the degree to which I have faced some of this crap. But I think it scares me because I start to think I have become a selfish, angry person if I am changing. But when I slow down or you point it out, I can see that I'm still a decent human being. But the guilt creeps in really fast sometimes and takes over."

At other times, I am not as successful in keeping my interpretive balance. An example of how guilt quickly clouds Todd's outlook and how it can influence my interpretive direction came in a recent session. Todd was telling me a story about how his wife had asked/told him to help move her office. She had been angry and upset, telling him, "you have no idea how stressed out I am, and I need you to start to look at how you never help me with anything. Sure, I have the company's workers to move me, but a good husband would be here to help me when I need it! But if you don't care, that's fine. I can find someone else." Now in tears, she added, "I always have to do everything by myself; I guess you don't care about me and don't love me! Fine, if that's the way it is, then don't bother me with your selfish bullshit. I don't need you anyway!"

This was a fairly typical interaction with his wife, and Todd responded in both an old way and a new way. He told her that he is always helpful, so it is unfair for her to talk to him so abusively. At the same time, Todd told her he would call in sick to his job and spend the day helping her out, thus going back to his guilt and sacrifice. On the day of the move, there was a crisis at Todd's job, and he told his wife he had to stay to deal with it. She was being professionally moved by her company, and there were plenty of people assigned to help her out in any manner she might need. Regardless, she became furious and yelled at Todd, telling him that he always let her down and obviously doesn't love her. Todd told me in detail about how he felt very upset, stating, "I'm hurting her and letting her down. I feel so guilty and frustrated over not being able to help her!"

I interpreted and explored Todd's intense depressive feelings and phantasies of guilt over letting his wife down and hurting her. This was very productive. Todd discussed his guilt with great emotion and brought up memories of feeling bad over not being able to help out his father at the family business when he went off to college. My line of interpretive exploration was accurate, helpful, and integrative. The more we went down this road, the more he seemed to work through this guilt over his sense of helplessness and inability to heal, calm, or help his needy object.

However, I felt we were missing something. I realized that what we were successfully working on was a passive version of his feelings and phantasies. I was interpretively colluding with him by avoiding the more active aspect of his guilt. Once I realized this, I interpreted that he was deflecting us away from the harsher reality of his feelings. I said, "You say how guilty you feel about not being able to help your wife. I think what's much harder to share with me is that you *don't* want to help her. You actively don't want to and are glad to not have to. I think your anger is at her outburst, and you simply don't want to have to help her move." Todd said, "Well, I think you're right. But, isn't that really selfish?" I said, "That is where the guilt is. I think you dread having me realize that you have your own agenda and actually act on your own mindset sometimes. You don't know if I will still like or respect you."

Todd replied, "Yes. That's definitely still a work in progress. I think you will be ok with it during the times when I feel ok with it. But, when I feel shaky with it, I don't know if you could stand me being that way." Interpreting his realization of his projection, I said, "So, now you own that it is your own strength and independence as well as your doubts and anger that you put onto me. That makes us more equal than when you were making me the master who decides if you are a naughty, selfish boy or not. That is the same thing you struggle with in the marriage, but right now you are working it out here with me so you can take it on the road."

DISCUSSION

As Segal (1967) has outlined, a primary feature in the Kleinian approach to psychoanalytic technique involves a focus on interpretation, especially of the transference. And in the Kleinian view, anxiety and defense are always interpreted together rather than separately or with defense being explored before anxiety, as is common in classical ego psychology. Interpretive acting out, as illustrated by the case material, can include a deviation in technique, via an overemphasis on anxiety or defense. A common way that the analyst might act out within the interpretive realm is to become stuck interpreting the patient's defensive structure and thereby never getting to the actual anxiety that is occurring and shaping the transference. In this way, the analyst becomes part of the defensive structure and helps perpetuate it. In order to address best this constant threat, the analyst has to be looking for what Spillius (1994, 347) has defined as Klein's concept of the total transference situation. This means the "expression in the analytic situation of the forces and relationships of the internal world. The internal world itself is regarded as the result of an ongoing process of development, the product of continuing interaction between unconscious phantasy, defenses, and experiences with external reality both in the past and in the present."

I would state that the analyst's complete countertransference is one tool in better locating and understanding the total transference situation. Riesenberg-Malcolm (1995, 453) explains how the analyst's countertransference "can be used as a kind of sense organ to perceive certain aspects of the patient's feelings, which the patient either cannot express in any other way, for whatever reason, or which complement a more direct discourse. In order to understand and use countertransference in assessing the patient's material the concept of projective identification is indispensable." She goes on to state,

Thanks especially to Bion's, Rosenfeld's and Joseph's emphasis on the use of projective identification as a means of communication by the patient in the session, analysts have developed and refined the use of the countertransference in understanding the transference and the nature of the patient's internal object relationships, the affects and anxieties that predominate, and therefore the various ways in which the patient defends himself. All this forms the core of analytic interpretations.

This chapter has explored the ways that countertransference can pave the way to a better understanding of the transference and, therefore, more helpful and accurate interpretations of the patient's internal world. At the same time, this chapter underscores the ways that the analyst can be pulled into various forms of acting out that emerge via interpretation. Betty Joseph (1989) has pioneered the understanding of how patients will invite, seduce, corral, and demand us to become part of their core conflicts and unconscious phantasies. This can lead to interpretive acting out and the ongoing enactment of different defensive postures or pathological repetitions of self↔object relations.

Rosenfeld (1964) and later Joseph (1989) have described how acting out by the analyst is something that takes place in almost every analysis. Therefore, Rosenfeld notes the need for constant understanding and to consider it as something to minimize. But, since it is always present, it is also something always to try to learn from. Hanna Segal and Ron Britton (1991, 271) have stated:

It is likely that we are induced into unconscious enactments with some of our patients in more subtle forms since our "actions" may take place under the forms of apparently ordinary analytic activities (e.g., in choice of interpretation, tone of voice, turn of phrase, level of analytic activity). This too, however, can be monitored and elucidated if it can be seen as the emergence of an unconscious object relationship within the analysis.

Joseph (2003) and Steiner (2006) have written about the enactment process as it takes place within the interpretive field. Steiner (2006) points out the limiting or even destructive effects that interpretive acting out can have on the patient's ability to develop his or her own thinking and judgment. He goes on to point out how the analyst has to keep his feelings under control, remaining both involved and separate, in order to be engaged but also able to observe and assess.

Elaborating and expanding on Joseph's and Steiner's work, this chapter has focused on the analyst's potential for making interpretations that are actually vehicles for unconscious acting out. These interpretive entanglements are inevitable; thus the task is both to minimize and study them. In turn, their examination hopefully can provide helpful information about the nature of the analytic contact occurring in that clinical moment.

While potentially harmful if not recognized and dealt with, interpretive acting out can provide important clues to the transference and projective-identification climate that might otherwise go unnoticed. There may be, as illustrated in the case material, phantasies that involve fears, wishes, pain, and guilt, which the patient cannot bear to communicate or reveal in any way other than projective identification. Thus, the nature of how and when the analyst acts out interpretively may, if properly handled and understood, provide the only doorway into certain aspects of the patient's internal struggles, with which we can then attempt to assist them.

2

SLIPPERY WHEN WET

The Imperfect Art of Interpretation

IT IS RELATIVELY easy to come up with everyday examples of interpretive acting out. When a patient is talking about his or her intense feelings toward the analyst, the analyst and/or the patient may feel so guilty, angry, anxious, or persecuted that they engage in a defensive retreat or reaction. This may take the form of the analyst suddenly shifting from interpreting the negative transference to interpreting genetic material that focuses the patient's anger at his or her parents instead of at the analyst.

A supervisee provided an example of another sort of interpretive acting out. The analyst was telling me about her patient's disappointment, hurt, and anger over how the patient had felt brushed aside, ignored, and minimized by the analyst's comments during the previous week. The patient had been talking about some important feelings that were very difficult to share, and the analyst had attempted to make a transference interpretation. The patient found this jarring and out of touch with what she had been discussing, and indeed, there was not much of a connection between the patient's material and the analyst's interpretation. The next week, the patient was recounting this hurt and associated to her childhood experiences of being ignored and brushed aside. She said, "Growing up, my father must have turned away from me and what I was saying at least a million times. He would barely listen to me, even if I was obviously pouring my heart out. He would turn to something of his own concern, something about himself, over and over again." The analyst replied, "I wonder if that is what you feel I have been doing lately?" The patient responded, "There you go again, its all about you!"

The analyst's transference comments were, on the one hand, very much to the point. This patient has a habit of bringing up various feelings toward the analyst but strongly resists exploring them. The patient wants to feel in control of these uncomfortable feelings by not answering questions or elaborating on them. And, given what had happened in the previous week and what she had said about her childhood experiences, it also made sense to bring up the immediate relational situation. However, the manner in which the analyst voiced the interpretation and the timing of it, given what the patient had just said, were significant enactments of the betrayal that the patient felt at her father's hands. Basically, the patient said, "my father always turns my concerns into something about him"—and then the analyst turned that comment into something about herself.

No doubt, this analyst is currently stuck in a projective-identification dynamic in which she is acting out the role of a dismissive, self-absorbed father who doesn't see the importance of his daughter's thoughts and feelings. This is the next crucial point of work that both patient and analyst must undertake. They must discover, learn about, and change these underlying pathological dynamics that are leaking out in the therapeutic relationship, including in the analyst's style of interpreting.

Interpretations that accurately address one important area of a patient's unconscious conflicts but miss another equally or more important aspect of the conflict are partly a result of the fact that the analyst simply can't be at all places at all times. However, because of the patient's use of projective identification and sometimes because of the analyst's own countertransference, there can be a subtle seduction to focus on one side of the conflict rather than another. This draws attention away from the more frightening or overwhelming aspects of the conflict that the patient isn't ready to tolerate.

There is a basic to and fro inherent in the interpretive process that is necessary in order to keep pace with the patient's shifting and mutating phantasies. This constant hunt to discover and translate, via interpretation, the source and meaning of the patient's internal state is always in motion, because of the defensive strategy employed within the transference, which usually relies heavily on splitting and projective identification. Also, there is never a singular, unitary phantasy to uncover. Phantasy states are naturally composed of multiple, interlocking, overlapping, mutating elements of conflictual desire and anxiety. This shifting inner landscape shows evolving complexity during periods of integration, growth, and change, making interpretation a complicated art form aimed at a moving, developing target.

In our efforts to establish analytic contact (Waska 2007) with patients, we are in extremely close, intimate proximity to their unconscious visions of themselves and their objects. We have to get close to the fire to understand why and how it burns so brightly and destructively. In doing so, we often end up scorched ourselves.

Another metaphor that helps to clarify this issue is that our patients have confined themselves to a psychological prison cell, and to discover how and why they have sentenced themselves to that particular prison, we often have to enter that cell too. In the process, we may at times end up incarcerated with them. These are the moments in which acting out in the interpretive process may be inevitable but critical to notice, understand, and disengage from. Again, projective identification is often the underlying culprit, contaminating the interpretive process. We then are left to struggle with and learn about what is being communicated to us in this turbulent way and gradually find a manner to interpret it without playing it out in a pathologically repetitious cycle.

CASE MATERIAL

I met with Cathy for an initial consultation. She had lost her husband in a car accident, five months earlier, two months after they were married. They had bought a new home and were planning to start a family. After his death, Cathy started a new job and plunged into it with intensity. She said this was because it "was a real opportunity to go up the ladder quickly" and that she "needed to start making money fast, to pay off all the mounting bills, since now she was the sole provider." My impression was that she was using the job and "the ladder" as a manic defense to avoid the crumbling feelings of massive grief and loss.

Cathy spent most of the interview telling me about the concrete diffi-culties she was now facing after her husband's death. She told me about her endless frustrations with lawyers, the various memorial services that seemed to "never end," and the complicated travel plans she had to negotiate in order to attend all of them. Cathy described her new job and hoped that "maybe it will provide enough money that I can find a way to pay all these bills." She listed all the bills that they had shared but that now she was responsible for. There were complicated commu-nications with all family members on both sides about many matters, in-cluding financial ones. She didn't know if she wanted to try to sell their new home or keep it.

She related these descriptions and details with a nervous intensity, and at first I found myself caught up in it. I asked how much her mort-gage was and if she was going to get enough from her husband's estate to be able to pay it each month. I asked for some details about her meet-ings with lawyers. When she started telling me about her new oppor-tunities at the job and how she was positioned to move up the ladder quickly, I noticed that I was asking for details about her day-to-day job duties, mostly out of curiosity. This made me wonder why I was situated so far away from this woman's tragic story and her grief-stricken life. Why was I curious about what she did at her new job, when this poor woman had just lost her husband in a grisly car wreck? I suspected that I might be acting as a part of her defensive mask, acting out in my inter-pretive questions and colluding with her defensive system at first in a rather passive manner and then more and more actively.

Trying to reestablish analytic contact, I said, "I notice the one thing missing in our talk is your husband. Maybe it's painful to tell me how you are doing without him. You must miss him." Cathy looked at me intently and said, "I can't talk about him! That's one thing I don't want to talk about!" She began sobbing. "I'm so lonely without him. I don't know what to do. I work all day and stay busy, but then I come home, and the house is so quiet and lonely. I have to eat dinner by myself. I have to walk the dog by myself. I have to watch television by myself. I have to go to bed by myself. I miss talking to him, just talking! I miss him so very much!"

I had made an accurate interpretation to the level of her core anxiety and grief, instead of getting swept up in her manic defenses against this terrible loss. Now, we were back on track, working together in this sad and difficult task.

Betty Joseph's (1989) work on transference, countertransference, acting out, and projective identification is relevant to this case. In summarizing some of her contributions, Hinshelwood (1991, 300) states,

Central to her method is the close examination of the way that material emerges in the session. Again and again she gives vignettes of the way that taking up the simple meaning of some piece of material results in the analyst falling into a collusive acting out with the patient—the analyst, she says, is "drawn in" by the patient. What the analyst is drawn into is some situation which actually prevents the patient experiencing certain painful situations.

CASE MATERIAL

Analytic treatment with Robert demonstrated a much greater pattern of acting out or technical deviation in my interpretive style, because of this patient's massive use of splitting and projective identification.

Robert grew up in a very religious household. He and his siblings went to church often, studied the Bible, and went to church camp every summer. They lived in a community close to the church, and most of the church members lived in the neighborhood. Almost everyone Robert had contact with was part of this fellowship.

When Robert was three years old, his father left the family to be with another woman. Robert never saw him again. He says he doesn't remember his father and feels like his whole life was "really about being raised by my mother." Robert said he was "a good boy and did what I could to behave and do the right thing for the family and God." He reports that his older brothers encouraged him to be "a responsible man of the house and to always take care of his mother." When Robert was eight years old, his mother was diagnosed with cancer and started to weaken. She was soon unable to function around the home. She spent many of her days in bed or just sitting around the house in pain. She underwent treatment, but the prognosis was grim. She died when Robert was twelve, and Robert's oldest brother took over as head of the household. Over the four years of his mother's suffering, Robert dutifully stayed by her side, trying his best to care for her and do what she wanted.

Reconstructing this period of his life, Robert and I have come to understand that he felt obligated to care for his mother and never considered himself in the process. Robert sees this as normal and what any "good Christian son would do." I proposed many times over the three-year analysis that as a child he may have had mixed feelings about this duty, feelings that left him in a state of conflict that continued to follow him in his adult life.

On the one hand, I was presenting the possible other side of the coin to his adamant stance of simply being a good Christian. However, by stating it as a "perhaps you" instead of interpreting the way he seemed to need to have it be so one sided, I was making more of an interpretive enactment than a genuine exploratory comment. In other words, I was actively suggesting he had less than pure feelings, which might have been my reaction to his insistence of purity. In acting out this interpretively, I neglected to point out the possible defensive needs that he had to be always pure and to make sure that I knew and never doubted it.

When I made my "you probably felt conflicted" proposal, Robert could see what I meant and intellectually agreed with it. However, he quickly switched to telling me about how he was simply "being there for his mother and not being selfish." I think the taboo feelings and conflicted memories he carried about this tragic period were projected into me mostly as a way to expel and deny them. But he also wanted help with this emotional burden. Although Robert had a small but very conflicted interest in resolving this tangled attachment, he also supported his position with his emphasis on being Christian. I sometimes fell prey to this and found myself overemphasizing the idea that he really must have wanted to be outside in the yard playing as a child without the burden of caring for mother. I was forcing the one side of his split onto him, without giving him the room to work with the anxiety he felt—the anxiety that he could only manage with such constant splitting and projective identification.

Thus Robert rightly characterized our discussions as him standing for Christianity and me standing for hedonism. I would try to underscore the possibility that as a child and now as an adult, he was minimizing his desire for autonomy and might resent caring for others. He would fight back with Bible stories or by describing the benefits of the Christian lifestyle. He would tell me that he could see that maybe he was "a little one sided" but that I was telling him "to be too much like a non-Christian."

Robert was right. I had lost my interpretive way, in that I was simply advocating for the exploration of his defenses and pointing out his reactions to his unconscious desires and conflicts. But I was not taking the time to explore the burden of his guilt, the pain of seeing others as weak and in need, and the trauma of feeling like he had failed in caring for his mother and others. In other words, I was constantly interpreting one side of his internal world. This was accurate, but the singleness of mind with which I was doing it was evidence of my acting out. I was essentially judging him for not being more selfish and less Christian. And he felt that and told me. Melanie Klein advocated the combined analysis of defense and anxiety. Singling out one over the other can be a sign of interpretive acting out or, as evidenced by my interpretive stance, some type of collusion with the patient's projective-identification process.

When I heard Robert tell me of my error, I was able to reflect on his feedback and tried to regroup my interpretive efforts by now interpreting both sides of his lifelong struggle instead of just my one-sided enactment. But when I did so, he would get very concrete and begin to beat me over the head with ideas about the benefits of Christianity. In other words, he got even more one sided. We both were enacting this type of assault on each other's perspective on life rather than talking about the feelings that came up when we had to consider something outside of the realm of what seemed normal to us. Bit by bit, over the years of his analysis, Robert was able to consider and utilize other ways of thinking and feeling. But the closer we came to working on these phantasies and conflicts in regards to his mother or father, the more his projective-identification acting out occurred. To face his grief, guilt, and anger over his mother, father, and his lost childhood was too painful and unbearable to himself and his internal objects.

Progress was made—but in other areas. Robert's wife of twenty years had a long history of depression and hospitalization. In many ways, he had chosen someone that he again felt obliged to care for. Every few years, she would become so depressed that she couldn't work anymore, leaving Robert to scramble to pay the mortgage. Because of the side effects of her antidepressant medications, she has no sex drive. This obviously frustrates Robert a great deal, but initially he tried to assure me he was "understanding and patient" with her and "didn't want to ask for something she couldn't provide."

I interpreted that he was worried about being pushy and hurting her, so he tried hard to ignore his needs. He agreed but added that his needs were "something that can be set aside for the common good." I was frustrated by his blatant denial and his claim of purity and patience. Overall, I think my interpretations regarding his hidden and denied anger, desire, and conflict were accurate, but they were cloaked in countertransference frustration, which meant that I was acting out his unacceptable feelings by slightly overemphasizing them in my interpretation. I think this acting out alarmed him and made it difficult for him to take in my interpretations fully. It was too much, too soon, so he recoiled and became cautious about fully accepting them. In fact, at times, he fought against them and claimed the opposite.

Yet, over time, Robert was able to be more honest with himself about some of these feelings, and, in turn, he made important changes in how he related to his wife. He was more honest in his communication. He asked for more when he needed it and sometimes brought up his irritation when he felt she was "escaping into depression." Over time, he did the same at work, becoming more assertive and asking for what he needed. Also, he developed better boundaries, because he didn't feel as guilty about saying no. Overall, he tried to control others much less and didn't feel he had to be on guard at all times to make sure everyone was happy and free of conflict. However, he would routinely tell me that this progress was just his adaptation to "my non-Christian ways." It was too overwhelming for him to own this new independence, so he had to blame me for it. Sometimes, I interpreted this; other times, it seemed better to say nothing, to avoid possibly emphasizing the other side of his splitting process.

Robert felt that he was slowly being "brainwashed into being more Godless and more selfish." He told me that he could see the benefits of "this new confidence" much of the time, but he still felt it was a basic betrayal of his faith. The term "betrayal" struck a cord with me, and I interpreted that he felt any change we orchestrated was a betrayal to his bond with mother. Over the course of the analysis, he was lukewarm to this idea, agreeing in principle some of the time and disagreeing other times based on religious and "basic moral edicts."

Overall, my impression of what seemed to be the cornerstone of his emotional experience of life was his experience with his dying mother. But, as it was so difficult to own any feelings that weren't completely pure and positive toward her, we had a hard time ever truly discussing his underlying, warded-off feelings. I approached this topic from various angles, including his sense of guilt at having failed to care for her, his sense of survivor guilt, his anger at being restricted by her illness, his gratification at feeling able to care for her and be such a good little Catholic boy for his mommy, and his desire to take over his father's position. He would come close to these various conflicts but always shy away. When I tried to explore his retreat, he always justified it in religious terms.

The guilt around his not always wanting to be her personal nurse, savior, and bedside companion was equivalent to admitting he didn't care about her or her slow decline. In his phantasy conflict, Robert struggled with having to face that he cared not just more about himself than his mother but that he cared for himself *instead of her*. In his mind, it was an either/or situation: he had to choose between himself and his mother. It was a yin-versus-yang conflict, which was a metaphor he brought up at termination. This splitting dynamic led to primitive guilt too severe to bear, so he tried to avoid it by relying on projective identification, which allowed him to feel the false sense of being the responsible, moral, good Catholic boy who always put his mother, wife, and others first.

Robert's projective-identification process was intense and massive, but it was also subtle and well defended through logic and rational debate. I frequently took the bait when he tried to convince me of the merits of his religious stance. I would argue for the other side of the split rather than realize that we were now both involved in a defensive move. In some ways, I didn't want to bear the pain of having to try to be there for a dying mother, so I argued the benefits of being independent. At the same time, I was on the mark interpretively by frequently pointing to the manner in which he divided everything into "good and religious" versus "selfish and unethical." Unfortunately, I would sometimes act out the very thing I was interpreting.

Robert both did and didn't want me as a father figure. Over time, we explored how and why he kept the vision of his father out of much of his analysis. Unless I brought his father up, Robert never spoke of him. We explored his angry dismissal, in which he said, "I don't think my father had much impact on my life." This allowed him to push his father out of his mind and kept him from facing the pain and abandonment he felt. Also, Robert seemed to enjoy the Oedipal gratification of having his mother all to himself. He was actually proud of this and was willing to tell me how he "enjoyed being mom's little man and having her to myself." This Oedipal triumph was tainted severely by the fact that his victory turned into being with a sick and dying mother.

During the course of treatment, I interpreted that Robert both wanted me and rejected me as the father who could give him permission and guidance around his independence and anger. He let me be and seduced me into being that, especially around work and marriage situations. But, when we started to interact that way about his mother, it was too much to integrate. Having to give up his Oedipal victory and internalize his guilt and grief was too painful, so he aborted me as father and went back to the safety and power of his religious stance.

Unfortunately, at times I acted out the side of him that still felt angry and frustrated, that wanted to separate and be more his own person. While Robert backed off and went back to his religious-defense mode, I would continue to push as father and rally for independence and separation. This was equivalent to suggesting that Robert betray his mother, so he could not go along with it. Also, to admit to missing his father or needing him for advice or guidance was to realize how angry he was. "Life is unfair" and "I want father but I hate him too" were feelings that went against the Christian, idealized mother-union phantasies that he tried so hard to maintain. He avoided those feelings at all costs.

After three years of psychoanalytic work, Robert decided he wanted to terminate, for two reasons. First, he felt that he had learned a great deal from my "secular approach" and felt he had "made important changes in his life that left him feeling better about himself." The other reason was that he had seen a television program about a Catholic psychologist who teaches people how to use the Bible and church teachings to overcome their psychological problems. He bought a book by the man and told me, "he speaks to me in a way that really makes sense. I want to try that side of the fence now."

At first, Robert told me about it in a way that prodded me to feel jealous and forgotten. I held myself back from reacting to the jealousy and instead tried to use it as information about my internal state. I interpreted, "Maybe you want to see if I can understand that you want to find your own way without hurting me in the process." He responded, "I was surprised you told me last week that you thought I could benefit from continuing for a while. I know I asked for your honest opinion, but I was sure you would agree with me." I discussed with Robert how it seemed that he convinced himself that we would be on the same page as a way to avoid his fear of us having differences. I said, "And if I don't agree with you, you have to face the feelings of wondering if it is ok to leave on your own accord, sort of making your own way in life." He agreed and said it "made him worry about hurting me but that after a while he decided I would be fine." I pointed out that this situation with us might bring back feelings about separating from his mother and him having to work that out one more time. He told me, "I feel ok because I am still pursuing help, but from another avenue."

Here, I think he meant that he felt guilty for going out on his own, away from his treatment and relationship with me. This way, he was able to feel less guilty, by thinking of how he would still be in treatment and in a relationship with the new Catholic therapist.

On our last day, Robert told me that he felt he had learned a great deal and had discovered ways that his experiences with his mother still shape him. Nevertheless, he said he was going to try "the other way" for a while. I pointed out that he might be more comfortable keeping me and the Catholic therapist apart as two very separate approaches and that seeing things as more of a possible blend or mix might be a bit frightening. Here, I was addressing the splitting that he used throughout the course of the treatment to keep his internal world and objects safe and controlled. Robert responded by telling me how "in his life there is the yin and the yang. The yin and yang have to stay separate for the colors to stay vibrant." I asked, "What does it feel like if they are mixed together?" He said, "It would be a loss; something would be sacrificed. I think it is better to keep them separate so that both remain vibrant, not blurred or washed out." I was listening very closely to this. Here, Robert had come very near to consciously describing his internal conflicts.

Before leaving at the end of the last session, Robert showed me a picture of him at age ten, dressed in religious clothing. He told me how his mother wanted him to be a priest, and when he was ten years old, he went to a Catholic summer camp where they encouraged the children to consider the priesthood and allowed them to try some of the daily activities a priest might do. They were allowed to wear religious robes at one point. Robert told me how he got homesick and had to leave after three days but that he also "felt dedicated to the cause" and wanted to stay to "learn how to start becoming a man of God." I interpreted his loyalty to mother. He felt the conflict of wanting to stay with her and take care of her but of also wanting to be a man and find his own way. I interpreted that he may also be feeling that conflict with me. Robert said he was "afraid I am disappointing you and making you unhappy. But, perhaps evidence of our work together is that I feel ok to go ahead and leave anyway." I said, "that sounds like a touch of grey, a blending of yin and yang." Robert nodded.

Summarizing this case, I think there were many unnecessary and sometimes harmful interpretive enactments. These frequent moments of interpretive acting out were sometimes avoidable but seemed to be the result of my ongoing reaction to the patient's strong reliance on splitting and projective identification. Perhaps another analyst might not have fallen into these pathological cycles as often or as severely.

However, I think that this was the arc of this patient's treatment, given his internal conflict structure more than external circumstances. Overall, I think this patient benefited greatly from his analysis but left with a significant aspect of his unconscious struggle still intact. That said, his day-to-day functioning, overall happiness, ability to experience life in a full and engaged manner, and way of relating to others were all greatly enhanced by his treatment.

CASE MATERIAL

Francisco was a twenty-six-year-old man who came to me for help with his relationship. He had been seeing a woman he met in college. They were friends in college but had become sexual on occasion. This friendship with sexual overtones continued for the past four years. From his description, she was a volatile borderline woman with a drug addiction and unpredictable mood swings. For example, she would become suicidal and extremely depressed, begging for his help and support.

Very quickly, this would turn to her being angry and belittling him. She would yell at him and tell him he was worthless.

When they had sex, she would initially be "really into it." But by the next morning or even right after sex, she would tell Francisco "what a crummy lover he was" and compare him to "all the other hot studs she had slept with that were so much better."

When I started seeing Francisco, he was clearly unhappy about this relationship but was primarily suffering with guilt and fear of rejection. He felt very guilty about not wanting to "be there for her" in her hour of need. He wanted the sex to continue, because he was convinced she "was the only woman who might ever want to be with me." In fact, she was the only woman he had ever had sex with. He was convinced that his penis was too small and his sexual techniques inadequate. He thought that while she tolerated this, other women would not. This was part of his guilty, devalued phantasy, which kept him in this sadomasochistic relationship. He always tried to please others and avoid conflict, and he dreaded the next unpredictable turn, in which he could disappoint and possibly be punished with rejection, criticism, or abandonment.

Growing up, Francisco was one of three brothers in a family where "everyone loved each other and family values were important, but there wasn't too much emotional communication." When Francisco was four years old, his next-oldest brother died in a car accident. His father made an illegal U-turn and was hit by a truck. "The family grieved for a short time, but my parent's religious faith helped us move on with life." When Francisco was sixteen, he was driving his youngest brother back from the store, made an illegal U-turn, and was almost hit by a truck. He remembers his parents "being terrified" when they found out.

Francisco never said much about how he felt during his childhood or his impression of what psychological stamp may have been left by it. But, in my countertransference, regarding how he acted with me and how he talked about his day-to-day experience with others, I had the idea that his parents were overwhelmed by guilt and grief but never talked about it. Francisco was left to worry about them and perhaps feel responsible for them. In fact, his mother was hospitalized for depression several times, but nothing was ever said about it.

My working hypothesis was that he was overwhelmed by a sense of guilt and worry for the object and had to find a way to make sure the object was happy and healthy, even if it meant sacrifice and suffering for him. Part of this phantasy seemed to be that if he couldn't prevent the object's unhappiness, he was to blame for it in the first place. Therefore, he imagined he would be punished, usually by rejection. So his girlfriend might say she was "very depressed and was thinking about using drugs and needed someone to be there for her. If no one shows up, who knows what I will do." Francisco would feel that if he didn't personally save her, which might mean taking an immediate plane flight to where she lived, he would be the cause of her depression, overdose, or suicide.

When Francisco thinks of dating other women, he becomes overwhelmed with a combination of guilt and fear. He is guilt ridden to think that if he leaves her she will feel abandoned. He is sure he could cause a relapse or worse. He is also very intimidated that if she finds out he is dating someone else, even though they have not really been dating for over a year, she might become furious and seek revenge on him and the new girl. Finally, he is worried that if he does find a new girl to date, the new girl might be just as abusive and volatile as his current girlfriend. He is reluctant to date under these kinds of perceived threats. Better to stay with the demon he knows than to meet a new one. Better to stay lonely and alone than to feel responsible for tragedy and suffer the consequences.

I noticed myself having certain feelings in the countertransference. When Francisco told me stories about how this woman was so dominating and abusive to him, I found myself thinking, "What a victim, what a weakling. Boy, she really controls him." Also, I had the impression that he was holding back emotionally with me, waiting for me to set the tone, giving me the option to be the leader. I interpreted this idea of him giving me the power. Francisco responded, "I don't want to piss anyone off. I do anything to avoid conflict." This began a useful discussion of how he feels that we and all his other relationships are always on the brink of collapsing into conflict.

Some of this phantasy came out in interpersonal aspects of the transference. He told me, "I hope I used the waiting room switch the right way." I told him he must be scared that if it isn't the right way—my right way—then he is in trouble and our relationship has sprung a critical leak. He agreed and said he didn't want to hurt anyone's feelings, and he noticed himself "very stressed out always trying to figure out what people need or want." My impression of him waiting for me to tell him what to do with his life was validated when he told me how his last therapist "gave me pointers on dating and advice on how to make friends and leave a good impression."

As the analysis proceeded, I had to be careful in how I made my interpretations, as I could easily fall into this same trap of being his guide, telling him what to do and how to please me. I felt that it was important to interpret how he was prodding me to be a guiding parent who eventually took over and dominated him. Once I had become that, he felt guilty and scared about disappointing me.

Unfortunately, in making these types of interpretations, I was in fact doing that very thing! Francisco heard me as instructing him on the right and wrong way of being when I said, "You want me to take over and show you the way, so we don't have any conflict. You are scared of what will happen to both of us if you are more independent and outspoken."

In other words, he easily took my interpretation as advice to be more independent and outspoken, and by doing so, he could please me and avoid conflict. My interpretive direction was correct but also became washed into his particular projective identification–based transference. Therefore, I was frequently making interpretations and then having to interpret the way he was selectively using them to shape us in his mind.

We are always walking a line between correctly interpreting the patient's unconscious phantasies, selectively focusing on one aspect of the phantasy and avoiding another, or playing out a role within those phantasies. The outcome to our interpretive efforts is often a product of the patient's projective-identification process.

Over time, Francisco has settled into being "a watchful eye" over his tendency to be the slave in relationships. He comes to me now reporting his latest findings and the times when "I caught myself doing it again." On the one hand, this is helpful and productive. He is now using a more reflective observation of himself to change his patterns and slowly understand himself. It makes sense for me to accept his latest findings and help him explore them more. But again, this type of interpretive stance is also a collusion with his phantasy of needing to please me and make sure he isn't being a bad boy in my eyes. I interpret how his bringing me reports of how he has been bad turns him into a bully and turns me into a critical policeman watching over a guilty little boy trying desperately to please me by admitting his crimes. Francisco was on alert at all times, trying to be whatever he thought he needed to be to "get under the radar." Intellect, control, and rationalization were his conscious approaches to dealing with life.

In his analysis, we continue to explore how he still tries very hard to avoid any conflict and always adapt to those around him to make sure all of his objects are "ok and not pissed off." We have worked on this in the transference, where Francisco consistently tries to be my good, obedient little boy who tries as hard as he can to learn, change, and freely associate. He is quite skilled at controlling me and making me feel like I am getting exactly what I want or need. I have, at times, been tricked into thinking we are doing wonderful analytic work when in fact it was a bit of a Trojan horse, in which he sneaks in his real self, which he experiences as dangerous and bad, within the cloak of the best little therapeutic Boy Scout.

In the transference, Francisco makes everything into a logical report of facts, in which he is either succeeding or failing in his therapeutic goals. In his obsessive focus on how to fix himself, he becomes the facsimile of the perfect analytic patient. I interpret this, letting him know that I see his efforts to please me by being the perfect little boy, to win my praise and avoid my wrath. Francisco is very good at being this hard-working analytic patient, so I find myself coming close to agreeing with his punitive, demanding approach. In these moments of acting out through the interpretive countertransference, I end up essentially saying, "Yes. It's good you noticed yourself about to repeat your old behavior again. You caught yourself. We have got to keep a close eye on that bad boy side of you and help him to get in line!" It is also tricky, because when I confront him on this type of transference situation I am, on the one hand, correct in pointing out how he is trying to manipulate me and avoid my wrath. But, in making that interpretation, it also feeds into his transference phantasy of me now saying, "Hey! I caught you doing something bad and wrong. You had better change that and become the good little analytic boy that I want you to be."

Overall, as the treatment unfolds, I have been able to find my analytic balance and maintain a more healthy degree of interpretive contact with Francisco, even when he is deep into one of his obsessively factual reports on his current behavior at home or work. I will interpret, "is this

story for me, for your girlfriend, for your boss, or for you?" This more
balanced type of interpretation then opens up a moment for Francisco
to stop and consider his intention. Often, he is able to see that the story
is for me: a gift or a peace offering. Then, he is able to slow down and
consider what he really wants, which in turn creates a degree of anxiety,
conflict, and guilt. We are then back on track, examining and exploring
his phantasies and core internal struggles.

Recently, Francisco reported how when talking on the phone with
his girlfriend, she became abusive and told him how angry she was that
a mutual friend hadn't bothered to visit "when she really needed it."
She was cursing and very angry about it. Francisco, "doing it a totally
different way," told her she needed to calm down and not sound so angry when she talked with him. She told him to "fuck off" and hung up.
Francisco told me he was very proud that he was "able to tolerate" being
hung up on without immediately feeling guilty and trying to call her
back to apologize and make it his fault. He then told me how he later
called up this mutual friend and told her that she might want to call her,
since she was so upset.

In response, I interpreted that he fell prey to his guilt. He felt he had
to apologize, make her feel better, and hope she would take him back
under her wing after he made the outreach call to the mutual friend.
Francisco was silent for a bit and then said he agreed, but he added that
the time between "his victory and the call was way longer than usual."

On the one hand, I was right in my interpretation about his guilt and
wanting to make up to his girlfriend. But Francisco wanted to focus on
his victory for a while. I think this was legitimate but also served as a
defense against his self-blame for simply taking a bit longer before he
once again succumbed to his guilt and had to make up for it by running
errands for his angry girlfriend. I felt I was correct in my interpretation,
but in doing so I became part of his scolding superego. Yet if I merely
focused on the victory, I would be stroking him like a pleased parent,
much like the treatment he wants from his sadistic girlfriend. I tried to
interpret all of this, but it was a slow and complicated matter.

By and large, Francisco's analysis shows a gradual but progressive
movement forward. Yet, along the way, there is this zigzag of acting out
by both parties, a projective-identification system that creeps into the
interpretation process. However, we are plodding our way through it

and managing to find useful and insightful moments that seem to lead to change and growth.

CASE MATERIAL

Mike grew up as an only child in a very religious family. His parents went to church several times a week and often made reference to God in their day-to-day interaction with Mike. They stressed the importance of being a loyal follower to God. Mike's father was a fairly distant figure in his childhood. As an adult, Mike tries to get close to him by discussing business, the only thing his father seems to be interested in. His father runs a delicatessen and has always wanted Mike to join him in the venture. He wants Mike to lend him money for expansions or remodelings and hopes Mike will help him invest in opening a second location. Mike feels harassed by this but also very guilty about not doing what his father asks. He doesn't want to hurt his father's feelings, so he never tells his father about any major purchases, for fear of being scolded for "wasting his money" instead of pooling it with father.

In many ways, Mike has broken away from his father and pursued his own life. He is a successful architect and makes a great deal of money. However, his father thinks that this is "some kind of crazy upscale trend that won't survive the ups and downs of the market like a deli." I interpreted that Mike feels guilty for growing beyond his father and feeling stronger and more manly. He tries to hide his success and sabotages it in various ways, such as by getting into fights with his boss, or he punishes himself by working long, lonely, exhausting hours.

Growing up, Mike's mother was strict and controlling. He remembers longing to be close to her but always being afraid of her moods. She would "fly off the handle and beat me for minor infractions or just because she was having a bad day." Mike tried hard to please her but felt he failed when she would yell at him. His father rarely interceded. One of the main topics in Mike's analysis has been his desire to be with a woman but how his intense fear of not being "man enough eclipses that wish. If he is able to interact with women, he makes himself out to be just a friend, to avoid the fear of being too manly and aggressive.

He is also afraid of being rejected outright and humiliated. He imagines himself "just having his way with a woman" but then in reality becomes submissive and passive. Then, he sabotages the relationship in some way, ending up feeling "like a real loser." I have interpreted this same dynamic being alive in the transference.

Mike had taken a break in his analysis when he had to relocate to Paris for work. There, he found an apartment for well below the market price, "a real steal." He felt confident and victorious about it. This led to him actually decorating it, in contrast to his last apartment, where he slept on the floor and had no furniture except a kitchen table.

However, this prize of an apartment was the only bright spot in his time there, as he felt trapped in a miserable job with long hours and a difficult boss. He made no friends and rarely went out. Mike wanted to move back, as he missed me and his family, but he felt humiliated to admit it. He had envisioned the trip as him going off to the big city after separating from his family. He was all grown up now and his own man. Now, he felt he had to return with his tail between his legs.

Once back, we worked on all these issues, and Mike told me that he had managed to keep the lease on his apartment in Paris and have it paid for each month by his old company, which used it for visiting consultants and board members. Mike was happy that under that agreement he still had the key and the lease, which meant that he could visit Paris once or twice a year and have a free place to stay.

This all seemed like something Mike was proud of and felt like he had achieved with manly skill. But, like many aspects of his life, he also felt so guilty about it that he managed to find a way to make it complicated, frustrating, difficult, and even inaccessible.

In a recent session, Mike told me "how upset he was about his apartment situation." This was the projective-identification welcome mat. He had not said anything positive about the thing he valued, the apartment, in some time, and he was now starting to disguise it and present it as a failure instead of a victory. Unfortunately, I took the bait by listening and getting caught up in the details, which marked the beginning of my passive interpretive enactment.

Mike explained how a friend in Paris had suggested that they try to sublet the apartment to make extra money. This would, of course, be done behind the back of the company, but Mike had thought it was a potentially good idea, since he liked the idea of extra cash. However, his friend had become dominating and pushy about it and wanted to be in charge of the whole operation. They fought about the details, and Mike began to wonder if he should do it at all. He explained that he was now worried, because he had being using his friend to deliver the monthly payments and occasional forms to the landlord's office in Paris. If they were fighting and his friend refused to do that anymore, Mike wasn't sure how he would get the payments to the landlord without being found out to be an absentee lessee. If he mailed the monthly rent in, the landlord would be suspicious that it was coming from the United States. Mike described the details of this dilemma with a vengeance.

I became caught up in the whole story. I found myself off balance therapeutically when my comments focused on how he should maybe look into paying online, since there might be no trace of his address that way. Here, I was actively involved in interpretive acting out, promoting the enactment in my own way, adding to Mike's pathological phantasy state. Mike disagreed with that suggestion, arguing that the checks would still show the address of the home bank. We went back and forth about it, and after a while, I became frustrated and said, "Why do you have to put yourself through such agony, all for just a few days free room and board? This is a very high price to pay for that." Here, I was almost back on my analytic footing but then I again slipped off and added, "a hotel room would be cheaper." I switched from looking at the emotional and the symbolic to losing myself again in the concrete and literal.

Rightly so, Mike responded, "I hear you judging me and wanting to take away my thing that I feel good about, just like my parents seem to always do." I thought about his comment and replied, "I think you're right. What I said is a parental response to how messy, complicated, and troublesome you seem to describe the thing you actually feel very happy about. What I would like to say instead is that you are paying a very high emotional and financial price for your victory. I wonder why you can't just savor it in front of me without having to suffer or sabotage it?" Here, I was back on track.

Mike said, "It's like everything else. It's like my problem with women. I feel really guilty about anything that feels good. I think you or my parents will disapprove." Here, we were able to find our way back to his core phantasies, including these conflicts and fears regarding his object's disapproval over his victory. I said, "And you worry I won't understand or approve. I know you want me to approve and even be proud of your strength and manly ways. But I think you are afraid of my judgment and you feel guilty about the pleasure you have, so the way you end up telling me the story invites me to see it as a failure that I can judge. Sometimes, I take the bait. You must end up very anxious about sharing the joy this apartment brings and what that victory really means to you. Instead, I think you must feel you got away with something nasty and bad." Mike added, "And I should be punished for it!"

Now, we were on more solid clinical footing. Analytic contact was reestablished, and we were less influenced by acting out in the transference or in the interpretive field.

3

INTERPRETIVE ACTING OUT

Unavoidable and Sometimes Useful

THERE ARE MANY elements to consider when making an interpretation. One is the immediate transference situation. This is usually the
most useful road to take. However, whenever highlighting how the
patient appears to be using the analyst or the therapeutic relationship
in one particular manner, the analyst is also in danger of missing, ignoring, or minimizing other aspects of the transference that might be
as important or even more critical. In other words, one portion of the
patient's core conflict and phantasy life may be exposed while another
is more defended or withdrawn. So, often in choosing our interpretive
approach, we are accurate about one part of the patient's internal world
but missing another. Often, this is just the way it is. We can't expect to
be aware of all areas at all times. Our patient's phantasies are complex,
multilayered, and mutually contradicting visions of self and object that
shift and mutate. But, by trying continuously to be aware of what we
might be missing, there is less opportunity to collude with the patient's
defensive system in our interpretive efforts. Nevertheless, in making
interpretations, we invariably end up acting out a role in the patient's
pathological defense system, which is usually fueled by rigid and intense projective-identification dynamics.

Sandler (1976) was one of the first to point out how the analyst is
frequently pulled into realizing or acting out the patient's transference

phantasy. Ivey (2008) notes that enactments occur when the patient successfully recruits the analyst to feel and act in certain ways that will confirm their transference phantasy. I would add that confirming the phantasy may often be a simple repetition of prior object-relational struggles, but it can also be an attempt to create something new, a new object experience, not just a detour from old or current anxieties. In other words, motivations behind the projective identification–induced interpretive enactment can be quite varied. But the essential result is that the analyst is no longer functioning as an analyst; he or she is now part of the patient's inner stage of self and object relations.

Feldman (1997), Spillius (1992), and Steiner (2006) are among the many contemporary Kleinians who have explored this aspect of psycho-analytic work and have published their findings about how this unde-sirable yet inevitable process can be turned into something profitable to the treatment. Steiner (2006) defines interpretive enactments as verbal communications that transmit countertransference feelings and phantasies that are usually the response to transference and projective-identification pressures. The reason to try always to not engage in in-terpretive acting out is that it is a collusion with the patient's efforts to avoid and deny the pain, fear, guilt, and loss that they carry for them-selves and their objects. And the analyst may also be avoiding and de-nying the pain, fear, guilt, and loss they feel by being with the patient in the intimate and enduring experience that psychoanalysis provides. However, as this chapter will suggest, we can often recycle or mend something that seems broken or useless. That goes for both the patient's experiences and our own. In always trying to rebalance ourselves and learn from the interpretive mistakes that are eventually going to hap-pen, we also provide the patient with new perspectives of a fallible ob-ject that can forgive itself and work to rebuild itself, striving to learn and understand along the way.

Echoing my thoughts, Hinshelwood (2004, 1257) states:

Following Klein there is a view that the interpretative process aims at a modification of anxiety during the session, an accurate inter-pretation bringing about a reduction or change in affect which is palpable to the analyst. Second, Kleinian analysis emphasizes how the analyst is inevitably drawn into playing a part in the phantasy

activity of the analysand, and thus required to bring to conscious-
ness and formulate the role he enacted within the session. This
task dovetails with a conception of psychoanalysis as a joint learning activity aiming to produce new knowledge about the patient,
a third feature of contemporary Kleinian analysis which can be
traced back to Bion's notion of the K-link. The K-link itself becomes
a focus around which the dynamics of the session unfold, and it
can be resisted or attacked by the patient (and maybe the analyst).

The following case, an extensive write-up with a follow-up section,
will demonstrate the elusive nature of making interpretations. Clinically, we can be on target and helpful in our efforts but eventually also
end up participating in various enactments. By noticing these mistakes,
we can begin to sort out their origin, which is often a countertransference reaction to certain strong projections. By utilizing this information,
we can move toward making less-corrupted interpretations. As our interpretive efforts are less linked to acting out the patient's projections,
our interpretations become more helpful to the patient. In turn, the patient feels less anxiety and is less in need of utilizing projective identification so extensively to defend against his or her core anxieties. A
healthy and healing cycle is thus formed.

CASE MATERIAL

Beth came to see me after "things didn't work out with her other therapist." She told me that after seeing a therapist for two years and discussing her feelings about a man, Philip, who didn't want to make a full
commitment to being with her, the therapist told Beth "she should move
on, get a life, and forget that guy." Beth told me, "I realized that I had
gone to this therapist to try and resolve this messed-up relationship or
nonrelationship I have. I talked about it every week for two years, and
then she comes out and tells me what I should do. But it felt like that was
based on what *she* wanted me to do. Even though I know she was right,
I didn't like her trying to be like a friend and telling me what I should
do. From that moment onward, I knew this therapist was biased. It was
never the same. I think she must have gotten sick of me talking about

Philip and how he never wants to be with me. Also, there is this other woman that Philip seems to like more than me. I can't ever get her out of my mind. She's like the obstacle between me and him. She is this crazy, weird person who I think is madly in love with him, but he claims he only likes her as a good friend. Anyway, I always talked about how I was sure that in time, he would see the light and want to be in a fully committed relationship with me. But my therapist told me I was just fooling myself and that I should move on. I could see her point, but it didn't feel right. So, I stopped seeing her and here I am."

In the countertransference, I noticed myself thinking what a poor therapist this other person was and by how much she had missed the boat by not listening to the real story. The multiple aspects of Beth's conflict with this relationship had not been explored; instead, something became acted out in the therapeutic relationship. At the same time, I was aware that the particular way that Beth told me this story was part of a transference relationship in which she was, via projective identification, tugging on me to feel certain ways about her and her prior therapist. I tried to take these ideas and my feelings into account before making my next comment. In other words, I realized I could easily fall prey to siding totally with Beth and attacking her old therapist instead of trying to understand the underlying dynamics.

I asked, "You are hoping I will be able to listen better and accept you better without reacting or forcing my agenda on you?" Beth said, "Yes. I hope you will stay unbiased." All this was important information, as it gave me a reference point to watch out for in my countertransference. Indeed, in fairly short order, there were times in our sessions when I wanted to tell her to just move on, get a life, and stop dwelling and complaining about something she would never get in the end. But this countertransference reaction helped me understand something valuable about the internal struggles Beth was caught in.

If the countertransference is not acted out, it can provide vital clues to core conflicts that the patients are communicating in ways that are provocative but psychologically necessary at that time. Indeed, Beth was in the grips of feeling like she would never be able to reach the love of the object. Without it, she seemed to feel she would perish, so she hung in there and kept trying regardless of how hopeless it seemed. More than once I interpreted, "I am sure it is more complicated than just breaking up with him and moving own with your life." Beth exclaimed, "Exactly! I think I need learn how to live my own life better, but I have a lot of feelings that keep me where I am at." This seemed like a good sign: Beth was now reflecting on herself and her psychological issues.

However, she then added, "So, I am hoping you will tell me how to fix that." I was surprised at this turn in her way of relating. I interpreted, "Suddenly, you want me to be biased and tell you what to do. Maybe it's uncomfortable relating to me from your own identity. Maybe it's easier to slip into having me call the shots." Beth replied, "Damn, you're good. I know I do that. I don't want people to push me around, but I do easily fall into letting them." I added, "Letting them or even setting the stage for it, as you just did with me." Beth nodded and gave me the thumbs-up sign.

In the Kleinian approach, the therapeutic alliance is a result of engagement with the phantasy and transference as well as the interpretation of anxiety and defense. Here, by making helpful and balanced interpretations that addressed her core fears and defenses, she felt that I was able to understand and help her.

Beth was very polite and somewhat passive in the way she related to me. She was motivated to tell me everything that was on her mind, but she also needed me to ask her questions to prime the pump. I commented on this, and she said, "Well, I don't want to just say any old thing; you might think I am crazy or not following the rules." We explored this aspect of the transference and found she had phantasies regarding my reaction to her being more independent and having more of her own identity. Over time, we came to understand this as a way she felt she had to be passive and helpless in order to one day win my approval and love.

I interpreted that this meant she kept two versions of us alive in her mind. There was the meek and scared little girl who kept her feelings and needs to herself in order not to rock the boat while she waited to see if the superior object would one day notice her, appreciate her, and accept her. There was also the vision of us combined in a happy unity, where there was no conflict, she had the freedom to be herself, and I was accepting and understanding. This was the golden reward for all her waiting and suffering.

Sometimes, she would respond to my interpretations by saying, "Oh, you got me again. I need to pay more attention. I didn't even see that."

My interpretations were essentially accurate, but she used them to verify my role as a strict teacher and authority, whom she needed to please ahead of tending to herself. Sometimes, I fell into this by essentially telling her "it's ok, I'm not scolding you; I'm just making an observation." Here, I was falling into being a gentle, soothing father reassuring his scared little girl.

When Beth told me about her family history, I had a better understanding of what she might be trying to do with me in the transference and how she might be using her objects. Beth's grandparents lived in a remote Caribbean location. Her grandfather was a famous political figure and an extremely successful businessman. Both grandparents were very superstitious and regularly sought the counsel of local fortunetellers and mystics. After the birth of their first child, they consulted the mystics about the future of their new baby. They were told he would be a rich and powerful man and a positive influence on the family heritage. When they had their second child, Beth's mother, they also consulted the mystics. This time, they were told the child was a curse to the family and should be removed from the family after birth to minimize the risk. Specifically, they were told the child would cause sickness to the mother and financial ruin to the father. So, when Beth's mother was five, her family sent her away to relatives on another island. When she was ten years old, her parents took her back, because the relatives could not care for her anymore. Within a year of her return, the political climate in their country changed, drastically affecting Beth's grandfather's fortunes. His money was lost, and he was reduced to a managerial job that was an embarrassment to the entire family.

During the analysis, Beth eventually told me "she knew she needed to be honest if this therapy was going to work" and "confessed" that she was consulting psychics, asking them if Philip loved her. She was trying to keep the hope alive that Philip would transform himself from uncommitted and unavailable to focused and devoted. Beth was also hoping the other woman he seemed to be interested in was out of the picture.

I interpreted this situation, focusing on the elements I thought to be the foundation of her phantasies and internal conflicts. I interpreted that she longed for an ideal union with her distant object, but when I made my observations, she felt she was losing this ideal union. I brought her into an unbearable state of loss. By not being honest with me, she could keep her hope alive. I was put in the position as the one who kills the hope, leaving her abandoned and lost.

I interpreted that in the transference I was the harsh voice of reality, another obstacle that kept her from her beloved phantasy of transformed objects. I stopped her attempts to see if her broken, unavailable, distracted objects could be turned into focused, committed, caring ones. Beth could not look directly at her relationship with her boyfriend and see it for what it was: a disappointing, sad stalemate. It might change and become what she wanted if she waited and suffered enough. Beth did not want to face the loss, abandonment, and disappointment about what was really going on with Philip. Instead, she distracted herself by paying attention to the other woman. I commented that my voice of reality took that wish and hope away. Therefore, she didn't want to tell me about her feelings and instead spoke to the psychics, whom she hoped would tell her that her wishes were coming true. Finally, I pointed out that Beth wanted the psychics to tell her the other woman was bad and no longer in the picture, shipped away like Beth's mother was after the psychics said she was cursed.

While I think my interpretations were on target and helpful, I believe I was treading a fine line between being the helpful "voice of reason" and being a harsh "get it together and smell the coffee" voice of reality that ignored her deeper hurt and loss. In the projective identification–based transference, I think Beth was unsure if I was a helpful supportive object that she could count on permanently or a temporary figure that could easily shift into a rejecting punisher.

After Beth's grandfather lost his fortune, the family felt Beth's mother had led them into a life of shame. She was considered the outcast and lived under this shadow until she was eighteen, when she met a man whom she would marry a year later. Once married, Beth's mother had two daughters. From what Beth told me, her parents got along fairly well before she was born but that they started drifting apart soon after Beth's birth. I pointed out that Beth's unspoken belief was that she was a curse to them, much like Beth's mother had presumably been.

When Beth was five years old, she walked into her father's office and found him dressing up in women's clothes. Her father yelled at her to get out of the office, as if she had done something wrong. Over the next few years, her father would walk around the house wearing makeup and women's clothing as if nothing were odd about it. Beth also remembers her parents fighting and yelling more and more. During this time, her father was drinking to the point of being drunk almost everyday.

When describing her relationship with her mother, Beth told me, "I wanted to be able to go to my mother for comfort, but she was often more rejecting then my father. It felt like I could never do enough or that anything was ever good enough for her. She found fault with everything I did. I could play with my sister when I was really young. But, as we got older, she seemed to go her own way, so then I felt completely alone."

Beth told me that once she was nine or ten she "began realizing what was going on around the house much more clearly." Because of his alcoholism, her father lost several positions at his accounting firm before he was fired. He was then reduced to low-paying jobs as a contract worker to fill in when others were sick or on vacation. Beth said, "no one respected him anymore, and our family was filled with shame. We couldn't afford to stay on the island, so we moved to the States. My father found odd jobs with various firms but never really got back on his feet. When he was home, he was dressed up like a woman and was either drunk or walking around enraged and yelling at us. I felt like I could never be close to him. I kept waiting for him to change and be my father, but it never happened."

After Beth stopped crying, I pointed out that this resembled her current state with her boyfriend: waiting for him to change but feeling she could never be close to him. She agreed and said, "I don't like waiting, but I don't know what else to do." This sense of helplessness and lack of choice was part of her internal experience of herself and part of the transference.

Beth said she knew from age eight or nine that her mother was a drug addict and relied on the local doctor to supply her with pills, which she took every day. These were mostly narcotics, and she spent many days in bed, high on pills and "depressed about her marriage." This was "another way I could never rely on my parents or feel I could get close to them. My mother seemed to love her pills more than she loved me." Many of the analytic sessions were filled up with Beth's terrible sorrow, sense of betrayal, and loss over never "really having two normal parents who cared about their kids. They just cared about themselves."

In volunteering information about her family and upbringing, Beth presented two different feelings. One was pity and compassion for both her mother and father. The other central feeling was dread and disappointment. While she shifted from focusing on one and then the other, I had the consistent impression that she lived within both states much of the time.

When Beth was ready to move out of her home at age eighteen, feeling "she finally would be independent and not have to bend to whatever my parents' moods were," her mother committed suicide. Beth blamed herself, even though this was the result of her mother's lifelong depression and frustration with her marriage. In talking about her father, she also blamed herself. She said, "It was weird and strange. I always felt sorry for him and how he obviously didn't feel he had picked the right life for himself. We were a burden for him. He wanted a different life. I wish he had been able to find that for himself." In this way, Beth felt concern and sorrow for him but thought she had been part of what caused him to be so unhappy. She was convinced she brought him pain and frustration but never felt she could do anything to make it better.

At the same time, Beth felt "sad that I never had a normal father. My whole time growing up, all I would think about was why couldn't I have a normal father, not this angry, cross-dressing freak that made the family a hell on earth." Here, she felt more persecutory, angry, and hopeless feelings about being neglected and abused.

Beth told me, "I know my father loved me, and I could tell that because of how he treated me some of the time. But, overall, it was so far from what I wanted or needed." I interpreted that she was caught between several dreadful feelings. She had guilt for both her parents, in which she felt she caused them great grief. She felt sorry for them and wanted to heal them somehow.

She also felt the anxiety of the ultimate abandonment of her mother's depression and suicide combined with the threat of her father's rage. Also, I interpreted that she was caught in the guilt of being very angry about his cross-dressing and her anger at her mother's depression but also her feeling that she shouldn't lash out at such weak and broken individuals. Also, Beth seemed to feel that her anger had brought about their punishment and abandonment.

She responded, "Yes. You got it on target. All of it! And I was always in a state of terror from his combined drinking, his crazy paranoia, his cross-dressing, and his angry rage. I never knew when or why he would turn on me." She went on to describe her combined depressive and paranoid experience of him. "I always felt sorry for him and wanted to help him. But it was like feeding a starving wild animal and getting your arm torn off and eaten. He was that unpredictable. I never knew when this sad and troubled person would turn into the monster that pushed my mother to kill herself. I loved him, and he loved me, but it was in a way that was so twisted and insecure."

In the transference, some of these phantasies and memories took hold. When she was late to a session, she said nervously, "Sorry I'm late, but it's only five minutes." It was clear what she meant, so I interpreted, "you are trying to tell me or almost beg me, 'it is only five minutes, please don't punish me too much.' " I interpreted her fear of my anger and my rejection. In response, she went on to tell me how she is "always trying to please people and wanting to accommodate their needs but she ends up scared of failing and of what will happen." The fear of failure was the point when her phantasies shifted from very conflicted depressive concerns colored by paranoid anxieties to a more fundamental paranoid fear of reprisal and punishment.

This combined tangle of paranoid and depressive experiences surfaced in a rather profound way when she discussed her feelings about her father. In talking about her frustrations with her boyfriend and how she couldn't trust him to follow through or show her that he cared, Beth told me she can't ever get her hopes up for too long before they are dashed. I remarked that her initial hopes of finding a quick resolution to an "irritating boyfriend issue" had changed to her more intense sense of chaos and despair. She associated to, "I am so disappointed. I thought I had dealt with my father. Oh no! Not that again."

She continued, "I remember such sad and terrible times with my father. I remember when I was like ten or eleven years old and it was his birthday. I had helped my mother stock the refrigerator with all his favorite foods, and I had spent all day making decorations and cards for him. I dedicated myself to him that day because I loved him and wanted to show him love. I recall him coming home. He was in a terrible mood and started drinking and yelling. He ripped up all my decorations and threw everything out of the refrigerator onto the floor. I think he hit me too, but all I remember is running to my room and crying all night. I was terrified. No matter what I ever did, good or bad, he could turn into a monster." For Beth, even loving her father could make him upset and angry. Thus, love was linked to pain, fear, and suffering.

Here, I realized that even though my prior interpretations about her fear of me in regards to being five minutes late were accurate and helpful, I had missed another level of understanding. I had missed commenting on her love and loyalty to me and how in her mind she must have felt that love didn't seem to be enough to keep our relationship intact or allow me to forgive her for her lateness. I was on one side of an exploration but missed another side that was at that moment probably more germane. In doing this, I think I was slightly acting out the more fearful side of her conflicts and missing the more painful, sad side, which she tried to avoid most of all.

Beth's father died from complications from drinking when Beth was in her early twenties. She told me about his funeral. When she went to his home to pick out a suit for the burial services, she found a "handsome suit that he reserved for special events. When I saw him lying in the casket dressed in that, I broke down sobbing." In telling me this story, Beth was nearly hysterical with tears. She continued, "I realized that he finally looked like the father I always wanted. I finally had what I needed. He was a respectable-looking man with a calm look on his face. There was no women's clothing and no makeup. He was a man. He was my father." Beth paused and began sobbing even more, "But, now he was dead!" She explained that the tragic irony continued when she went back to his home to sort through a wardrobe of women's clothing, makeup kits, and a diary full of his angry ranting about how much he felt wronged by life and how he hated everyone around him. Beth said, "Reality hit, and it hit hard. This was who my father was, not the person in the casket."

One way that Beth's phantasies of harming the object and being harmed by the object combined in the transference was revealed in how much she withheld expressing her feelings to me. In relaying her stories about her upbringing, her troubled relationship with her boyfriend, or general matters about her day-to-day life, she tended to buffer, censor, or minimize the affective aspect of each story. Most of the time, this was an emotional cauterization of offensive, angry, needy, or assertive feelings. For example, she might be telling me about her frustrations with her boyfriend, some problems at work, or her memories of her family. But these were muted and lacked the full emotional stamp of her feelings and experiences. I interpreted that she wanted me to stand in as her guiding, empathic father who would finally be there for her and understand her. But I interpreted that this also meant she had to depend on me in a way that made her powerless and mute, relying on me to translate what she really meant and felt. This put her at a disadvantage, and she could never feel she was an equal that had the ability to find her own voice. I added that this way of relating to me was a repetition of how restricted and limited she felt with her father and of her current frustrating relationship with her boyfriend. In other words, she wanted me to tell her what to do and say, which initially might feel comforting and safe but soon would feel controlling and dominating.

Again, I think this was the right interpretive approach, but reviewing it, I also think I rushed Beth into growing up and being independent when she secretly wished just to be my little girl for a while. I was being a bit of a bully that way, possibly repeating her sense of not being able to depend on her mother or father as a little girl would. When I brought up these ideas later on, Beth told me, "it sounds like music to my ears to think of being that little girl who could sit on my father's lap without having to worry something bad would happen." She started to cry and said, "But something bad always did happen."

My ideas regarding the nature of my interpretive approach were validated in specific transference moments. I found Beth wanting me to reassure her that she was not harming me with her needs or making me angry by depending on me. She said, "You work so hard. You are always here when I come in." Her psychiatrist, who provided her with antidepressant medication, had an office in my suite. What she meant was that when she passed by my office every three months to see her psychiatrist for a prescription, she noticed that my lobby sign showed I was "in." I replied, "You must worry that you drain me and that I need rest from your needs. You care for me and are anxious that I might be hurt or angry with the way you need me." Beth said, "I do feel like that. Am I too much?" I said, "Let's talk about those feelings of me either being drained and hurt or being angry and resentful."

Beth was overwhelmed by grief, but it was unresolved grief stemming from the many emotional conflicts she felt in her corrupted and sometimes absent connection with her objects. When I noticed myself not very moved by her frequent sobbing, I was able to use my countertransference indifference to make a provisional interpretation to Beth about her sense of both loss and anger over her parents, which left her emotionally conflicted. She was sad and angry about the indifference they showed her despite the care she so desperately craved. Her sobbing was her desperation, and my indifference was her projected anger combined with her conviction of her parent's cold distance.

I also noticed that sometimes I was more interested in Beth's stories than in her affect. I realized that there was a triangular situation involving Beth, myself, and her history. Specially, I was more interested in the stories than I was in her; the stories were the obstacle between her and me. This repetition of her historical experience of always wanting to get to one or both of her parents and feeling it impossible to get through the obstacle of their desires (the drugs, the cross-dressing, the alcohol, the anger) and instead being left with their indifference was now a part of the transference and countertransference. Bit by bit, I was able to notice my feelings and phantasies and make interpretations that were more helpful to Beth. As a result, she was slowly able to re-own these unwanted psychological experiences and work though her conflicts about them.

This last matter is an example of my more successful interpretations and my avoidance of interpretive acting out. The countertransference was strong enough to effectively warn and inform me about the dangers ahead in the clinical moment. At the same time, the countertransference was not so strong as to pull me unwittingly into acting out and only notice it after the fact. Countertransference intensity is one of the many variables that can create interpretive acting out. If the countertransference disturbance is minimal, useful analytic contact can edge toward a disruptive condition but usually still remains intact, and the countertransference becomes a source of new knowledge and clues to the patient's otherwise unspoken desire. If the countertransference is too intense and uncontained, it can shift the analytic moment to a state in which the analyst acts out interpretively and later feels surprised, remorseful, and confused about how to find the way back to normal analytic contact. Of course, if the countertransference is subtle and minimal, the analyst may not notice anything amiss and drift comfortably and unwittingly into a pattern of interpretive enactment.

I noticed that Beth created triangulations with other objects, just like she had with me. This seemed to be a primitive Oedipal situation created by splitting, in which the other woman at work, the bad object, represented the obstacle to the ideal, good object (Philip), with which Beth wanted union. Beth always focused on the other woman, saying she "wanted her gone." I said that the woman symbolized the drugs her mother took and her father's cross-dressing, which were obstacles in the way to finding love and commitment from her parents and her boyfriend. She consulted psychics in the hope that the obstacles to finding love and soothing from her objects would be removed and that she would find a wonderful union with her objects. She would find care and satisfaction and finally be able to count on her objects.

My countertransference continued to guide the way, helping me both maintain my analytic focus and avoid interpretive acting out. I interpreted Beth's lifetime wish to have the unavailable object transform into the ideal, caring parent she longed for. But to reach this ideal, she had to strike a bargain in which she passively suffered with a broken, unavailable, or angry object while she waited and hoped for change. This projective-identification process included her subtle assault on me via her endless tales of missing her ex-boyfriend. Just like her last therapist, I ended up wanting to tell her to move on and quit whining. If I did this, however, I would shift into the angry, uncaring object. I interpreted that she hoped I could tolerate this projective-identification process and one day be transformed into the understanding, caring object instead. But, to achieve this, in the meantime she had to wait in pain and be a victim, all while giving me a taste of her anger and frustration.

Sometimes, I became a passive part of this process by acting out in the interpretive field. I would say things that simply went along with her stories of feeling frustrated. Instead of pointing out her masochistic stance, I would say something like, "You really miss your boyfriend and feel so lonely, just waiting and hoping. But, you feel he has a first choice before you, the other woman." While this was helpful from an empathic standpoint, I was also just rubbing salt into her phantasies about being helpless and lonely. In other words, I was confirming her phantasy of herself as worthless and second rate.

Other times, I more actively acted out. I said, "From how you describe him and the nature of your relationship with him, you probably could do better and would end up happier without him, but you aren't ready to take the risk." Now, on the one hand, I think I was accurate and helpful in pointing out her resistance to change, her anxiety, and her masochistic way of being in the world. But I was disregarding her internal conflict, fears, and her longing for a transformative experience with a disappointing object that might turn into a fulfilling, loving object. In this way, I became her disinterested father, ignoring her true needs and dismissing them as unimportant or weak. I told Beth to do what I thought best instead of being interested in what she thought, felt, and wanted.

Most of the time, I stayed on course, making balanced interpretations that were more in touch with Beth's overall emotional state. As I've mentioned, she really pulled for me to be a better parent than she remembered her father and mother to be. But I interpreted that this meant she had to be my inactive, helpless, and scared little girl, waiting for the time when, maybe, things would get better.

Examples of this transference phenomenon were abundant. Beth told me how she had been losing sleep for years because of her toilet running all the time. I felt a pull to step in and ask her why she didn't fix it and give herself a decent night's sleep. This would be the active form of interpretive acting out, in which I was the lecturing parent. When I did ask her in a less punitive way, focusing more on why she neglected herself so much, she responded by saying that she was worried the landlord would be angry, since she already paid such low rent. At this point, I detected a projective-identification pull on me to become the rescuing, caring parent who would stand up for her against the angry, uncaring landlord and provide her with an acceptable living situation. I interpreted that she wanted someone, me, to intervene for her and transform the unhappy situation into something better. But in the meantime, she had to be the passive victim who longed for a transformation but had to endure the lack of comfort until this magical moment occurred.

I interpreted her wish for me to be a certain way, her positioning herself between me and the landlord, and her bargain in having to be the victim waiting for the elimination of the obstacle to her desires. I thereby avoided the near pitfall of urging her to call the landlord, which would have been my interpretive acting out. Instead, I interpreted her desire for me to do that—and the potential fallout of doing that—which we came to understand as her punishment for asking for love and attention.

In exploring how she gave her power over to others in the hopes of being loved, Beth told me she hoped her "boyfriend" would one day decide he wanted to marry her and buy a home together. This was a part of her painful "on-hold" life, which had brought her in to see me. Again, she wanted change but also feared and resisted it. Beth began to tell me about how she was more able to "separate and draw some boundaries between myself and my disappointing boyfriend who was never really a boyfriend." In allowing herself to feel disappointed and take a stand for her own needs, Beth was making progress in separating from her phantasies of a broken, unavailable object for whom she was eternally waiting. Instead, she was now able to bear the thought of pursuing her own needs and obtaining what she wanted on her own, even if it meant saying goodbye to the disappointing object. This marked a significant move forward in her psychological growth and was a shift toward the healthy mourning over her prior disappointing and neglectful objects.

She also felt great guilt and a fear of rejection if she were to try to take care of herself. When I told her that I noticed how she was looking at houses for sale and was telling her boyfriend about it as if she was just sharing a story about finding a parking space, we talked about her desire for them to buy a place together but that she "didn't want to push the issue." After she finally discussed this with him and he said he wasn't ready for that type of commitment, she told him that she had started to look at other houses for sale and asked him "if it was ok for her to buy one as an investment for herself." He said, "of course." Beth told me how relieved she was, because she was sure that when he realized she was doing something for herself and being her own person, he "would drop me like a hot potato."

As a result of our working on this fear of rejection and punishment for taking care of herself, Beth was now able to enjoy the vision of "buying my own cozy home that I could call her own and be happy in, instead of being lonely in a broken-down shitbox of an apartment." She told me "I may not have Mr. X to keep me warm at night, but I will be ok. At least I have my little portable heater I can move into the bedroom."

I asked Beth what she meant about this small portable heater. She explained that her apartment heater had never worked, so she relied on a little space heater she moved from room to room. I told her I was pretty sure it is illegal to rent a dwelling without heat, so I was interested in why she would put herself through that sort of torture. Here, I was interpretively acting out by telling her it was illegal. This was a return to a stern, all-knowing parent who informed a naïve child of the proper ways of living. She told me, "I never thought about it much; I guess I'm used to being without. I think that's about my family, my past. I grew up having to be without, to be cold all the time emotionally." In investigating this, we discussed the same type of triangulation transference in which, via projective identification, she tried to enlist me as the rescuing, soothing parent who would stand up on her behalf against the unavailable, cold, and neglectful landlord/parent and help her remove the obstacle in the way of finding warmth and care.

Another example was later in the analysis, when Beth told me she had decided to "get rid of her old, broken-down television," which was "so blurry it was hard to tell what you were watching." She had endured this "piece of junk" for years, but now Beth decided she "deserved something that would give me pleasure." We discussed how her new, big television symbolized her new ability to throw away, grieve, and move past her former unavailable, disappointing, and broken objects and to not put obstacles in the way between her and her desires. Bit by bit we worked through these primitive Oedipal situations, which were part of the projective identification–based transferences that had activated my countertransference.

* * *

Jumping ahead to some six months later, some of the same issues remain, along with an evolution in her projective identification–based transference. One area of exploration has been around how she wants me and others to side with her against her adversaries. She won't refocus on herself and her own life until she feels that occurs. A frequent way this happens is when Beth becomes convinced that the other woman at work is up to no good and wants her coworkers, her boyfriend, and myself to side with her and "talk shit" about the other woman. If she feels that we do this for her, then she will simmer down and look at what she needs to do for herself and her own life. If she feels we don't, then she remains irritated and anxious. In the transference, this takes a particular form.

By setting up a story about this other woman in a certain evocative way, Beth pulls me into being on her side against her enemy. She will go on at length about the latest drama and I find myself interpreting her competitiveness, her persecutory anxiety, and her Oedipal fixation. I also make comments about how she wants me to understand how pushed aside she feels and wants me to come to her rescue to make it all better. I also interpret how she wants me to understand how difficult it was to tolerate her mother and how she wants me now to be a good, understanding father who comes in to straighten things out.

Now, I believe these interpretations were correct and indeed helpful. However, I neglected to realize that her stories were a controlling and defensive move that helped her avoid being with herself more and taking ownership of her own life. Indeed, she favored this Oedipal persecution state rather than spending time with her own success and independence. So, stepping out of this momentary interpretive enactment, in which I was shielding her from more disturbing internal conflicts, I interpreted that she was enlisting me in the fight against this other woman, and that gave us important information about her feelings and conflicts. But it also masked her anxiety about being alone with herself and feeling whole. I said, "You must picture yourself all alone without me in that place. If we fight together against your enemy and work on your anger and anxiety about her, you won't lose me. If you step out of the ring, you might feel lost and abandoned."

Beth told me, "I think you're right. I feel like something would collapse if I let go of the fight." Here, we were coming closer to usually well-hidden deeper phantasies and emotional states. Now, my interpretive line of investigation was more about this fear of collapse. It better matched her immediate state of mind than my first line of interpretation, which was correct in one way but also a colluding acting out that arose out of her defensive projections. Both produced helpful results, but one was more about the central phantasy that left Beth so disconnected to life; the other was a strong but secondary conflict. Since my first lines of interpretation were part of her defensive projections, they were not *as* healing or integrative as my comments about her "collapse." Just as every transference move is not completely defensive, not all enactments are completely destructive or useless. Often, much of what happens on both sides, to the patient and the analyst, is a complicated mix of defensive maneuvers and direct engagement with core psychological issues. The patient and the analyst are often lagging behind or rushing ahead in their efforts, but hopefully we find our way back to the main path more often times than not and stay on course. Interpretively, this course is bound to be crooked and lurching but hopefully consistently pointed in the right direction.

Over the course of the next several months, I tried to focus on this "collapse" phantasy. I interpreted that she wanted me and others to side with her deeper laments, fears, and anger over her parents, whom she now projected on me and others. I interpreted that unless I step up and tell her that her parents were wrong in how they treated her, tell her the girl at work is bad, and tell her that her boyfriend should treat her better, she will not grow up or own her own life. In other words, I was focusing on this rebellious little child saying, "I won't grow up until everyone admits how bad they treat me. I will sit here and do nothing until you give me that!" Beth replied, "Absolutely. But even then I won't believe you, and I still won't grow up!" I responded, "I guess you want it from the horse's mouth: a direct apology from your mother and father." Beth was quiet and then said, "yes, but it's too late. They're dead," and broke into tears. Here, she was beginning to face the loss and mourning that she usually shunned. My interpretations at this point were more on target, with much less acting out by Beth in the transference or by me in my interpretive stance.

Over time, the core dynamics we worked on shifted, and the projective identification evolved once more. At times, I was again pulled into interpretive collusions. In a recent session, Beth told me she was glad to be back from her vacation and was proud of how she is "less tangled up in noticing the other woman and less into racing around in my head about her motives and what she might be up to." Beth offered many examples of this success. I found myself making interpretations about the transference, in which I commented about her being happy to see me again and bringing gifts of her successes to share as well as wanting me to understand the difficulty she has separating herself from this feeling of the other woman blocking her. I made interpretations about envy, Oedipal conflict, competition, and persecution. Finally, I pointed out how she wants me to be proud of her, like a father who could be aware of her needs and achievements instead of his own narcissistic chaos.

All of these interpretations felt right, and, judging from Beth's responses and associations, they were helpful and produced therapeutic progress. We were exploring and working on important emotional material. However, I noticed that we were still very much involved with this other woman, given the amount of energy we spent talking about how Beth wasn't involved with her and wasn't thinking about her anymore. I pointed out that we were in fact still obsessed with her, but these interpretations, while correct and helpful, also had an element of defensive detour in them. I began to realize that through projective identification, I was colluding with Beth to focus on one area of her issues to avoid another area of greater importance and greater anxiety.

I noted that this same process had occurred in Beth's story about her coworkers. When her coworkers had asked Beth if she had a good time at the recent company picnic, Beth thought they meant "how did you cope with being around the other woman at the picnic," so she was very quick to tell them she "was no longer involved with that bitch and had no reason to be discussing her. She's not worth the mental bandwidth." With me, she very casually and discreetly mentioned that she had attended the picnic with her boyfriend, and afterward they had spent the night together. But then she quickly went on to talk about the other woman and her recent frustrations about her.

I made interpretations about how she put her drama in front of me so I would overlook her pleasure and success. Beth told me, "you're right. I try and stay with the other stuff, the drama and the craziness. It feels strange to tell you about the good times I am having and the peace and quiet." I said, "Maybe you would feel lonely and out of touch with me and others if you focus more on your own needs and pleasure. It's like you're drifting away without me, all alone. The chaos is a way to stay in touch with me."

Here, I was thinking of her need to control me and others as a method of being attached, to avoid abandonment. I think I chose this more paranoid-schizoid line of exploration because of her previous feelings and phantasies regarding the persecutory woman at work and her retaliatory attacks on her. That was the immediate emotional climate at that moment, but here I had fallen behind a bit. Beth was now within much more of a depressive crisis. She revealed this in saying, "it isn't that I will be all alone. I think I have to focus on my parents all the time in my head. If I don't keep going round and round with them in their crazy state, they will collapse. My mother will kill herself, and my father will have an emotional breakdown." At this point, Beth began to cry. She said, "this was confirmed when I was eighteen and I disagreed with my mother and told her we should move and start a better life. I went off to college at the same time, leaving her for the first time. I was unhappy with the way our lives were going, and I told her so. The next day she killed herself." Beth was quiet and sobbed for several minutes.

For the rest of that session and the next few sessions, we explored these phantasies and fears. We discussed and I interpreted how she needed to use a third object, the woman at work or other people and issues, to focus on, in order to save the second object from collapse. I pointed out that she, as the first object, was then tied to the constantly chaotic third in order to preserve the safety of the second, but this meant she could never feel attached to the second, since she had to always stay focused on the third. To say it another way, it was dangerous to concentrate on her pleasure and her needs because that could cause the collapse of that object and leave her forever alone.

Indeed, Beth clarified this when she said, "I will be punished if I concentrate too much on me and not enough on you." Here, I was on target interpretively, without much interference from my own countertransference or her projections, and Beth was in tune with her deeper conflicts and able to share them without much defensive posturing or retreat. We were working through her unconscious phantasies.

The next session she came in and said a few things before sheepishly asking me if we could change the time we met on one day. She explained that she had a work meeting at that time and it "would be much more convenient if I could make the meeting. Would that be ok?" I told her I thought we might be able to make that change but that I was very interested in how she was feeling about asking me. This led to a productive exploration of how she had worried about asking me, because "she didn't want to put me out, but her manager had told her she needed to make the meeting from now on. So, I guess I don't want to disappoint either one of you. If I am too pushy, who knows what will happen." At that moment, I felt that her immediate anxiety was more on the side of disappointing and hurting, so I chose to lead with that. I interpreted that she was trying to prop up both mother and father (me and the manager) to avoid our collapse. In doing so, she was now caught in the middle and had to sacrifice her needs to make sure we were not hurt or killed. Here, we were working through this pre-Oedipal triangular funeral or her desperate effort to prevent one.

Next, I took up the other side of her comments. Beth said she didn't know what might happen if she was too pushy. I turned to her sense of aggression. "You said you could be too pushy, like you will overwhelm me and be a bully." Beth replied, "I just think my expectations are too high. Maybe, I just want too much, and that will make me seem like a bully." She went on about this for a while, and I interpreted, "you are worried you are too aggressive and hungry. If you feel you demand too much or expect so much, then it makes sense you worry I will get hurt in the process. So the more you want something, the more you see me in danger. Then, you probably try to deny whatever you want to save me, but that leaves you hungry and empty." She said, "That fits pretty well. I don't want to be empty, but I don't want to hurt you either." Here was another core dilemma for Beth, and my interpretations were in line with them at that clinical juncture. I added, "We are starting to see how you end up putting yourself in the middle of two angry and hurt people and then feel guilty, anxious, and scared. You try to control, fix, and please, but it never really works. It just leaves you scared and alone. But to change that means you have to face the power of your own identity and face the loss of people not being exactly the way you want them to be." She said, "That is what I want, but it feels like we have a way to go!"

Today, Beth is still working hard to understand, accept, and change many of her internal feelings and phantasies regarding herself and her objects. She has made remarkable progress and no longer sees herself in the same narrow and confining manner. Nor does she feel as captured and weakened by the historical links to her parents and her deep and painful disappointments with them. Finally, she is much less inclined to wait for a lacking, rejecting, or unavailable object to finally notice her and transform into a loving, caring object that is committed to her. Beth is now able to accept that she lost out on fundamental important experiences with her family but that she can still find strong, meaningful bonds with others to share reciprocal, rewarding relationships with.

Her initial Oedipal phantasies were strong and drew me to make interpretations directed toward those elements of her phantasies. These interpretations were helpful and healing but also not fully comprehensive. Later, I was able to see the need for other interpretations that focused more on pre-Oedipal anxieties related to loss, aggression, and primitive guilt. Her fear of the object's "collapse" and her plight of being alone without any object at all—except perhaps a crippled or dead object that shifts into a vengeful, angry ghost demanding revenge and threatening abandonment—were phantasies that left Beth convinced that passivity, helplessness, and secret masochistic manipulations were her only choices. We are now working our way through and past these internal conflicts.

4

ENACTMENTS, INTERACTIONS,
AND INTERPRETATIONS

BIRD (1972) HAS established that the transference is present in the analytic setting from the beginning. The analyst may or may not be aware of it, but the transference is alive at all times, shaping both the patient's view of and relationship to the analyst and the analysis. Waska (2004, 2005, 2006) has noted that projective identification is often the core element of many transference states, and thus it is present from the beginning of the treatment up to the last moment of termination. Therefore, there is an important technical interplay between projective identification and analytic contact. The role that projective identification takes in a particular analysis, the manner in which the patient relies on this dynamic, and the way that the analyst interprets it influences the growth or decline of analytic contact.

Numerous analysts have established that projective identification is a constant pressure and influence on the external object of the analyst (Joseph 1989; Segal 1973; Spillius 1988; Young 2006), and, therefore, it plays a major role in shaping the therapeutic relationship and the quality of analytic contact. Unless it is noticed, understood, and interpreted, there will always be some degree of acting out of unconscious material from both parties. Thus, it is to be expected that every analytic moment can be a potential acting out by and between both parties as well as a potential opportunity for interpretation, working through, growth, and change. Transformation always includes repetition, and psychological shift always comes out of an echo of the past. Phantasy and reality coexist, as do the external and internal.

Sometimes, there is a misunderstanding of what Kleinians mean by the clinical term projective identification. Mitchell (1995, 80) illustrates this misconception of Klein's early thinking when he states:

> The patient, in the deepest recesses of his unconscious, imagines a profound form of interaction between himself and others. It is crucial to remember that for Klein the interaction never actually takes place, it is fantasized. Projective identification is a defense mechanism like any other defense mechanism; it takes place in the mind of the patient, and the analyst discerns its presence by discovering its workings within the patient's associations.

In recalling her supervision with Melanie Klein, Hanna Segal (2001) pointed out that Klein always envisioned phantasy interacting with the environment. Segal states, "I emphasize in my work, following Klein, that the work is trying to see the interaction (between reality and phantasy). There is no such thing as pure phantasy."

When Mitchell continues examining projective identification from his theoretical perspective, he does eventually arrive at a more accurate overview of the Kleinian concept. Unfortunately, he never ends up giving Klein herself due credit. He writes:

> It was a short step, however, from projective identification as a fantasy of interaction to projective identification as an actual form of interaction. The focus was still on uncovering the deepest contents of the patient's mind, but, with the interpersonalization of the concept of projective identification, the contents of the patient's mind were now often to be found in the analyst's experience. This step was accomplished in the work of Bion and other of Klein's analytic descendants, and it has developed, in the past few decades, into one of the most powerful and fascinating tools for the study of interaction in the analytic situation. The interpersonalization of projective identification moved the Kleinian approach directly into a study of the interaction between analysand and analyst; the framework became dyadic.

(Mitchell 1995, 80)

Mitchell seems to want to make the interpersonal aspect of projective identification his discovery. However, Melanie Klein and her current followers, including the author of this book, have always viewed projective identification as having an interpersonal aspect, which, in fact, is frequently the core element of the transference↔countertransference situation.

Stein (1990) has described the basic elements that distinguish between Melanie Klein's intrapsychic positions. The paranoid-schizoid position (Klein 1946) embodies the fear for the survival of the self against persecutors and a primitive sense of guilt that produces fear of revenge from the object. Loss of the object and feelings of guilt for harming innocent objects highlight the depressive position (Klein 1935). Waska (2002, 2004, 2005, 2006) has rigorously examined the nature of patients who are psychologically caught in both arenas, struggling within a state of persecutory loss. Each of these three internal experiences—that is, Klein's two positions and the state of persecutory loss—is fundamental for the type of projective-identification situations outlined in this chapter. The intensity of such phantasies is often so great that the patient is unwilling, at least initially, to engage with the analyst in exploring it. Rather, they do their best to position the phantasies within the analyst, having the analyst take them for either temporary safekeeping or permanent entombment. The strong efforts at orphaning these unthinkable phantasies and feelings often bring the analyst into some degree of acting out of the discharged aspects of personality. Unless interrupted by regular interpretations that focus on both the transference and the nature of these unclaimed phantasies, analytic contact is difficult to establish, and the patient is usually unable to make significant change or find true self-acceptance.

These types of difficult analytic situations are often held within the global grip of the patient's intense reliance on projective identification as a method of survival in what they experience as a hostile and confusing world. Projective identification has a rich history in the Kleinian theory and practice of psychoanalysis (Waska 2004). In this chapter, case material will be used to show that when patients go beyond the use of projective dynamics for communication, learning, and empathy, certain provocative, manipulative, and seductive interpersonal dynamics emerge. When anxiety and aggression dominate the patient's phantasy life and when intense internal conflicts shape their intrapsychic world, interpersonal acting out often emerges. In other words, external interactions with the object are colored by the intense internal interactions with various phantasy objects.

Steiner (2000) has outlined certain aspects that occur within the transference, when projective identification holds sway over the relationship. He notes that the reception of certain projections can provoke action on the part of the analyst, either in defense or in retaliation. I would add that sometimes the analyst reacts under the illusion or justification of love, guidance, or even the setting of limits. When the analyst is able to avoid "excessive action" (Steiner 2000) and instead is able to utilize his normal capacity to feel and think, he is in the therapeutic position to decipher what the patient is trying to do in his or her projective stance. If the analyst can gradually find meaning in the projective web within which he finds himself, he can use interpretation to facilitate some degree of integration to the discarded fragments of the patient's mind. What was before an orphaned phantasy, something unbearable that must be gotten rid of at any cost, can now be assimilated and integrated as a healthy and helpful part of the patient's inner life.

This chapter will take a Kleinian perspective in examining patients who are often lodged between the paranoid-schizoid and depressive positions (Schafer 1994). They are captured by painful and frightening phantasies involving persecution, guilt, loss, anger, and anxiety. The following cases and the group of patients that they represent involve borderline pathology of some degree, with both paranoid and depressive transference states. Steiner (1979) discusses that the analyst's difficulty with such patients includes the formidable task of containing intense projective-identification dynamics, that is, shouldering the symbolic function for the patient until he is capable or willing to internalize his orphaned and expelled object-relational phantasies.

CASE 1

Susan worked in a doctor's office but longed to find a career in the music industry. She played several instruments and enjoyed songwriting. She described her life as "a list of empty relationships and boring jobs," which left her feeling "empty and helpless in her march through every-day life." She came to see me to address a lifelong feeling of "not know-ing what to do or how to get from A to B." Susan told me she grew up with a mother who not only told her what to do all the time but literally did everything for her. Far beyond the age when she needed help with get-ting dressed, organizing her room, or doing her homework, her mother would still do it for her or, at the very least, tell her how to do it, every step of the way. In the analytic treatment, Susan explored how this forced dependence and what she felt was a "complete lack of an independent or encouraging role model from her father" left her to experience life as an "empty path devoid of direction." Indeed, over time, Susan acted very directionless, hopeless, and helpless with me. Bit by bit, this left me feel-ing uneasy and sorry for her. I felt the urge to step in, tell her what to do, and show her how to find direction in her life. Fortunately, I noticed my discomfort and even pity for Susan and stopped short of becoming another mother who did everything for her. Instead, I began to interpret this aspect of the transference and the projective-identification inter-action into which she seemed to draw us. This gradually led to fruitful explorations of her phantasy conflict: she wanted the security and close-ness of depending on me to show her the way and guide her through life. But this sort of dependence and the forgoing of her own autonomy also meant that she had to endure the empty, hopeless state she was so used to suffering from. I interpreted this bittersweet compromise or bargain she had created for herself and for us. Gradually, we were able to use this focus as a map from which to work from and move toward change and integration.

CASE 2

Erik, in his first session, presented himself as a very agreeable, moti-vated man who wanted help in understanding his inability to manage his anger. At our first session, I was running late by approximately four minutes. Erik knocked on the door very softly. I opened it, and he said, "I am here for my six o'clock session, and I don't know what to do." I asked him to come in. He told me about himself in a very articulate manner, outlining his own insights and ideas about his recent struggles with his temper and his lifelong passivity, which he traced to living with his volatile, angry father, who wanted everything his way. At the end of the session, I thought Erik's would be an interesting case, one involving someone who wanted to look into the deeper meanings of his problem. It felt promising; we would be an effective team, working together to find answers and create change.

At the exact minute our next session was due to begin, as I was about to open the door connecting my office to the waiting room, Erik knocked in an aggressive, loud manner. I noticed myself wanting to scold him and to lay down the rules about how he should behave in my waiting room. I had the urge to act like a dominating father. I pointed out that he seemed to be taking a different sort of approach this time. He quickly said he was "just practicing being assertive" and then launched into telling me how he was now "ready to hear what you think is wrong, what your assessment is, and what your plan of action will be!" He went on like this for a bit, reiterating this demand for immediate answers and fixes. I felt the urge to put him in his place, as his father possibly had. For a moment, I found myself defensively telling him he "wanted me to spit out an instant formula, like he had put a quarter into the machine and was expecting his magical solution to pop out." I then regained my analytic balance and began interpreting what appeared to be his aggressive demand and his devaluation of everything we had done so far. I said, "You say you want the answer now, as if we hadn't spoken before. Your demand cuts off the helpful discussion we had last time, which opened a road to eventually finding your solutions." I also pointed out that when he displayed this demanding temper with me, he saw it as merely being "assertive and proactive in recovery." We were able to explore his fluctuation between passive and aggressive and how his role as dutiful son/patient and mine as authority/father in the first session had now switched, with him as the dominating father and me as the son under pressure to perform and please. This case, which was only just unfolding, already showed projective identification as the possible core of Erik's transference. He is acting out his splitting and projective phantasy, and although I am noticing his invitation to join the party, I am mostly able to keep my therapeutic balance, observing and investigating, gradually interpreting and translating his conflictual phantasy state.

CASE 3

Danny, a diabetic in analytic treatment for over three years, came late to a recent session. In the matter of ten minutes, he managed to tell me that he had forgotten to take his insulin; overslept through a lunch date with his new girlfriend; neglected to turn in his project at work, which meant that he might be put on temporary probation status; and that he had almost been ready to go to the gym last night but had ended up staying home and watching television instead, but that he felt bad about that, as it had been over a month or two since he had worked out. For Danny, this is a not uncommon type of announcement. Throughout his treatment, he has consistently done issued catalogues of his misbehaviors, and, early on, I was guilty of acting out the roles of disapproving parent, the parent with advice on how he could take better care of himself, and the parent who holds his tongue while junior runs amok. Over the years, I have been able to catch myself and come to an understanding of the dynamic that colors our relationship. We have made significant progress in grasping the unconscious motivations behind this projective identification–based transference↔countertransference interaction. In this particular example, we were quickly able to notice the return of this invitation to judge, criticize, and educate as part of Danny's desire for a particular form of pathological parenting (Waska 2007). Danny looks for the comfort of depending on my common sense and guidance but pays the price of being eternally naïve, dependent, and weak. As the treatment continued, we discovered that his vision of equality and mutual interdependency amounted to a frightening mix of intimacy, love, lack of control, persecution, and loss. Over our three years together, we have only been able to reach this level of analytic progress and psychological growth by accepting and examining the rather consistent level of projective identification–based acting out that we both fall into.

CASE 4

With Marsha, there were certainly projective-identification processes at play. But they lacked much interpersonal acting out, making them much harder to notice. As I did not detect any major form of countertransference in myself most of the time, I lacked any red flags to guide me. What clued me in was by simply looking, as an analyst always is, for any parallel process in the therapeutic relationship that mirrored the patient's material and associations.

An example of this more subtle form of enactment, which I believe to be always present until found and worked with, involved one session in the second year of Marsha's analytic treatment. Marsha was exploring her history of always feeling guilty about being happy, especially when she imagines her object to be in pain or less than happy in any way as a result. She was doing an excellent job of examining and exploring how she tries to magically fix and please her object but, upon failing to do so, puts herself down instead. In this second method of controlling her internal world, Marsha believes that, through her pain and suffering, the object will feel better and not blame her for being happy. As she spoke about these feelings and thoughts, she mentioned how she sees me as also needing her magical rescue and healing and how she is "now painfully able to not do that as much as before and instead take the risk that we are both going to be ok."

This was genuine analytic progress. However, I also realized that Marsha was consistently critical about this progress, saying, "well, I now understand X, Y, or Z. But why haven't I fixed it yet? I'm really slow about how I work on this stuff, just like I plod along at work." It took me a few moments of being a passive participant in this devaluation before I was able to interpret how she was uncomfortable to be feeling proud and happy in front of me with her new insights and growth. I interpreted that she had to denigrate herself because she was unable to find anything to fix in me. In this way, we were able to examine and work through how Marsha was able to make progress in her phantasies and conflicts but by doing so felt compelled act them out with me in the very same moment. Her acting out and my passive participation was subtle but still an example of how ubiquitous projective identification is and how frequently it is the master of the transference↔countertransference situation until both parties can notice and work with it.

CASE 5

Betty was a woman in her thirties. She had married at sixteen and had a daughter shortly after. When her daughter was ten years old, Betty visited the United States and decided to move there. She left her child in Europe, with her family. I was struck by how lacking in emotion she was about it. When I pointed that out, she assured me that her family was very loving and that she felt confident that they could give her child a much better upbringing and more financial security than she could. Betty said, "I had ten good years raising her. I miss her sometimes, but I know she is happy and taken care of." In Europe, Betty had worked as a dancer at a ballet company. She initially hoped to pursue that career in the United States. She had done quite well in the company but had never achieved any major status. In fact, Betty was so exacting and demanding of herself that, had she not emigrated, the company director would have fired her. Rather than simply following the required routines of the company, Betty had established her own strict notion of how and when she should train and how certain dances ought to be executed. She told me she was "just trying to do a good job and push herself to be the best dancer she could be, but the director didn't see it that way. He thought I was being difficult and strange, not being a team player."

Betty ended up working at her local post office once she moved to the United States and never did much to pursue her dance career. She felt aimless and confused, "not knowing what direction to take or if anything really had meaning. The idea of failure seems so close." The more we discussed this area of her life, the more I had the impression that Betty had never really felt connected to dancing. Instead, it was the arena for intense phantasies of control, perfection, and self-judgment. Once Betty felt that she had failed at dancing, she quickly moved on to other career possibilities, not ones of personal interest but ones she thought she could be perfect at. What we discovered, over many months of analytic exploration, was that there was always a moment in time when she was genuinely interested and excited about a new direction or idea, but that would rapidly be extinguished by her demands for success and then her dread of failure. The post office job served as a place to pay the bills while she obsessed about what her "proper career choice" would be.

When I asked her what the proper choice would be, Betty said she wanted to do something that "made a difference" and that would "provide her with a way to excel." I interpreted that it seemed like "excelling" meant a self-imposed trap, in which she never did enough to please others or satisfy herself. This demanding phantasy quickly became a major piece of the transference as well. Betty was very anxious when she asked me what she should call me: "Doctor," "Doctor Waska," or "Doctor Robert Waska." I asked her to tell me about her immediate thoughts and feelings and she told me, "well, I want to be respectful, but I'm not clear what the proper title would be. I want to make sure I do the right thing." Hearing this, I perceived a dual anxiety regarding persecution and intimacy. Trying to address the leading edge of that anxiety, I said, "It sounds like you feel afraid there could be trouble between us if you don't do the right thing." Betty replied, "I don't want to do the wrong thing and make you think I am uncaring or rude." I said, "So, you could hurt my feelings by not doing it right." "Exactly," she answered. "If I don't show you I really care, you might not want to waste your time with me." I interpreted, "so, if you don't find the perfect way to relate to me, I would be hurt and retaliate by rejecting you." Betty said, "of course." This type of do-or-die phantasy plagued her in most aspects of life and certainly shaped the ongoing transference situation.

Next, I interpreted, "you are caught between several formal ways of addressing me. I wonder if that shows us that you are uncomfortable feeling closer with me and therefore need to keep a strict distance." Betty said, "I want to keep things neutral and to not have us get into any 'iffy' situations." Noting that the tone of what she was saying seemed to imply a fear of intimacy, I said, "Being in this room alone with a man makes you feel like things could easily become iffy?" She replied, "Every time I have ever tried to have a relationship with a man, it ended up being more than I really wanted. It gets too serious and intimate. I don't want that to happen here. I don't want you to be one of the guys." I suggested that unless she kept things under tight control and felt successful at doing things the "proper way," our relationship could easily sour, she could lose control, and one of us would act improper. Betty said, "You summarized my life right there!"

This exacting and demanding outlook was the treacherous way that Betty tried to gain closeness, acceptance, and care from me. However, this was part of a projective-identification dynamic that alternated with another phantasy. Betty also saw me as an object not to get too close to, because of her ideas of seduction, persecution, and lack of control. Britton (1999) argues that borderline cases differ from cases of hysteria because of the former's focus on knowledge rather than love. I believe that there are patients, like Betty, who struggle with a combination of these conflicts, constantly being pulled by phantasies involving the loss of love and the quest for knowledge of their object as well as by the fear of intimacy and the defensive need to never know about themselves or their objects. An example of this overlap is my projective identification–induced countertransference with Betty. I felt both controlled and constrained by her need to know and need to be right but also important and special, from her need to please me.

Steiner (1979) has outlined how the borderline patient feels fundamentally rejected by his or her object and relentlessly searches out ways to regain this basic bond. This can emerge as a demanding transference, as the need to know answers before ever learning about a problem, or as a more narcissistic approach, in which others are seen as not providing what the patient feels he is entitled to. In this last situation, the patient who feels rejected and then entitled suspects that the analyst is deliberately making him suffer by having to learn and think on his own, without the analyst doing all the dirty work for him. Often, regaining this sacred space with the idealized maternal object is seen as contingent on pleasing the object or at least not causing trouble of any sort. This creates a very polite, independent, or distant transference that avoids any issues of substance that could become messy. Also, separations of any sort are experienced as unbearable and often seen as retribution, revenge, and sometimes warranted, given how inferior the patient sees himself.

These same patients will react intensely when they feel that they have succeeded in their demands. They believe they have become arrogant, greedy, or overbearing and dread the consequences of having harmed or angered their object. They may also feel that the closeness that they have finally achieved is suddenly too much, seeing it as cast upon them by their object. They then flee from this imposed intimacy and forced knowledge. Change is seen as something that is being demanded of them, even though they were the ones demanding answers and growth a minute before. The persecutor becomes the persecuted; the guilty party becomes the judge. They feel trapped and as if they are a puppet of the analyst, who wants to control them. Without the knowledge, intimacy, and power of the analyst, these patients feel empty, cold, and despairing, overtaken by loss, persecution, guilt, and anxiety. Once they have access to their desired object, they become overwhelmed and need to escape its confinement, seeking independence and freedom. Only then does the cycle repeat itself. Betty was a patient who clearly fit most of these demand↔retreat criteria, both with herself and her objects.

Throughout the treatment, Betty pulled me into a variety of projective-identification cycles. One variation had to do with her setting up situations in which her dread of my judgment and criticism came to pass. One example occurred early in the treatment. After we spent the session discussing several important points and arriving at a few helpful insights, she stood up to leave and asked, "So, do you have any assignments for me?" Feeling a bit irritated by what seemed to be a dismissal or devaluation of the work we had just completed, I replied, "We're not in school, so I don't have homework to give you. I will see you next time to continue exploring things." Immediately, I became aware of several things. During the session, we had been discussing her experience of her father as rigid, demanding, and controlling. Now, as she was leaving, she seemed to place a demand on me that felt controlling, and she was also asking me to become a rigid teacher-father who handed out assignments. By not giving her an assignment, I let her down, and she felt rejected. My stern, sarcastic remark probably made her feel chastised as well. But, had I given her an assignment, I would have infantilized her and made myself into a powerful, controlling father. Fortunately, we were able to explore this successfully during the next session, but it was interesting to realize how quickly I took the bait when Betty offered it. Since that is not my way of reacting to all patients, I believe it had more to do with the particular projective-identification dynamic that she en-

listed me into: she attempted to construct a one-up-one-down relationship in which she could feel inferior to and like she was failing to please
the object.

Another example occurred when Betty told me that she had learned
that her insurance company would give her several free sessions if she
had a new problem, one different from what she came into treatment
for, but for this to happen I would have to tell the insurance company
that Betty had suddenly developed a new condition. Betty said, "this
would be great, because money is tight right now and I'd rather not pay
for this out of my pocket if I don't have to!" She said this in a way that
sounded arrogant, as if she was belittling her current condition and our
treatment in favor of a crafty way to beat the system. Instead of simply
interpreting that, I momentarily became defensively punitive. I said,
"You seem to want to milk the system by getting me to tell them you
have a brand new problem or condition. But the fact is that you don't."
This sort of acting out and debating went on for awhile, with me being
the disapproving father, pointing out her lack of honesty, and her pushing back, insisting that she did have new problems and that the insurance company "could well afford to give away some of its blood-stained
profits." Fortunately, I quickly realized what was occurring and began
interpreting it. I pointed out that the way she presented the story to me
almost guaranteed a negative reply. I interpreted that, on the one hand,
she worked very hard to keep me as a neutral, genderless object that
wouldn't seduce or judge her. But this defensive phantasy often crumbled, revealing her view of me as easily hurt and resentful or her current view of me as a controlling, critical parent. I interpreted that these
views were aspects of her inner self that she placed onto me at times.
Betty fluctuated between crying and "feeling reprimanded and put in
my place" to "seeing how I can sound entitled and edge you toward being the person I dread you might be."

Yet another time the dynamics of projective identification seemed to
take over and temporarily dominate the transference↔countertransfer-
ence was during a period when Betty was dating a series of men. It was
a testimony to her growth and courage that she had gone on these dates
to begin with. She normally felt so poorly about herself that she would
make no effort to date but then would feel that she must be unlovable,
because she never had a date. Betty came into the session proud and

happy to tell me about how her recent date had gone. She described a wonderful dinner, some dancing, a walk through the park on the way back to her house, and a warm, sincere embrace at her doorstep. At the same time, Betty said that her date had told her that she asked so many questions about his life that he "felt on the hot seat." The next day, Betty left a lengthy message on his answering machine, telling him she had a wonderful time and that she looked forward to their next date. Later that day, she received a reply saying that he was "glad to have met her" and that he "appreciated meeting someone as direct and open as she was." He ended with, "thanks again, I will call you."

As soon as Betty finished telling me about the message, the excitement and pleasure she had initially shared with me evaporated. Suddenly, she broke into tears and told me how she was convinced this "was a thanks-but-no-thanks message." She was sure that "the tone and content of the message was clear. He didn't want to see me again." Betty cited different ways that she was sure she had "blown it" and "had somehow managed to once again alienate someone and sabotage my life." She sobbed and told me "it was hopeless. I will never get it right." This was a moment of projective identification in the clinical situation, in which I felt a psychological and interpersonal pressure to react to her way of relating. The interaction she constructed in that moment was designed to draw me in, in several ways. Her phantasy and object-relational conflict unfolded in the transference relationship. I found myself making small suggestions about how she might have come on too strongly with this man. I gave her reassurances about how things sounded very positive and how it was too early to make any negative judgments. On the one hand, I gave Betty the message that she had performed well with her intelligent dinner conversation and that she should be rewarded for it with another date. On the other hand, I gave her the message that her formal follow-up message was a disappointment and that she would be punished for it. I became the persecutory object, scrutinizing her every move, exactly as she usually did for herself. In response, she felt hopeful or hopeless. All this acting out was limited to one portion of one session, but it was intense enough for me to fortunately notice and begin exploring. I told Betty that I noticed we were engaged in these dynamics and interpreted that this type of interaction seemed to limit us to a par-

ticular sort of parent↔child relationship, in which she was pathologically dependent on my grading of her behavior. Betty replied, "I know
that one pretty well. That is the way my mother always was with me!"
She went on to discuss various examples of this from childhood. Then
I interpreted that perhaps Betty was anxious and uncomfortable being
a mature, grown woman with me, feeling confident in sharing with me
her sense of victory and desire. I pointed out that she had related to me
in this independent yet close and excited way when she began the session. There was success and victory in the air. But then she had quickly
extinguished it with attacks of doubt and judgment. Betty agreed with
me, saying it was "a hard thing to do, to be a fully developed person, an
equal." But she added she was nevertheless sure she had "screwed up
once again."

A similar scenario occurred when Betty was thinking about a new career in the field of local politics and decided to do some volunteer work
to explore what the work was really like. As with the date, she started
by telling me of her excitement and hope and about the new and interesting things she was discovering as she looked for possible volunteer
positions. But once she actually made some calls and set up some inter-
views, the flavor of how she presented herself and how she related to
me shifted to a more obsessive debate, in which she presented me with
two options and essentially asked me to tell her what to do. Betty told
me she couldn't figure out if she should focus on the "more drab, boring,
and secure internships that could easily lead to an actual boring, secure
job" or the "more creative, flashy internships that were scary because
they could lead to jobs that you could never count on for security." Betty
said, "I want you to tell me how you see me as far as how I would fare
in each category, given my illness. Do you think I will be more emotionally stable in the future to take on something creative, or should I just be
content with the run-of-the-mill positions I am finding?" I said, "You are
inviting me to say you are sick and can't get better, so you better accept
your fate." Betty started crying. "Yes. I believe I am not able to change,
at least fast enough or significantly enough to have something special in
life." I interpreted that this doom-and-gloom approach and the way she
wanted me to join in with "assessing her sickness" was possibly a way to
avoid exploring her own desires. She could not risk me seeing her as a

creative, capable woman who needed me but could do fine on her own as well. Instead, she projected her creativity, intelligence, and strength onto me, encouraging me to treat her as a weak, incompetent little girl in need of direction.

Another example of Betty's transference phantasies occurred when I received a message from Betty over the weekend. Betty acted out aspects of her phantasy that engaged me interpersonally, but, in this particular instance, I was not fully seduced and was able to maintain my analytic stance.

Betty's message said she was feeling depressed and despondent, "not feeling like anything meant much anymore." She added, "I realize this is an intrusion into your time and I don't expect you will call back when you are having your own life, but if you by chance have a spare moment and want to, I would appreciate the call." This conflicted, complicated message was typical of Betty's internal struggle and of the transference view she held. I called her back and talked to her about how she felt lonely and how she thought she had "completely ruined her chances with a new boyfriend." What came out in the phone call was that Betty thought I was probably at a conference related to psychology or in my office, busily writing some professional article. When I investigated this further, it became clear that this was a safe, controlled way to have me be in her mind. I interpreted, "if I am doing something official, then maybe I can tolerate you calling and you can justify your needing me. But if you don't control me that way and let me live my life, maybe just having fun on the weekend, then you can't imagine me tolerating your needing me." Betty started crying. "Yes. I'm afraid you would be furious that I am overstepping your boundaries and intruding on your space. I'm really sorry!" I replied, "It seems you would rather decide ahead of time that I am offended and angry rather than risk having to see if I am willing to care for you and understand your needs."

Over the course of this phone call and the next few sessions, we explored Betty's phantasy of breaking the rules, needing too much, making mistakes, and me retaliating. Gradually, we saw how she was cruel and intolerant of any sort of need or deviation from her own prescribed norm and thus projected that image onto me. Also, Betty dreaded that I was injured by that level of hunger and aggression in her. In this example of our analytic work together, the pull was for me to reassure and convince her that I was not inconvenienced by talking with her. I was not seduced by that projective-identification tactic, because her self-attack was so severe and her phantasy of me and my reaction was so caricatured that I could keep my mind clear enough to interpret the dynamic rather than act it out with her.

During the end of the first year of analytic treatment, Betty exhibited this same sort of fear of her own projected demands. Like the last example, the phantasy was so concrete and one-sided that I could maintain my therapeutic stance rather easily without being pulled into performing any particular role in her projective-identification experience for very long or at all.

Ten minutes after our session was due to begin, I received a call from Betty. She was crying and very anxious. She explained that her car was in the shop and that she had planned on taking a taxi to my office. However, she forgot that our appointment that day was during rush hour. There were no taxis available, and the one she finally flagged down brought her to the appointment with only five minutes remaining in the session. In those five minutes and the next few sessions, she expressed intense remorse for her "ultimate stupidity and complete lack of competence." I interpreted that she was trying aggressively to convince me of how bad she is. I suggested that not casting us into that frightening place might leave her feeling even more exposed and at risk. She said, "That would feel like chaos, completely unknown. But, this is certain. I know for a fact I fucked up big time!" I also interpreted that she was not allowing us any room to explore this "mistake" and was forcing me either to forgive her and reassure her immediately or condemn her outright. I said, "Without me intervening and convincing you that I forgive you, you seem to overwhelm yourself with guilt and won't stop attacking us with judgment and demand."

This interpretation is in line with Steiner's (1998) ideas about how projective identification, if it lacks a protective envelope, container, or boundary within the self↔object relationship, can cause intense guilt and anxiety that escalates uncontrolled. Reparation or a sense of understanding and tolerance is unavailable, because the ego's attacks continue unimpeded. Betty seemed to be caught in this inner struggle, where there would be both the destruction of object and severe retaliation from the object, and she felt like she couldn't stop inflicting the very thing that brought on these frightening consequences. She placed me in a position to either confirm these destructive phantasies or create an internal foundation that could tolerate, detoxify, and translate these attacks. At times, I was hopeful that she would gradually internalize this emotional filter as her own. At other times, I felt like she was merely testing me over and over again to see if I could maintain the filter or if I would transform into the disappointed, angry parent she dreaded.

Another aspect of the transference, as shaped by projective identification, had to do with how Betty related to me in a one-sided, serious, pessimistic way. I felt a pull to be the lighthearted, humorous one who always found a ray of hope in Betty's gloomy outlook. This became familiar enough that I was able to interpret it and explore with Betty why she needed to hand over that aspect of herself to me while leaving herself with the dark, static side of life. Also, we looked at how this dynamic was an attempt to make me be reassuring to her at all times, providing security and the sense that I didn't take her plight seriously. These discussions led to another piece of the transference: she was so concerned about and attentive to whatever I thought, felt, or wanted that she rejected any thought, feeling, or desire she had. Without a slavish dependence on me and my opinion, she was empty and lost. We looked at how she tried to take aggressive control of the object, which in turn left her feeling powerless and out of control.

During the second year of her four-times-a-week, on-the-couch therapy, Betty spoke a great deal about her trouble with men and how she saw herself as always drawn to the same type of man, someone unavailable and distant. This was reflected in her long-time affair with a married man who had always promised to leave his wife but continually failed to do so. While seeing him, Betty was also dating another man who was always busy with work, and, when they did spend time together, he often spoke of how he missed his last girlfriend. The more time that Betty spent discussing her troubles with dating, the more it seemed like she was searching for advice and direction on how to date more successfully.

During one session, Betty was talking about "what her boyfriend had done to her." I commented that she often connected with men in a way that left her passive and put them in a position to lead her around. Betty asked me what she should do about that. I started making small suggestions about how to be more assertive and how to look out for red flags in the beginning of a new relationship. Fortunately, I noticed myself participating in this projective-identification dynamic and began interpreting it. I said, "You are demonstrating this way of relating in *our* relationship. You are asking me to guide you and tell you what to do. Therefore, you end up passive, with a man who will tell you what to do and lead you around." Betty immediately associated to her father. She said, "My father never was a mentor for me. He never showed me the way. I feel I lost him in that way; he was never there for me. I wish he had been there for me." Betty cried. I said, "Without the sense of him there to guide you, you must have felt lost, waiting to be shown the way. I think you are looking to me for that guidance now, but to gain that with me or other men, you have to become lost and passive and allow me to take over and tell you what to do. In the end, that may not feel so great. You never can see yourself as strong and smart, and your relationships with men have to be one sided, with one person calling the shots and the other person hoping it turns out ok." Betty agreed. "That certainly describes my experience with these last few boyfriends!"

A similar transference situation occurred during a time when Betty dated a man who was pushy, domineering, and volatile. It was clear that she was intimidated by him, but she was reluctant to act on her own behalf. She let him lead her around, which left her fearful, frustrated, and sad. We had talked about this dynamic a great deal, and at one point Betty described a situation where she had "felt bullied" by the man. She said, "at that point, I asked myself, what would Doctor Waska want me to do?" I pointed out that this was a double-edged sword. On the one hand, she was showing an eagerness to understand herself and to be aware of how she was relating, instead of just going along with her familiar self-destructive way of relating. On the other hand, I noted, "when you say what would I want you to do, you are making me into the next bully in your life who will tell you what to do. I think you are afraid to have your own ideas because they might be different than mine, and you picture that causing trouble, pain, and punishment." Betty replied, "I see what you mean. It is more comfortable just to wait for you to give me my next assignment. I think I might mess up or do it wrong on my own." I added, "And you worry that if you make a mistake that way, I might be angry, and our connection would be broken." She rolled her eyes. "How do you know me so well?"

This case material is meant to illustrate how common projective identification and the resulting levels of acting out from both patient and analyst are in psychoanalytic treatment. Interpretations are most effective when they focus on the current moment and the ongoing here-and-now details of the dynamic as it plays out in the transference↔countertransference situation (Schafer 1994). The analyst may have to contain the projections for some time while exploring how and why the patient deems those aspects of himself to be so unbearable. Other times, interpreting these projections and phantasies as they occur is helpful in showing the patient that they are not as destructive, evil, or exciting as the patient fears (Schafer 1994). Since acting out is inevitable, the analyst does best to observe the early signs of such activity and to seek to understand the underlying meaning so as to better interpret the core phantasy conflicts that the patient feels most burdened by at the moment.

SECTION 2

Difficult and Jagged

IMPERFECT CLINICAL SITUATIONS

5

KLEINIAN COUPLE'S TREATMENT

A Complicated Case

THIS CHAPTER INVESTIGATES how a Kleinian psychoanalyst works with couples. The number of individual patients in classical psychoanalysis, as defined by the use of the couch and the frequency of sessions, has declined dramatically in the last forty years. Research within the psychoanalytic community finds the typical analyst spending the majority of his or her clinical time treating couples, families, and low-frequency individuals. Given this contemporary profile of private practice, it is important to understand the technical issues involved in treating our actual caseloads. At the same time, it is valuable to study the more complex and difficult cases in our day-to-day practice so we can better understand how to refine our theory and technique. This chapter uses extensive case material to illustrate how Kleinian clinical concepts are utilized in couples work and to demonstrate the confusing, humbling, and trying nature of the therapeutic task. Whether in individual or couples work, we often face very resistant patients who challenge us in a variety of ways and bring out our own imperfections.

Melanie Klein's discoveries strengthened and expanded Freud's clinical work and have become a leading worldwide influence in current psychoanalytic practice. Key Kleinian concepts include the total transference, projective identification, the importance of countertransference, psychic retreats, the container/contained function, enactment, splitting, the paranoid-schizoid and depressive positions, unconscious phantasy, and the importance of both anxiety and defense in the interpretive process. These and other clinical components of the Kleinian approach have become commonplace in the literature and have been adopted by many other schools of practice. It is easy to forget that object-relations theory and technique was Melanie Klein's discovery. The Kleinian approach regarding total transference, countertransference, and defense are just as important in couple's treatment as they are in individual work.

In broadening Klein's work, I have written (Waska 2007) about the use of Kleinian techniques in all aspects of clinical practice, with all types of patients and in all types of settings. Whether family therapy, couples work, or once-a-week individual therapy without the analytic couch, the goal of what I call "analytic contact" (Waska 2007) is the guiding principle. Analytic contact is less tied to external factors such as the use of the couch or the frequency of visits as it is to the production of a clinical climate for the understanding and modification of the patient's deepest phantasies. Analytic contact is about gaining a foothold into the transference and into the core phantasy states tied to the patient's feelings, thoughts, and actions. Continuous moments of analytic contact, when fostered and maintained, create a psychoanalytic process by which psychological change can occur. This is the vehicle for internal shifts and psychological integration for both individuals and couples.

In the Kleinian method, projective identification is the blood that circulates through the body of the transference (Grotstein 2007). It is always present, and it shapes the nature of phantasy, defense, and transference. Therefore, it is always a focus in interpreting the clinical climate and the nature of the here-and-now anxiety that pushes the patient to relate in one manner or another. In working with couples, the dynamic of projective identification is even more pivotal, and it operates as the cornerstone of the couple's pathology and marks the path to growth, change, and healing.

Viewed from the Kleinian perspective, couples utilize projective identification as the primary vehicle for defense, communication, attachment, desire, and aggression in their relationship to the analyst and to each other. As such, projective identification constantly shapes and colors both the transference and countertransference. For analytic contact to be established soundly, these three aspects of the clinical situation must be constantly explored, investigated, interpreted, and worked through. With couples, these elements of the clinical interface are often more difficult to locate, interpret, and work with, because there are essentially *three* patients in the room: both parties as individuals and the couple as a unified entity.

KLEINIAN COUPLES TREATMENT

By the time couples show up for treatment, they are usually operating at a fairly chaotic and often primitive level of psychological organization. It is common to hear statements such as, "things have been like this for years but now it's gotten worse. We're thinking of getting a divorce unless something drastic changes immediately." From statements like this, we can see that we are also up against problems that have been in place for a long time, with both parties quite used to operating in that manner. From a psychoanalytic perspective, we understand that they want change but also resist change and are even prone to fortifying their pathological pattern of relating, because of various unconscious fears and desires. Usually, there is an urgent demand placed on the analyst for drastic changes immediately, even though both parties are internally cautious about relating differently. All this makes for very difficult, frustrating, and confusing treatment situations.

From a Kleinian perspective, the internal world is structured around paranoid-schizoid (Klein 1946) and depressive phantasies (1935, 1940), and it fluctuates back and forth between them in a balanced and growth-oriented manner. However, pathological conflicts can bring about a fixed paranoid or depressive state, with an overreliance on certain corresponding defenses or pathological organizations (Steiner 1993). Other patients seem to be oversaturated and unprotected from the ravages of both psychic states and rapidly oscillate between them in a desperate and painful state of mind (Waska 2009).

Certainly, the therapist's critical function is to translate and interpret the couple's pattern of mutual transference and unified projective identification throughout the treatment. However, the nature of that pattern may be so intense and/or the nature of one party's internal conflict so overwhelming that the focus on the couple's conjoint signature must be dealt with alongside of each party's individual dynamics. The transference to each other, each party's transference to the analyst, and the couple's unified transference to the analyst are all important factors in couple's treatment. However, the immediate here-and-now phantasy, anxiety state, or defensive posture of either singular party often takes precedence. Often, only in the later stage of successful couple's treatment can all these factors weave together and interpretations focus primarily on the unified couple's conflict, with a back-and-forth, healthy dialogue between both parties. Because of these typical clinical conditions, often a period of specialized individual treatment for one or both parties is conducted under the umbrella of couple's work.

One issue in treating difficult, disturbed, and impulsive patients in either individual or couples therapy is finding a way to help both parties through their initial hostility and panic. In individual work, the analyst's own efforts at containment are sometimes not enough to keep the patient from fleeing. One advantage of couple's treatment is that it can offer an additional protective psychic envelope for the more fight-or-flight-oriented individual. The party who is most prone to this attack-and-retreat pattern can feel temporarily buffered by the presence of the other party and protected from frightening phantasies of the analyst and what treatment may symbolize. This protection can be experienced as an Oedipal comrade that stands against the opposing parent or as a more primitive pre-Oedipal partner who is willing to join in the fight against the dangerous analyst. Either way, the party who would normally terminate prematurely has a sense of containment that helps to sustain partial contact with the analyst without being overwhelmed by immediate internal conflicts and projections.

Again, for some time, the primary focus may have to be on one party rather than both, if that party's emotional turmoil is so great that a three-party dialogue is impossible. This idea of one half of the couple providing a necessary holding environment for the other half is only possible if the first party is able and willing to do so for the latter. Otherwise, the latter might experience the refusal as a narcissistic wound, a demand, neglect, or blame. Alternatively, the first party may find this task in line with his or her own masochistic or guilt-ridden phantasy and easily become the latter's caretaker, to avoid having his or her own identity. However, the opportunity to give to the other party and try to understand and contain his or her suffering can sometimes be very enlightening and healing for both members of the couple.

Overall, this situation of one party providing a temporary psychological buffer for the other as he or she becomes acclimated to the treatment setting is reminiscent of Rosenfeld's (1954) work with psychotic patients. He noted the initial importance in more difficult cases of a family member or friend being present with the patient and/or needing to conduct the sessions in home or hospital settings, so that a sense of containment and safety is offered to the patient until he or she can come to see the analyst in a less dangerous way.

As noted, the Kleinian approach, as well as my specific technical goal of analytic contact, considers transference, countertransference, and projective identification to be the key elements in all forms of treatment. The moment-to-moment emergence of each party's phantasy regarding self and object is to be collected, contained, translated, and interpreted in a consistent, here-and-now fashion. As mentioned, attention to one party's immediate psychic state can also be beneficial to the other party. I have written (Waska 2008) about the value of each party witnessing the other party's emotional conflict and the gradual hope and healing that takes place as a result. To see your partner work on their deepest wishes and fears or, alternatively, having your partner supportively witnessing and listening to your own painful struggle is a potentially transformative element for both parties.

To witness your partner's efforts to overcome their personal anxieties and conflicts and to see their attempts to make reparation to the object can help you realize that you were not being personally attacked. This frees up the space to find an inner confidence, safety, and self-identity separate from the other.

An example of this came in the third year of couple's work with Mark, a borderline man prone to angry outbursts and demands on his wife, Mary, to give in to his infantile tantrums. These behaviors grew out of his phantasies of neglect and entitlement. His wife had been scared of him for years, trying to please him to avoid conflict and accepting his demeaning behavior as a personal truth about herself. As a result, she was depressed and felt weak and ugly. During a recent session, Mary told me, "Mark was nasty to me yesterday like I am used to, but this time I was able to step back and realize he has a emotional sickness. I felt bad for him but knew this ugly moment was all about him and not about me. I didn't take it personally. I remained myself and sadly watched him change and wilt, but I stayed strong and still."

This was a great moment of progress. The idea that there is a mutual nature to the relationship is rarely encountered in the beginning phases of most couple's therapy. Usually, one person takes the other person's actions in a highly personal manner and reacts accordingly. One or both parties usually do not imagine a mutuality or criss-cross pattern of any type. Rather, it is the experience of me versus them, how I failed them, or how they failed me. The essence of Kleinian couple's treatment is to help both parties come to grips with how they both contribute to a mutual projective-identification process that produces a series of predictable relational phantasies and interpersonal transactions. Before reaching this important and challenging stage of treatment, often significant and ongoing individual focus is needed. Of course, hopefully both stages are happening simultaneously, but often it is more of A, then B, then A, then B, before it becomes an A+B=C process.

CASE MATERIAL

To examine some of the ways that modern Kleinian theory and technique are useful in working with couples, I will present the first three sessions with John and Jane. Currently, the diagnostic picture is one in which Jane seems to be operating more in the depressive position. She displays a pattern of controlling and dominating her object, and she then feels guilty about and sad for her hurt and weakened object. She makes restitution by caring for him and tolerating his retaliation. This masochistic behavior leaves her feeling neglected and without a partner.

John, on the other hand, seems to be more of a libidinal narcissistic personality (Rosenfeld 1964) or a thin-skinned narcissist (Britton 2003); he strives to prevent separateness. John also exhibits destructive narcissistic traits; namely, he tries to destroy the separate object if it does not provide the services he demands (Steiner 2008). Segal (1997) sees this distinction as more blended, and she cites the manner in which life-affirming relationships and healthy self-love are experienced as part of the life instinct but violently attacked by the narcissistic personality, who is fueled by envy and the death instinct. The degree of John's primitive conflicts and his intense use of projective identification created a very difficult clinical situation. Far from optimal and certainly not successful in the end, this case helps illustrate the often challenging aspects of our work with hard-to-reach individuals and couples who both desire our help and understanding but push us away and limit our ability to think with or for them.

SESSION 1

I met with Jane and John after they called me for help with "better communication." At our first meeting, I asked them both to sign my standard informed-consent form and explained that the treatment is confidential except if they use insurance, which they were. In order to use insurance, one of them would have to qualify for a mental health disorder diagnosis, which may or may not affect them somehow in the future. The form also discusses fees, cancellation policies, and my possible use of case material for teaching and publications. Immediately, John said he "had an issue with the mental health disorder thing." I proceeded to explain this matter in more detail, as they had not read their insurance policy and their HR department or insurance carrier had never informed them of that fact.

Now, I think it is healthy and normal for all of us to be upset that this is actually an issue in our national health system. Nevertheless, many patients experience this problem in specific ways that can help us begin to assess them. I would be interested if the couple felt it was a third-party intrusion, an Oedipal invasion into our privacy. Or they might take it as an "us-against-them" type of moment, in which we would all feel like victims of the insurance company. Other patients see me as the bad guy and blame me for putting them behind the eight ball. Still other patients might apologize for putting me in the middle of such a mess and immediately make amends by agreeing to sign the consent form without

protest. These reactions would all be seen as part of the total transference situation (Joseph 1985) and the beginning of a particular projective
identification–shaped clinical moment (Spillius 1992).

Jane said she understood the matter, but John sat there looking very
tense. Jane asked, "You are uncomfortable with it, aren't you?" I took
this as a sign that Jane could operate in the depressive position long
enough to witness John's anxiety and not be overly persecuted by it or
become overly panicked to make it all better. "Yes. I am uncomfortable,"
he replied. John proceeded to get fairly heated about it, telling me how
"unfair and unreasonable it was."

Some patients tell me they understand and proceed, others elect to
pay out of pocket to protect their privacy, and some patients, usually
borderline or narcissistic ones, become so anxious, controlling, and defensive that they break off the treatment. Here, I was worried that John
might terminate. I felt as if he was directing his anxiety and anger at
me and the treatment setting and interpreted the anxiety and defense
that I perceived. I said, "You are feeling like you will be exposed and
controlled or that taking the risk of seeking help and sharing yourself
with me will end up coming back to haunt you. So, you are angry with
me about it." Here, I was making an analyst-centered interpretation
(Steiner 1994), in which I let the transference projections stay with me
as a method of containment (LaFarge 2000). John said, "I am not angry
with you. It just seems ridiculous to seek help and then find out you will
be punished for it. It makes more sense financially to simply pay for it
out of pocket."

I was struck by how he switched from a more persecutory experience and a negative transference to this more controlled, intellectual
stance. This new stance kept us separate from the bad object (the insurance situation), but it also denied any contact between us, whether positive or negative. He went from a combative approach to backing down
and becoming seemingly adaptive or even submissively reasonable. Was
this was part of a fragmented or splintered aspect of his internal world,
in which angry objects alternated with passive submissive ones? This
would indicate a lack of whole-object integration (Sandler 1990).

After they wrote me a check, I asked them once again to sign my
form. Jane signed it and handed it to John. He read it closely and began
to sneer. Jane said, "It's all standard. Just sign it. It's fine." He shook

his head, rolled his eyes, and signed it. Here, Jane took the leadership role, managing John's anxiety and anger and directing his behavior. I noted this as one part of the overall role relationship they presented as a couple. Sandler (1976) notes that there is often a tie between countertransference and role responsiveness in the treatment setting. In Kleinian couple's treatment, I extend this idea not only to apply to patient and analyst but to apply to both parties of the couple as well. I wondered if Jane, as part of a two-party role-relational pattern, had reacted to or acted out John's need for a container and thus became his supportive envelope in that moment, creating boundaries and redefining his anxiety.

I asked John and Jane what brought them in to see me. Jane seemed uptight, irritated, and looked at John to answer. He appeared sad and a bit confused. After a moment, he said, "I think we have been unable to communicate and don't have a lot in common." He added a few more vague variations of this. He seemed distant and disengaged, which felt slightly sadistic and withholding to me. I asked him for more specific feelings, thoughts, or information. In the countertransference, I felt irritated and wanted to get tough with him—to get him to hurry up and spill the beans. I reflected on how he was withholding from me in a passive and vague manner, which invited me to speak for him, to push him to speak out for himself, or simply to be cross with him. Here, I was trying to be aware of both the transference and my countertransference, an important technical element of Kleinian technique, and what appeared to be a projective-identification process that seemingly combined narcissistic elements of hostility with a primitive request for communication and understanding (Rosenfeld 1983).

John and Jane commented that "things were at the end of the line in a lot of ways." I asked for details. They said things had gotten to "the point that we were considering everything." I asked if that meant divorce. Jane said, "Yes. We talked about it." John said, "Jane brought it up." She said, "I feel like things have gotten so estranged, so separate, that we need to consider that as an option." I said, "So, you have felt you may want to leave him." She nodded. Here, I was confirming that she held a mixture of feelings that led her to want a divorce and that she was the active agent of that wish. She was able to own those difficult feelings and share them with me and with John.

I asked John what he was feeling. His answer was interesting. He said, "Jane brought it up and I told her if that is what she wants, I would go along with it." Then he fell silent. Here, I was aware of how teasing, withholding, and submissive he was being. He was giving up, giving the power to Jane, and thus making her out to be the bad guy. And, instead of taking my invitation to be a part of the immediate moment in the room, he subtracted himself from it and focused only on Jane. I said, "You don't want to have an opinion about it? It seems you quickly agree to a divorce to please her, but you are not sharing with me what you really want or don't want." Here, I was interpreting the transference based on my countertransference reaction. He said, "If that is what she wants, I want to give that to her."

I was struck by how John wanted more from Jane on the one hand but also gave over so much of himself. In this way, he could follow her lead and be under the umbrella of her power and guidance. But the tradeoff was this passive, masochistic loneliness and a lack of power or participation. I interpreted, "you are leaving yourself out of it, as if you don't have any feelings. The result seems to be that you don't matter or don't even exist." Here, I was interpreting the result of John's overreliance on projective identification, which left him as just an empty shell. He replied, "That is right. If she wants that I will go along with it."

This was an interesting moment. I had put my interest and focus on him and had attempted to include him in my thinking, and he responded by excluding himself and pulling away from me. I wondered if this was the same dynamic that was alive in the marriage, one in which he excluded himself but wanted to be taken care of at the same time. As a result, Jane felt pushed away, angry, and hopeless. In paying close attention to how John responded to my interpretations, I was in line with the current Kleinian approach to interpretation, in which listening to and understanding the patient's response to the intervention is just as important as making a correct interpretation (Spillius 1988).

Throughout this session, I was collecting the pieces of the couple's projective-identification process in order to contain, organize, translate, and eventually interpret it. By "collecting," I mean that I use my countertransference to notice and gather the various strands of projective acting out that seem to be occurring between the couple or between them and myself. I am assuming that this scattered, projective breakdown is part of if not the central problem in the relationship. In other words, the way in which they relate to me is no doubt the way they relate to themselves and to each other. Also, the way I may act when stepping into an enactment can also be a reflection of their basic conflicts.

Since John and Jane operate in a psychologically scattered manner, I must collect the pieces as I find them and try to make sense out of them. This sense making is part of the containing process (Bion 1962), in which the projection into the analyst is kept for a period of time before being returned in modified form, transforming alpha elements into beta elements that feel safe, understandable, and nourishing to the patient (Segal, 1977; Kernberg 2003). This containing process is a translation of action, phantasy, and defense into something bearable, knowable, and speakable. It is a way for the analyst to make sense out of something that previously made none and to find a way to interpret the material in a new way that provides knowledge and opportunity for change. Of course, part of this containing involves protecting the material from attacks, until we can understand why they must attack it and prevent it from growing into something more healing and balanced.

Part of what each person does with the analyst's interpretation has to do with the witnessing function of psychoanalytic couples therapy as practiced from a Kleinian perspective. When I make an interpretation, each party will be carefully watching and witnessing what the other party does with that interpretation. Each person will have a personal meaning or phantasy attached to how their partner reacts to the interpretation.

As we proceeded, both Jane and John told me of how, after twenty years, things had become stale and empty. Their three children were now in college or working. Jane was still at her management job at a technology firm; John had retired five years ago. They both agreed that they used to "have much to focus on together and projects to take care of, but now there was not much to talk about." I said, "It sounds like you both were used to working together on projects like your children, work, or house matters, but without that you don't know if you have anything to share. I wonder if you are not used to simply sharing yourselves with each other instead of focusing on other things." Here, I was introducing the idea of a mutual defense or retreat (Steiner 1987). They both agreed and told me how keeping their mind on the kids or work "had worked for years, but without it there isn't much else to relate about."

I felt confident about my interpretation, but, at the same time, in the countertransference I couldn't picture why they didn't have anything to say to each other. I was not sure what they meant. I took this as some type of projective-identification dynamic, which inspired me to ask, "Surely there is plenty to talk about; why don't you just talk to each other?" I thought this could be the frustration one or both felt and the demand one or both felt too. I made a note to myself that they may be looking to me to be the repository, purifier, or spokesperson for these uncomfortable or unformed feelings (Joseph 1988).

In what seemed like an answer to my countertransference sensation, John brought up that "what he did during the day wasn't really enough to spend the day chatting about. I spend a good deal of time gardening and cleaning up around the house but I don't think I could spend more than five or ten minutes talking about that!" Again, I felt pulled to intervene and ask why it was up to John to be the one to have something to talk about. This countertransference feeling made me suspicious of what was not being said between John and Jane. Somewhat enacting this, I asked Jane, "So, you don't feel like you have much to share with him either?" She said she could talk about work, but she wanted something "more mutual. I wish he felt comfortable bringing up things to talk to me about so it isn't one sided."

John replied, "I guess I wish you would retire too so we could spend more time together." Jane said, "Well, if things are so boring and stagnant, I don't want to be home." Here, I thought I caught a glimpse of the harder, more hostile side of Jane. John replied, "I want you around so we can do things together, like go to the beach." She said, "Why don't you ever go to the beach yourself and then tell me about it later?" He replied, "I don't want to do things by myself; I want you to be there too." At this point, I felt a shift in the climate between the two of them. What seemed to be emerging was a particular manner of relating, in which more and more John seemed like a lonely little boy wanting the company of his mother. Jane now was acting like a mother who felt henpecked and was telling her son to run off and play on his own. I felt like the leading anxiety in the room was coming from John, so I addressed my next comment to him.

In psychoanalytic couples treatment, this is always a tricky moment. Jane was irritated and anxious about being put in this mother role and not having anything else for herself or from him. By attending to John instead of her I was somewhat enacting her neglectful phantasy, that John, as usual, receives all the attention. Unfortunately, we can't be in two places at the same time, and thus there is a fair amount of enactment almost built into the process of couples work. Modern Kleinian theory (Ivey 2008; Feldman 1997; Spillius 1992; Steiner 2006) has discovered enactment as a universal and generally unavoidable aspect of psychoanalytic work and interpretation in particular (Waska 2009). Kleinians attempt to minimize the enactment in any given interaction but realize it is probably an aspect of each session to some degree. Thus the task is to understand it and to try to utilize it. I tried to integrate this clinical reality in my next comment.

I asked John what made it so hard for him to go to the beach during the week and then share his pleasurable experience with Jane later in the day, giving her something and showing her attention. John told me he "didn't get much out of being on his own" and would prefer to do things with Jane. I then asked why they were not doing more things together on the weekends, which would offer a chance for more connection and something to share and talk about. My question was based on my countertransference frustration, which pushed me to keep coming up with ways for John to venture out on his own. I took this to be part of a projective-identification process, so I tried to avoid being pulled into it. Therefore, I was left with the obvious; they were not spending time together when they could. When I brought up the idea of doing things together on the weekends, their answers were telling, showing their unique individual experiences of it.

Jane said she "would like it if John brought up ideas like that, but he seems to never want to do much. So, why would I retire and sit at home and do nothing and have nothing to talk about?" John replied, "Well, there is a history to that. I used to try and bring up ideas and things to do, but she is quick to shoot them down." At this point, we had to stop the session. I interpreted, "you are both suddenly showing me a specific way that you relate, which is much like an irritated mother feeling tired of helping her child along and hoping he will grow up soon. Jane, you want John to give to you, because you are tired of giving to him. On the other hand, John, you seem like a lonely boy who just wants some company and feels neglected and unappreciated. And you both want me to understand each point of view and side with it. Instead, let's try to understand how and why this is the way you end up relating, even though it is painful and drives you apart."

Here, I was interpreting that they were involved in a particular projective-identification match based on motives we were not yet aware of, although I was certain that it both defends against something and fulfills something. I also mentioned that they want me to side with them in the transference but also want me to understand and help them. Here, I was interpreting the communicative, hostile, needy, and competitive aspects of projective phantasies.

In this first session, I employed standard Kleinian technique to treat a couple in distress. Overall, using the psychoanalytic method helped me to identify various anxieties, phantasies, and internal object relations that had become externalized, causing relational destruction. Theoretically, one encounters couples where both parties are in the paranoid-schizoid mode, both in the depressive mode, or in a mix of both. Clinically, I find that people in relationships are always drawn to that which they feel anxious having. In other words, a person is drawn to others who seem to have traits or aspects of personality that the person wishes he or she had but feels is unobtainable in some way. These might be aspects of personality he or she wants but is too anxious to own, so the person has to borrow them from the object or hide them within the object. People pick partners in whom they can deposit or expel aspects of themselves that they deem unwanted, dangerous, or toxic. In these ways, projective identification is the basis for most relationships; each person sees the other as containing that which is longed for, not wanted, or intolerable. By association, the person feels their partner completes them or provides a necessary function. Even if both parties are operating within the same psychological realm, be it neurotic, borderline, or psychotic, a balance is achieved in which each party plays a certain role for the other. A particular dynamic pattern is established, and the two partners fit together like a nut and a bolt. Of course, it is when this interface becomes destructive, stops working, or is overly active that we see the couple showing up in our office.

SESSION 2

The second session with Jane and John was intense. They walked in, and I immediately noticed the two ways they were relating with me. Jane made a point to say hello and smile, being social and polite. John looked depressed, much like last time. He walked past me in a detached and withdrawn manner, mumbling "hello" in a perfunctory manner.

I asked about changing our appointment time for the following week, as I would be out of town. Jane said she could make it; John looked unresponsive. I asked him if it would work for him. He said he would have to think about it and then was silent. I asked him what he had to think about, noting in myself a feeling of irritation mixed with a desire to drag the information out of him. John looked over at Jane as if to say, "I don't know if you (Jane) can really make that time," but he didn't seem to ponder his own schedule. Then he said he wasn't sure if the time would work, "so he would have to get back to me later." Confronting his vagueness and the way he seemed to be putting his conflict onto her, I asked, "not sure it would work for you or for Jane?" He said, "for me," and fell silent. Addressing his negative transference in the moment, an aspect of Kleinian technique, I interpreted, "You don't sound like you want to be here, now *or* next week."

John said, "Yes. I am unsure. I don't see too much progress," and then fell silent. Pulled into his invitation to be the active bully with the passive child, I said, "I don't either. We've only met once, and I don't know you or what is going on in your life. So there is no way for us to make any changes yet." He said, "Yes, but I expect some progress instead of nothing." Realizing that I was now participating in a projective-identification enactment, I tried to regain my therapeutic balance and made an interpretation aimed at establishing analytic contact. I said,

"You want something, some change, but it looks like you are also unsure if it is worth your while." He was silent, but this time in a way that seemed to be in the affirmative.

Next, I made a transference interpretation aimed not only at underscoring the transference between John and I but, more so, at exploring the nature of the marital problem. I said, "I wonder if this way of you not saying much and then me having to pull it out of you happens between you and Jane as well." Jane replied, "Yes, this is exactly what happens, except you are being direct about it, confronting him." I asked, "What makes it hard for you to do the same?" She said, "I think it is part of a cycle that's been in place for many years now. We are both so worried about hurting the other person that we never say what's on our minds." Assuming that she felt safer saying it was both of them instead of owning the anxiety herself, I said, "You see him as pretty fragile. Do you have some angry feelings that could hurt him?"

Here, I was interpreting both her depressive anxiety of hurting her object with her angry feelings and her vision of her object as weak or fragile. Jane replied, "Yes. I do see him as fragile. I think John has been depressed and sad for a long time. He has gone through a great deal and I don't think he has been able to work through it or share it. He lost his mother recently, he retired a few years ago, he has health issues, and he drinks when he gets down. I think he has been suffering with depression for some time now, so I find myself being very careful in what I say, but I also end up feeling frustrated and angry."

Meanwhile, John was silent. He said nothing after Jane was done, maintaining the same distant and withdrawn stance. I asked him what he was thinking as he listened to Jane. He said he disagreed with her and didn't know why she was saying what she said. He told me that he was not depressed at all. I asked him about how he was coping with everything she mentioned. John said, "These are all normal matters, and I'm just moving on. Things happen, and you have to move ahead."

Again, my countertransference warned me that I felt like pushing something in his face, making him admit some feelings. I tried to take this as evidence of an expelling projection and made the following interpretation, "You are trying to not feel anything about the loss of your mother and these other matters, but that is difficult, since they naturally affect you." He said, with sadness in his eyes, "My mother was the best human being in the world. She loved me and did everything possible for me. I will always miss her. She was perfect. But you have to move on and live life. That's the way it is." I said, "It must be hard to cope with losing someone so special and wonderful." He said, "No. It is just part of life. You move on."

Here, I really felt like shoving his grief back at him. I thought he was not just retreating from his own grief and collapse but that he was getting rid of a sense of pressure and pain that he could not bear and felt overwhelmed by. The hostile nature of my countertransference led me to believe this was not just part of himself he was trying to expel but some sort of aggressive object he needed me to take on (Alvarez 1993). I interpreted this as again a projective-identification method of expelling and retreating by asking Jane, "do you feel he is keeping something from you when he says that?" She started to cry and said, "I am tired of not knowing what is going on with you. I miss the time years ago when we did share feelings with each other. I hate having to keep my feelings to myself to protect you and make sure I don't make you more depressed. I miss you, and I miss us." She was weeping. John was silent and staring ahead. He looked sad and overwhelmed but also stubborn and withholding.

I said, "How are you feeling?" He said, "Great. I feel fine." I said, "You feel great while your wife is crying?" Jane added, "You don't feel great. I know you're miserable and depressed and have been for years. But you won't talk to me or anyone about it." After a minute of silence, John finally said, "You both are entitled to your opinion, but you're both wrong. I'm not depressed. The problem is that when I do try to share something or have an idea, Jane doesn't want to hear it and says no. If I bring up something, she puts it down." Then he fell silent. I asked him if he could tell me what he meant. He said it was a "theme and was always happening." Again, he fell silent. I said, "You ration your words, only giving me a bit of your feelings and then shutting down. Could you give us an example?"

Here, I was interpreting the sadistic control he displayed and the defensive posture he took, isolating himself in silent safety. John said, "Well, recently I suggested a place to have lunch, and even though we were both talking about lunch, you immediately said no to my idea. I had thought about it and felt it was a good choice, and you completely ran over it. I put myself out there and made a suggestion. Do you think I came up with that idea lightly? And then you slapped it down so quickly."

In listening to him, it seemed he was being genuine for once and sharing his hurt feelings. At the same time, it seemed he was operating at a very childish level: he had worked hard to come up with his restaurant suggestion, and now his nasty mother had thrown it out with the garbage. I asked Jane what she was thinking and feeling. She said, "I remember the situation. We were going out to lunch, and I thought it was no big deal. We were just going to grab something, or so I thought. I suggested fast food, and when he suggested more of a fancy place, I snapped at him. I think I was just rushed, tired, and hungry, so I snapped. John, I apologize. I didn't realize you had put so much thought into it and that it was so important to you. I hope you will try that sort of thing again so I can try to respond differently."

Diagnostically, it was helpful to see how Jane was able to respond to what John was saying without feeling attacked or too guilty, so that she didn't need to attack back or engage in any form of manic reparation (Segal 1998). She was able to stay in the depressive position from a more healthy perspective, have a sense of the object's experience, and still feel intact herself. She was able to be a separate and different entity without too much anxiety, except for her dread about making him more depressed with her anger and need.

John replied in an adversarial manner. He said, "Why would I keep trying? This is what always happens, and I don't want to try. There's no point. When you have been turned down and criticized for so long, you don't want to try again." Here, I again felt that he was acting like a hurt and pouty child who doesn't want to make an effort out of spite. I said, "Maybe by talking here about these matters and how this pattern happens, we can find some ways to change it." He responded, "We have talked about it before, and it never worked. Why would it work here? I don't think I want to." I said, "We're out of time, but maybe we can start by talking next time about how hopeless and resigned you feel." Here, I was making an interpretation of his affect state and his transference but also tried hard to contain the urge to tell little Johnny off. These countertransference feelings were instructive, as they were probably part of a projective-identification pattern in which Jane acted out some of the critical feelings I had to contain and then John felt he was being put down and picked on. My countertransference led to an interpretive acting out and my potentially helpful comment in reaction to his devaluation of me and the treatment. Often, the analyst may react to the pressures of projective-identification hostility or withdrawal by offering false reassurance to stave off the hopelessness being directed at the analyst (Joseph 1982; Alvarez 1993).

SESSION 3

Two themes emerged in John and Jane's third session of Kleinian couple's therapy. On the one hand, there were moments of genuine dialogue, reflection, and potential. However, this rapidly crumbled into John being stubborn, withholding, and withdrawn. Jane or I were left to take the lead and fill in the gaps.

When we started the session, I asked both of them what they were feeling or thinking. I usually say "what" rather than "how," because it emphasizes the internal rather than the external social pattern of "how are you" followed by "fine." John said, "Well, I'm still waiting, just like last time and the time before, for you to facilitate our communication. That is what we are here for." He both wanted my attention and was demanding it in a particular manner. By asking both of them what they were feeling, I was offering my attention and concern to him, wanting to know about him. He then seemed to discard this care and invitation in favor of a demand that I cater to him and actively take charge, which left him passively hanging at the breast demanding nourishment. But this stance ultimately makes him powerless, alone, and empty.

In excessive projective identification (Segal 1974), the individual attempts to place all of his or her needs and painful conflicts into the object, as a way to avoid any hostility, anxiety, guilt, or fear. But this leaves him or her depleted and dependent on the object in a helpless, one-dimensional manner. Excessive desire and projection is followed by a retreat from taking any of it back, because the object now seems full of overpowering, unwanted, or destructive properties. Also, this type of projective identification is part of a narcissistic demand for the object to take over the basic functions of the self. In all these ways, John seemed to rely on this psychological mechanism to rule his objects and defend against them.

There were several specific moments in this session in which John talked more and shared more than before but then attacked his own message and the listener as well. He would bring up how he felt that Jane was "in charge of everything and never gives me a chance to choose anything or make a decision." Then, he would fall silent, and Jane or I would have to take over and dig into him for information. Finally, he said there were "four areas in which I feel you are too much in charge and I am not. The house, the finances, vacations, and activities." Jane thought about it and replied, "I think you mean I can be too controlling. I think you're right. I have a habit of taking over and not letting you have a say sometimes. I want to work on that, but I need your help in showing me the ways I do that. If I am less controlling and you talk more, maybe things will work out." John was quiet and then said, "You are good about the house; you have picked out many nice things and make sure it is kept up and organized. I have most of the say in the money department, and I think that works ok for both of us. We don't go on too many vacations, because we haven't really planned any. Most of the activities we do I enjoy, so that is alright for the most part."

Here, John was neutralizing and exorcizing the emotional hunger and anger he felt with intellectual logic and counterattack. When I pointed out how he risked putting himself out there for a moment to reach a connection with Jane but then pulled back, denying his own lament, he was quick to say, "I don't know what you mean. We are pretty equal in those areas so I don't think there is a problem." To this I felt prompted to say something like, "Hey, you do have problems, and you do feel controlled and unhappy!" But this would be me pushing his hostility and grief back into him in a violent way, which would only verify his view of the object and his need to defend and retreat. Therefore, I tried to interpret just that. I said, "You seem to have risked putting yourself out there, and now you are taking it all back. I wonder what you're feeling in the moment?" He said, "Nothing. Everything is fine. I'm not taking anything back. I don't know what you're talking about." Here again was a tricky moment in which I could easily become the angry mother dealing with my pesky child, becoming snappy, like Jane.

This type of scenario occurred many times during this session. John would say something, usually brief and general, and then fall silent. Jane or I would have to ask him questions or fill in the blanks. Then, he would say we were wrong, were "putting words in his mouth," or that I was "acting like a typical therapist." I interpreted, "you are holding back, being more quiet. Then, I have to try to solve the mystery by filling in the blanks or asking you questions. That makes you feel like I am controlling you or putting words in your mouth. But if you stay silent and withdrawn, I will have to take over and do the speaking. Then you feel dominated and unimportant. That is the pattern in the marriage, and it is coming alive here in the room." Here, I was interpreting the transference, shaped by projective identification, and the parallel dynamic in the marriage.

At that point, Jane was nodding her head in agreement, but John told me, "You're completely wrong." I asked him, if that was the case, to tell me what the right idea was. He was silent. I remarked, "Here, again, by being silent you push us into you being the little boy who won't talk. I am the parent who tells you what you are thinking and feeling. You are silent, and I'm grilling you. We have to see why you're reluctant to fill in the gaps or let me and Jane know what is going on, so we don't have to question you and end up acting like your parent." He said, "That's bullshit." He was silent, and we were out of time.

So far, this has been a very difficult treatment situation. While John and Jane consciously want something better out of their relationship, the nature of their unconscious object-relational pattern in the marriage has kept them in a rigid, frozen cycle of pathology. He withholds, retreats, and attacks from the vantage of a neglected little boy who is angry that his ideal object is not providing his needs. Jane is angry, controlling, and feels that she is never given to and is always put in the position of being the responsible one and the caretaker.

The excessive use of projective identification makes victims of gratitude and love. Because of his intense reliance on and hostile utilization of projective strategies, based partly on his demand for the ideal mothering object who never fails or fades, the desired power, love, and union that John wishes for is injected into the object and sealed off from his reach. This creates anger at and envy of what looks like the object's greater wealth and refusal to give or share, which in turn leads to a destructive attack on the object and its resources, which eliminates joy and gratitude (Klein 1975; Roth and Lemma 2009). Thus, the ability to feel for the object constricts. The ability for compassion and relational fulfillment is limited and distorted.

John's grief over the loss of his "perfect mother" may be part of this intense standoff, in which he is a little boy insisting that his mother find him and care for him. Then he becomes angry when he discovers that she is not ideal, has her own needs and opinions, and has died and left him. As a result, John has adopted a "leave me alone/no trespassing policy" and now lives in a "love me and hold my hand NOW/leave me alone and stop controlling me" zone. I think this, combined with his envy, represents a clinical manifestation of the death instinct (Grotstein 2000; Segal 1993; Waska 1992), in which his spite, fear, and guilt over the source of life and pleasure being outside of himself leads to an attack on that which is separate or different. Eliminating difference, change, or growth becomes the method of maintaining the tie to the object and a way to defeat and deny any dependency on the object.

This type of clinical, internal conflict came out when I made another interpretation about how he seemed to want me to be his guiding, active parent while he remained passive and lost, but that desire also left him alone, controlled, and angry, so he had to distance himself from me and Jane to avoid this care/control struggle. He said, "That is your opinion and I don't agree with it. You are entitled to your opinion, but you are wrong." I replied, "Yes. That is my opinion. But, you won't share your feelings and thoughts so we can coexist. By not sharing your feelings, you make my idea the only one in the room, and I become the bully. Let's see if we can find a way to be equals instead of being so lopsided."

SUMMARY

Our best opportunity to help couples is when we can assist them in becoming aware of and working through their core unconscious object-relational conflicts. Using the transference and countertransference to interpret these internal states of fear, guilt, persecution, hostility, and desire creates moments of analytic contact. When these moments build into a continuous therapeutic thread, a genuine psychoanalytic process takes hold. As psychoanalysts, we are always examining what fosters or prevents these moments of analytic contact and how to better maintain them.

Working as a Kleinian analyst, I do my best to make analytic contact with the couple's unconscious object-relational world, gradually providing them with a way to understand, express, translate, and master previously unbearable thoughts and feelings. My goal is to make contact with their deepest experiences, so that they in turn can make contact with their fullest potential.

This particular case example demonstrates these points, in that I consistently made the therapeutic effort to establish analytic contact with both of them. But this case also shows the real-life, rocky, and often unsuccessful aspects of psychoanalytic work with hard-to-reach individuals and couples. John chose not to return after that third session. His wife continued and has been working with me on her own psychological conflicts for the past six months. Her treatment is going quite well despite being strained and slow, because of her guilt over wanting to focus on her own happiness. The couples' treatment with me was the third or fourth failed attempt they had made in the last five years to work on their marriage. Each time, John had told the therapist that he thought the therapy was useless and terminated. This was the first time that Jane elected to continue herself.

Overall, in trying to establish analytic contact from a Kleinian vantage point with Jane and John, I think I did some solid clinical work and tried my best to build a psychoanalytic connection with John. Along the way, I participated in various enactments and struggled with my countertransference. I think I helped him as much as I could and as much as he would allow me to. Hopefully at some point he will eventually reengage with me or another analyst. In the meantime, I hope my work with Jane will both benefit her and positively affect John as well. For now, John remains in a state of depressive anger and combative anxiety, lost in his internal world and without any objects to turn to that he trusts or can feel equal to. I am left with a bit of sadness and frustration—perhaps a parting projective communication from John that allows me to understand his tormented world a bit more.

6

SUCCESSES, FAILURES, AND QUESTION MARKS

MOST ANALYSTS ENCOUNTER a wide variety of patients in their private practice, and many of these individuals present complicated and difficult transference situations. Projective identification is often the primary vehicle in which persecutory and primitive depressive phantasies play out in the interpersonal and intrapsychic realm of the transference. With the more regressed and defensive patient, there can be chaotic and confusing moments in which acting out by both patient and analyst is common. The analyst can easily stumble within the countertransference, falling into a mutual object-relational enactment. The tool of analytic interpretation is most crucial with these difficult patients. Interpretation of projective identification and the defensive manifestations of the death instinct are crucial to the resolution of core transference conflicts. With these hard-to-reach cases, the analyst must try to work on his or her feet and consistently interpret the in-the-moment relational situation, since the flow of interaction tends to be rapid and unpredictable. This chapter examines these issues with five cases, starting with the most troubling and then moving to less vexing but still stormy and less-than-ideal analyst situations.

Once again, these cases illustrate the often vexing, suboptimal circumstances we face in a typical psychoanalytic practice. Countertransference enactments and interpretive acting out are common with the hard-to-reach patient, as are short, erratic, and stormy treatments that often end with either a disquieting thud or a quiet but painful whimper.

It is difficult to find one profile of the typical patient a psychoanalyst sees in private practice. However, I think several elements are commonly found in the makeup of this average patient we see in our daily work. I am not focusing on the one or two cases of five-day-a-week psycho-analysis on the couch that fits the standards of our training institutes. Research has shown that the vast majority of trained analysts have only one or two cases of classically defined psychoanalysis in their caseload at any given time in their career (Waska 2005). The major bulk of our work, throughout our careers as analysts, involves fairly disturbed indi-viduals who attend sessions one, two, or three times a week, sometimes on the couch and sometimes not. I prefer to see patients on the couch and as frequently as possible, because it seems to work best. But this is not always possible.

My typical analytic patient is an adult in their thirties or forties who has grown up with one parent commanding the attention of the family in a destructive manner. This might be because they are volatile, vio-lent, and controlling. Or one parent might be alcoholic, depressive, or psychotic, leaving the children worried, sad, angry, and confused. Other times, the two parents are embedded in a narcissistic relationship in which all they do is fight or bicker with each other, to the exclusion of caring for their children. Sometimes, loss through death of a parent or divorce leads to an unhealthy focus on the remaining parent as weak, suffering, or pitiful. Some patients recall the stress of seven or eight sib-lings combined with preexisting tension in their parents' marriage. In addition to these historical burdens, external stresses such as financial troubles, childcare difficulties, and health issues are often present in our patient's background.

Psychoanalysts are acutely aware of how external trauma and the dif-ficulties of the real world always combine with unconscious mental pro-cesses, with the mind attempting to find ways of coping, organizing, bal-ancing, and filtering the unwanted, painful, or unbearable feelings and phantasies. The combination of these internal and external factors, as well as the manner in which phantasy mutates them over time, is what patients bring to us and what patients share through the vehicle of the transference. The interaction of internal object relations with external circumstances is constantly producing, through phantasy, new and ever-changing psychological perspectives that then interface with day-to-day experiences in life to produce more internal and external cycles.

LITERATURE REVIEW

Assorted papers throughout the psychoanalytic literature explore patients who are difficult to treat. These papers usually concern borderline patients able to sustain a treatment process but who nevertheless provide a problematic and frustrating experience for the analyst. More sparse in the literature are theoretical or clinical papers that examine patients who are unable to work past certain severe transference states and who repeatedly act out and display self-destructive patterns of interpersonal and psychological relating. These patients often terminate prematurely after stormy, combative transference and countertransference conditions.

Primitive experiences of loss and persecution are usually at the core of many of these difficult cases (Waska 2002). For other hard-to-reach patients, a core mix of paranoid and primitive depressive phantasies drives the ego to rely on the death instinct and destructive cycles of projective identification as the principal method of coping (Waska 2004, 2005). The majority of all these cases have suboptimal analytic results. Some analysts would term these treatments to be failures. I see them as cases in which both analyst and patient strive for moments of psychological clarity within the darkness of the patient's lifelong chaos. These moments are hopefully cultivated, sustained, and enlarged. This is possible in some cases but not in others.

Wolman (1972) presented a number of views about what constitutes an analytic failure or success. This effort was revisited in Reopen and Schulman's (2002) collection of psychoanalytic perspectives on the concept of treatment failure. Important work has been done in looking at the analyst's contribution to therapeutic failure, including countertransference problems and counterresistance (Strean 1993). Cartwright (2004) has discussed the importance of transference interpretations in the treatment of those patients who give a direct or veiled threat of termination.

While usually not a point included in the psychoanalytic literature, most analysts struggle with a caseload that includes many quite disturbed patients who leave treatment early on or abruptly abort after being in treatment for a period of time (Waska 2005). Frayn (1992), Hoffman (1985), Piper et al. (1999), Reder and Brown (1999), Reder and Tyson (1980), and Van Denburg (1992) are just some of the psychoanalytic researchers who have examined the common problem of early dropout in analytic therapy, be it in once-a-week, sitting-up conditions or a five-days-a-week, on-the-couch setting.

HARD TO REACH AND HARD TO UNDERSTAND

I will present case material to illustrate some of the more difficult patients we meet in our analytic work. These are patients who need the exploration and dynamic internal change that psychoanalytic therapy offers but who are often very hard to treat with the analytic method. These individuals typically have a hard time separating their transference feelings and phantasies from reality, and they often terminate or abort the treatment very quickly. For these patients, reality is experienced as too painful, frightening, and ultimately disappointing. The ego must find ways to maintain ties to phantasy objects that seem to offer more than reality can. These objects are invariably the mother or father one wished for but never had. Anger, sorrow, guilt, and loss are so tied up with these wishes that the phantasy ends up being as painful and frightening as the reality one tries to escape. This is usually when the patient enters treatment, seeking to disengage with these troubling feelings, phantasies, and self-destructive behaviors. Of course, this patient is unconsciously not just trying to give up allegiance to this object of pain, rage, guilt, and betrayal but is also reluctant or outright refuses to give up ties to this object, because it also brings about hopes and wishes for love, comfort, attention, and acceptance. This push/pull dynamic is an important aspect, if not the pivotal aspect, of the transference and the projective-identification process that often defines the transference. I believe we can see our most difficult cases as struggling with these issues. Through the dynamics of projective identification, these patients act out their internal experience of being held hostage to the worst of mental states.

A mental dynamic such as denial can be used for positive, growth-oriented mental capacity. It can help the ego reach new levels of creativity and self-expression. Or pathological denial can get the ego into trouble with reality testing and self-destructive acting out.

The death instinct can be understood as operating in this manner, a shrinking from all growth capacity and a force that leads the ego to be a victim to its own potential. A part of the ego attempts to nullify, corrupt, or destroy other parts of the ego, which typically are more life affirming and drawn to the idea of union and idealization with a positive supportive object.

This antichange, antigrowth stance is typically entwined with different degrees of acting out and pathological uses of projective identification and splitting. The death instinct, as I think of it operating within the transference, is a state of mind in which the patient's ego is trapped within a fissure of internal chaos, persecution, and phantasies of unforgivable badness that create terrible feelings of loss and dread. The ego has yet to emerge from a regressive paranoid-schizoid position but also has the burden of premature depressive anxieties, fostered by external and internal factors. Therefore, unsolvable depressive phantasies and paranoid states make up the person's moment-to-moment psychic experiences. The death instinct, by definition, is the ego's best attempt to deal with this no-man's land of unresolvable pain and fear. It is the withdrawal from contact with any self- or object-related experiences of change, growth, reflection, or creativity in the hopes of avoiding further difficulty. It is a stubborn, play-possum stance. To help these sorts of patients, the analyst must be able to tolerate and contain difficult periods of acting out and ultimately assist the patient in facing overwhelming experiences of loss, persecution, betrayal, and lack of control. For these hard-to-reach patients, guilt and dread work together, fear and rage combine, and demands for power coincide with pleas for mercy. I believe I am describing a very specific variation of a psychic retreat (Steiner 1993).

The proper treatment of such patients involves most of the traditional aspects of normal psychoanalytic work. In addition, the analyst must be able to not only interpret the transference in a consistent manner but also interpret the often intense reliance on projective identification. This overuse of projective identification creates more of an interpersonal and interpsychic focus on the analyst and fosters more than the usual amount of acting out, enactments, and countertransference impasses. At the same time, the patient's more depressive conflicts make them feel vulnerable to overwhelming object-related anxiety, which is often more internal and therefore not as obvious in the transference. These phantasy states need to be interpreted not only as direct transference references to the analyst but also as frightening, uncomfortable inner experiences fought in private. Sometimes, the interpretation might be about how the patient is ashamed, frightened, or reluctant to share these inner conflicts with the analyst. Therefore, the transference would be of a misunderstanding, judgment, or shock from the analyst that the patient must avoid. The interpretation could begin there and eventually focus more on the actual internal phantasy conflict. At other times, it would be more accurate to interpret the deep phantasy conflicts the patient is privately struggling with and then tie these in with the analyst-patient relationship secondarily. This is in line with what Steiner (1994) has termed analyst-centered versus patient-centered interpretations. In other words, paranoid patients make the immediate transference issues more easy to notice and interpret. As those are worked through, the deeper phantasies this transference is based on can be worked through. Depressive patients tend to need their internal states discovered and worked with before the actual transference relationship with the analyst makes more sense to discuss.

I will begin with some examples of more profoundly intense and difficult treatment experiences to show the thorny and stormy moments that make containment, clarity, and interpretation hard and at times impossible. The nature of the patient's phantasies, the resulting transference state, the pathological reliance on projective identification and acting out, and the strong clinical presence of the death instinct make identifying and working with the deeper issues of loss, sadness, grief, rage, and dread very chaotic.

CASE 1

Mr. A was referred to me by a colleague who told me he was "a real handful" after meeting with him for a fifteen-minute medication assessment. He told Mr. A that he needed ongoing psychotherapy and gave him my name and number, knowing I was willing to take on difficult cases.

Mr. A was a forty-year-old man who had been thrown out of the house by his fourth wife after he relapsed using cocaine and attempted to rob a grocery store. He was arrested and was acquitted on a technicality. Mr. A was raised by an alcoholic father and an abusive mother. His mother, who had been married six times, would beat Mr. A as a child to the point of leaving him with black eyes and split lips. He had been a heavy drug user most of his life but had managed to stop for several years until his recent relapse. He told me the relapse was brought on by a fight with his wife about her recent affair. Mr. A had also had a history of cheating on his wife.

During the first session, I met with Mr. A and asked him to have a seat. I told him we would start each session with the payment of fees and a discussion of any business or scheduling issues before we would discuss what was on his mind. I emphasized that both business matters and emotional matters were important and that we might learn something from the way he approached either one. Mr. A paid for the first session and we scheduled the next appointment. He began telling me about his upbringing, his drug history, various sexual issues, the details of his four marriages, and his plans to build a new home. This was all done in a scattered, disjointed manner that seemed to reflect his inner experience of life. During this session, he casually mentioned that he might move to Europe and would be leaving in two or three weeks. He made no mention of how this would affect our meetings. I brought this up, and he said he wasn't sure about the move yet, but he if he moved he would be returning for business and we could meet then. I noted his lack of attention to our new relationship and my countertransference feelings of being treated like an appliance that could be replaced. When I asked Mr. A about how he felt being separated from his wife, he replied in the same indifferent way, "Oh, it's cool. I haven't given it much thought. I'm doing my own thing right now."

At our second appointment, Mr. A was thirty minutes late. When he arrived, he came in and immediately began telling me details of his past, his upbringing, his current business plans, his ideas about why his wife was so angry with him, and a variety of other topics. Again, it felt like he was backing up a dump truck and releasing a pile of debris over me. I said, "I'm interrupting you because I'm curious what made you late today. You didn't say anything about it." Mr. A mentioned taking the wrong exit, having to go around some back roads, and then look for parking. Then he jumped right back into his verbal flood of material. While I was listening, I also recalled that he had not paid me or brought up our schedule.

After a few minutes, I said, "I am very interested in what you are bringing up today. Before I can really focus on that, we need to take care of the fee and look at scheduling our next visit since we left it open last time." Mr. A acted as if he hadn't heard me and continued telling me details of his wife's affair and his last affair. At that point, I felt, in the countertransference, that Mr. A was acting like a self-absorbed drug addict who was just going to take from me without any idea of giving back. This feeling, combined with the fact that he was probably moving to Europe in a week or two and would abort the treatment, left me off balance from my analytic stance. I acted out these feelings and phantasies by saying, "Mr. A! I need you to stop talking for a minute so you can take care of the fee and we can discuss our schedule." He ignored me and kept talking. The session was ending, and I was feeling tense about being used. I voiced these feelings by saying, "Look! You need to stop for a minute and take care of business. Please pay me the fee now." Mr. A said something about how his wife "had screwed him over" after his relapse and how he "got into debt after the last big drug deal." Then, he said he only had part of the fee and would need some of that money for the bridge toll. I told him to give me what he could, keep enough for the bridge toll, and pay the remainder next time. Looking back on this, I felt like I was part of a shady drug deal at that moment. He gave me a portion of the fee and then continued his scattered, confusing monologue. I must add that I am almost sure he was not high on any drug at this point. This behavior was instead a psychological enactment. At the very end of this session, we agreed to meet one more time, as he informed me he was indeed moving to Europe the following week.

A few days later, I received a call from Mr. A. He told me I "was fired" for being "way too interested in money and ignoring my needs." I attempted to speak with him about what I thought had happened. I told him, "we agreed to deal with the fee and schedule at the beginning each time. When you didn't, I was put into the role of stopping you and asking you to give me money. Then, you felt offended." Before I could finish, he cut me off and said, "fucking right, Doc! I *am* offended, you asshole. You're fired!" Then, he hung up.

One thing that impresses me in this clinical material is the way in which the transference was demonstrated solely through the patient's and analyst's acting out. Mr. A's interpersonal actions pushed me to have matching interpersonal reactions, and this created a particular relationship of narcissistic dismissal, demand, contempt, rejection, and abandonment. There were several times during both sessions that I could have pointed out how Mr. A seemed to be relating to me, but I choose to comment only on the concrete interpersonal behavior rather than the possible unconscious meaning it may have had. This is a specific denial of the transference/countertransference by both patient and analyst, and this phenomenon is common with these difficult patients. The treatment often remains stuck within the acting out, and the patient, as Mr. A did, usually terminates early on.

CASE 2

Like Mr. A, this next case started out with some level of acting out and denial of transference/countertransference on the part of both patient and analyst, but the case moved past that to a mutual contact with deeper material. At that point, the analyst was able to begin making analytic interpretations.

Mr. B came to see me after he began experiencing extreme bouts of anxiety when driving. Whenever he had to drive somewhere, especially long distances, he felt he was going to pass out and crash the car. After extensive medical tests, he was referred to a psychiatrist for medications and then to me for psychological assistance.

During the initial interview, Mr. B told me about his symptoms and how they affected his life. I asked him to describe other aspects of his life, and he began telling me about the difficult years he spent taking care of his father. His father was elderly and suffered from mild dementia. Then he fell and broke both hips. He was confined to a nursing home two hours away from my patient's home. While Mr. B had a brother who lived minutes away and who could have visited and taken care of matters, the brother was also an alcoholic who would barely answer the phone, let alone be responsible to help others. So for a period of three years, Mr. B traveled back and forth to the nursing home to visit his father and take care of legal and financial matters.

Mr. B's mother was long dead, and Mr. B and his father were not very close, because, as Mr. B put it, "my father was a good man, but very angry and self-centered, which only got worse with the dementia." Mr. B's driving and anxiety problems started about a year after he began traveling to visit his father. Even though he often had to pull over to the side of the road to gather himself when overwhelmed, he kept up "his responsibility" and often drove there two, three, or four times a week. After three years of continued medical problems with his hips and deteriorating dementia, Mr. B's father died of a heart attack in the nursing home. I saw Mr. B one year later. The anxiety had now spread beyond driving and followed him into elevators, stairwells, tall buildings, and airplanes.

I asked Mr. B, "given your difficult relationship with your father and your alcoholic brother, the time it took to drive down all the time to the nursing home, and the whole stressful nature of that period in your life, I wonder if you felt a bit of anger and other feelings toward your father on the drives down to see him?" I based this interpretation on my impression that Mr. B may have felt such a mixture of anger, resentment, guilt, and loss during that time and that his anxiety was the result of these repressed feelings, creating a mental compromise of sorts. He didn't want to drive to see his father but felt guilt about that feeling, so it was easier to believe that his anxiety attacks prevented him from making the drives. This academic assessment was fortified by my countertransference. I had noted during the session that, on the one hand, Mr. B wept while expressing grief for his dead father. But, on the other hand, he also seemed irritated when answering some of my questions. It was unclear if he was irritated at me for asking particular questions or if the questions triggered something that brought up tension. Of course, both possibilities were important to keep in mind.

Mr. B answered me and said, "Oh yes. I drove down there feeling all sorts of things. I was angry at my father many times for all sorts of things." I said, "do you think that your anger toward your father over those three years turned into anxiety? In other words, sometimes you wanted to pull over or turn around and not go to see him. Since you love him and wanted to help him out but also got angry sometimes and didn't want to go, you were in a conflict about it. Maybe the anxiety was a way your mind made that decision for you?" Mr. B said, "You know, I never thought of it as clearly as you just put it. But I have wondered about something like that. Yes. I think my anger toward my father has something to do with my anxiety." He then went on for a bit, talking about the difficult times dealing with his ailing father, the onset of his father's dementia, his brother's drinking, and his own personal troubles with his wife, his finances, and his job.

We were out of time, and I confirmed the next visit. Mr. B looked at me and said, in a condescending, demanding, and irritated way, "So! How is this going to help anything? I can talk like this to my friends for free. Can you tell me how you are going to make me feel better?" I gathered my thoughts and replied, "we touched on a great deal of intense and uncomfortable feelings today. I think you're backing off from them right now and that's ok. We can continue to look at all your feelings and see the connection with the anxiety. I will see you next week."

In making my interpretation, I had several choices. I could have tried to explain how analytic therapy works. This would have been a reply to his actual question, but he clearly did not ask out of simple intellectual curiosity. He was upset and slightly agitated, and that was the way the question emerged. I could have interpreted his treating me in a condescending manner and linked it to his anxiety. Or I could have pointed out that he was treating me like he perhaps felt treated by his father and brother.

While all these options were valid and important to use at some point in Mr. B's treatment, I choose to engage with him at the level that seemed most alive in the moment. I thought he was reacting to the connection he had made to intense and uncomfortable feelings, and he reacted by putting me down. He was suddenly more in touch with the frightening, unacceptable phantasies that the anxiety had covered over before. He was more in touch with the hateful feelings toward the objects he loved. This was hate toward objects that were damaged, dying, or dead: his father and brother. This phantasy state, a set of ideas, feelings, and unconscious relations between self and object, was what brought Mr. B to treatment in the first place. I thus made my interpretation at that level.

This interpretation was aimed at the affective, intrapsychic level of the moment; the interpersonal aspect, the condescending and demanding attitude, could wait for another day. Both are elements of the total transference (Joseph 1985), but the analyst needs to engage with the element most alive in the analytic moment. If we hadn't ended the session at that very moment, I think I would still have made the comment I did and then would have listened to what Mr. B had to say in return. Then, I would have probably said something like, "I notice you're talking like you feel irritated at me. Is the anger toward your father that we talked about alive in the room between us right now?" But, for now, the fight-and-flee reaction he had was best addressed with a clarification of what he was feeling and how that might be causing him to react. Also, to bring up more direct transference elements at the very end is to not give Mr. B enough time to process the comment, reflect on it, and respond. At best, he could either ignore it or become defensive about it.

The agitation Mr. B displayed was similar in many ways to the outbursts Mr. A showed. However, with Mr. B, both analyst and patient were able to tolerate, process, and work with it in a way that allowed the analytic journey to continue, rather than to create a standoff or an abrupt termination.

CASE 3

Mr. C was a thirty-year-old gay man who felt "pushed around, controlled, and ignored" by his boyfriend. They had been living together for six years. We began by meeting twice a week, ostensibly because he was unsure if he had the time or money to meet more often. I interpreted that he might also be anxious to make a deeper commitment to me and the analytic treatment, but this was largely brushed off with intellectual ideas about time and money. Mr. C used logic and concrete thinking a great deal of the time. I suggested it might make him feel more in control to use only logic to relate. He agreed but felt it was "important to have a handle on things."

Mr. C was a police captain. Based on how he described his career, I made interpretations about how skilled he sounded at the job as well as how the tightly controlled and in-charge nature of the job seemed suited to his need for control and a sense of security. At first, Mr. C would reply with a comment to the effect of, of course he was good at his job, since he was an "in-charge, take charge" kind of guy. But after a while in the analytic process, he was able to share his more vulnerable side. He told me he often felt like an "outsider" and that compared to the other police chiefs and captains, he felt weak and inferior.

Before a holiday break, I informed Mr. C that I would be away for one week and that I would see him on the Monday I returned. Mr. C replied, "I won't be in on that day." This was said in a no-nonsense way, as if it was not really open for discussion. I asked why. He said he wouldn't have time to renew the authorization he needed from the insurance company. This was also said in a matter-of-fact way that left no room for discussion. I said that it seemed he had plenty of time to obtain the authorization, so perhaps there was something else going on. Here, my interpretive approach is similar to how I handled Mr. B. I could have brought Mr. C's attention to how he was being controlling and limiting with me in the moment, but I felt that this transference stance was linked to something that we didn't understand yet. So I decided to follow the trail a bit more, hoping to find the source of his tension. I think either approach is fine, but in the clinical moment, it seemed more to the point to investigate why he was treating me a certain way than to focus on how he was treating me. In this way, it is probably more accurate to say that I was trying to understand his phantasies and their accompanying affect states rather than focus on how he was relating to me interpersonally. Both are aspects of the transference, but one or the other is more appropriate to interpret at any given time.

Mr. C stuck with his insurance story, so I repeated my interpretation. I said, "I can understand you are concerned about having the insurance all lined up, but since that would be easy to do with one phone call and they're available seven days a week, I wonder if you're having some kind of feeling about either me leaving or about coming in to see me next time." Here, I was more specific about the possible transference anxiety he may have been having. It slowly came out that Mr. C wanted to have the day off to be with his family for the extended holiday period. I said, "you must feel like being honest with me isn't a safe approach, like I wouldn't approve of what you want to do." Mr. C told me he "needed to find the right stance to make sure I am not shot down." He went on to say he felt he needed to make sure he was "on solid ground" and to not "leave himself open to trouble."

I told him, "it must be tough to be on the alert and have to stand watch all the time." He agreed and told me that being on watch "just feels natural." I asked him why he didn't picture wanting to be with his family to be a legitimate reason in my eyes to not make the session. In other words, I wanted to know his phantasy about me and my disapproval. Mr. C said he "needed to be polite at all times. It is important to maintain that good will." At this point, we were discussing and exploring both the core object-related phantasies he lived with as well as the in-the-room transference manifestation of those phantasies and feelings.

I interpreted, "you have some things you want and need, but you seem afraid of hurting me. So you are polite and say it is about the insurance. Can you tell me more about those feelings?" Here, I was addressing what I thought were primarily depressive phantasies about harming me or offending me. Mr. C said, "I make it a point to be polite and strategic because, you're right, I think I could hurt your feelings. But, I also think you could shoot me down. I don't want to be told off or told what to do or not do. I don't want to be told I will not get what I want." He said this in a way that was somewhat narcissistic but mostly fearful and paranoid. In other words, he was clarifying that while some of the anxieties were depressive, he also envisioned being rejected, shot down, and told what to do. This fear of domination, control, and deprivation combined with the other fears of harming me. My clinical impression at that point was that it was a complex phantasy of harming me and thereby causing me to retaliate by harming him.

I asked Mr. C if these sorts of feelings were familiar to him. This question seemed to unleash a pent-up store of traumatic memories from his past. Mr. C told me he grew up in a family where his mother was "very strict and into discipline, so we had to be nice and polite and always thinking one step ahead of what mother was up to." I asked for examples of this, and Mr. C told me about extreme incidences of abuse and trauma throughout his upbringing. These stories included Mr. C's mother chasing around his brother with a butcher knife for speaking disrespectfully to her. Another example included Mr. C's mother breaking a kitchen chair over his older brother's head for stealing cigarettes at the corner market. I pointed out that he probably still carried some fear with him from these experiences, which might explain how he was relating to me. Mr. C agreed. "I think it is a fear-based reaction." He went on to talk about how he often feels fearful, inferior, and anxious about his life and his relationships. Thus the exploration of his phantasies, the immediate transference situation, and his developmental background initiated important analytic contact, which led to exploration and working through.

CASE 4

Ms. D was a thirty-year-old graduate student in psychology; her goal was to become a psychotherapist. She was a very articulate woman and tried to engage me with intellectual and theoretical concepts. She came to treatment to better understand and stop her sexual acting out. She had a long history of going to bars, gyms, and sex clubs to pick up men to have sex with. This behavior troubled her, and, as she studied psychology in school, she could see more and more, at least intellectually, that her behavior was self-destructive. This became more of an issue when she started dating a young man whom she liked and felt comfortable with but not sexually attracted to. She felt guilty for continuing to go to bars and bringing home strangers behind her boyfriend's back.

Ms. D told me she thought that much of this acting out was the result of her upbringing, in which she felt "very judged by everyone." She told me, "I think I am just rebelling against that parental and societal injunction now." Her father was a minister of a conservative Baptist church in a small town, and as a child Ms. D heard volumes about the sins of sex and desire. Ms. D said she grew up feeling "very different than others and singled out for scrutiny." She felt "everyone always was looking at me or watching me. As a young girl and still as a teenager, I felt like an outsider and an odd duck."

From age ten to sixteen, she engaged in masturbation and oral sex with her brother, who was four years older. This finally stopped when Ms. D told him she didn't want to do it anymore. When I asked what this experience was like, she told me she "realized it must have had a profound effect on her inner phantasy life, her Oedipal dynamics, and

her object relations." This was one of countless times in the transfer-
ence/countertransference where I felt pushed away by a disconnected,
omnipotent, and above-it-all attitude. It also put me in an odd, defeated
sort of position, in that I felt there was nothing I could say about Ms. D's
way of relating without being attacked or accused of being insensitive.
For example, when I asked, "you're suddenly using a lot of intellectual
words to describe an intense emotional experience. Maybe it is easier to
talk in those terms than to feel the discomfort of those memories," she
replied, "why are you putting me down for how I talk? I think I did an
accurate job of describing my specific experience in that situation."

Over time, Ms. D took most of my interpretations in this manner and
started to see me as a judgmental priest-analyst who saw her as a sin-
ner with words, always speaking the wrong way. I made that very interpretation many times as well, only to have Ms. D tell me, "I guess if
I don't speak the way you want me to, you aren't happy. Why can't you
accept me for who I am? Isn't that your job? Why are you so demeaning
to me?" This paranoid, persecutory transference, in which I was now a
carbon copy of her critical father and the conservative church, made it
extremely difficult to work together.

There was also a sexual aspect to this transference standoff. I interpreted that she might be using words to provide security and safety from
the sexual confusion in her mind of two close, intimate, but nonsexual
people: patient and analyst. I interpreted that she might feel that we
were like brother and sister, and that could be both soothing and frightening. This was met with the same type of intellectual defense. She said,
"you must be thinking of the possible projection of beta elements into
a fragmented object. I think there could be something to that." I would
try to follow the thread of this and hope she would eventually come to
some feelings of her own, but it would instead become a very lengthy
and one-sided discussion of various psychoanalytic authors and their
most recent work on various topics. When I would make some minor
comment about how she seemed to be keeping us together yet apart by
this method of relating, I was seen as suddenly "finding fault with everything, again."

Over a period of six months, this same type of situation would
emerge. Ms. D would present an emotional issue, bring up a traumatic
memory, or speak about a difficult current problem. These matters were

given to me as a combination of facts, dry statements, and theoretical speculations. The more she spoke, the more logical and removed she became. When I made my first comment about how she was relating to me, she would reply in a cold, mechanical way, with more psychological jargon. She insisted that she was using the most clear and honest language possible, so it "was cruel of me to question her very personality." Often, spending time with Ms. D was like being read to from an academic textbook. If I didn't address this transference stance at all, often out of my countertransference frustration and sense of futility, Ms. D would simply continue to zigzag around from one issue to another. The topics themselves were important, but she sanitized and stripped them of any emotion or meaning.

Over time, I tried several approaches, but all of them met with the same rejection and claim of judgment. I would simply summarize the emotional content of what she was struggling with. I would ask her to tell me how she felt about the issues. I would make transference interpretations about her anxiety over what she might be feeling toward me. I made comments about the mixed feelings she must have had over sharing her personal issues with me. I simply stayed silent. Virtually anything I tried led us down the same path. Fairly quickly, Ms. D would summarize the situation in dense psychological jargon and then stop, apparently satisfied with her packaged assessment. I would share my predicament and tell her that I felt unable to find a way to connect with her even though I was trying every way possible. I suggested this might be a clue for us to understand something about her feelings or her view of me. She would respond by telling me I was always too critical and not able to "bring the clinical lens to focus on her selfobject injury and facilitate a transmuting internalization."

My clinical impression was that this type of transference, in which the analytic relationship was taken up in a very literal way without reflection and without the option to consider things from multiple perspectives, was a weapon against change. I think that while Ms. D wished for change in her external life, she dreaded what change might mean to her internal life and sought to keep a rigid status quo. Therefore, she erected an impenetrable shield against difference and growth. As a result of strong projective-identification dynamics, I noticed myself prodding her and firing multiple salvos of interpretations: could it be this, could it be that? This, I think, was an enactment of her phantasy of having sex with someone who should be close but not that close: her brother. And, in response, she kept me at bay and under her control with jargon and emotional distance. Also, I think she was scared that if she did reveal her inner self to me, I might be judgmental and see her as sinful and wrong, much in the way she felt judged as a child.

Unfortunately, Ms. D stopped seeing me and contacted another therapist whom she said "seemed to know how to work from a more internalized schema perspective. I need that. You haven't been able to make contact with the inner child that needs maternal and paternal nourishment and a sense of being held within a container." This is indeed what I think Ms. D wanted and needed but, by the very way she described it, was unable to allow that degree of vulnerability and change with me. I hope she finds this "transformative experience" with the next therapist, but I have a hunch that there will be a repeat of the difficulty that we had.

CASE 5

Mr. E was a forty-year-old man who came to see me for help with severe panic attacks he had been suffering from for about six months. He was a very independent, overly confident man who said he usually took care of any problems that came along but realized he might need "the temporary assistance of a professional." I commented that he sounded like he just needed help with a flat tire and then he would be back on the road, in control again. Mr. E said, "and what's wrong with that, Doc?" I replied, "Nothing's wrong with it, but that kind of way of seeing things, being very independent all the time, may be an initial clue to understanding you and the problems you're having."

Mr. E has two brothers and two sisters. He described his father as "a raging monster most of the time and an ok guy some of the time." I asked what he meant. Mr. E's father had an extremely violent temper and at least once a week would destroy furniture, punch holes in the wall, and break dishes. All the children would scatter and run upstairs to their rooms, and Mr. E's mother would hide in another room. Other times,

Mr. E's mother would take all the children to stay at a friend's house for a day or two. Mr. E's father would be intensely remorseful, fix the house back up, and take the family out to dinner or a movie. Everything would seem wonderful for a few days, until he would again violently tear apart the house, screaming threats and obscenities. Throughout his youth and teen years, Mr. E remembers always focusing on the day when he would be able to leave that frightening mess.

When Mr. E was eighteen, he left home and began working several jobs. He met a woman his age and promptly got married. They had two children almost immediately and, sadly, she became more and more belligerent and violent, much like Mr. E's father. She would tear up the house and rage at the children and Mr. E, sometimes physically assaulting him. He left the family when he was twenty-three years old and moved to another state to start over. He developed a severe drug problem through much of his twenties but still worked hard at various menial jobs. He gravitated toward landscaping jobs and enjoyed the work. At age thirty-three, he was hired by a landscaping company that respected and promoted him for his skills. Mr. E was able to stop using drugs, all on his own. By the time he was in his late thirties, he was fairly high up in the landscape company and felt very proud and confident about his achievements.

Roughly a year before Mr. E came to see me, he was terminated from his job after a larger company bought the landscape company and eliminated many of the employees. This was a terrible shock to Mr. E, who felt betrayed and ambushed. There was an instant feeling of hopelessness and despair that he was unfamiliar with. "I never allow myself to feel vulnerable or accountable to anyone. I'm my own man! This was out of the blue and a feeling I didn't want but couldn't control," he said. Then, he added, "what sort of techniques do you have for me to get rid of it?" This was said in a controlling, use-me-and-then-move-on kind of manner, so I said, "you want to get rid of this stuff right away, so you're telling me to fix you like a car that needs an oil change. Maybe it's uncomfortable to look at it in a deeper way, to be more in touch with your feelings and to have to depend on me for a while." Mr. E laughed and said, "the last thing I'm going to do is depend on anyone. I gave that up before I was ten years old. If you are going to survive in this world, you do it on your own. The world is made up of greedy, nasty people who just look out for themselves, and if you are naïve and weak, you get screwed. That's just the way it is!"

The transference relationship was quickly set up to be one in which Mr. E looked to me to be a convenient appliance that was there to serve him. This was in place of what sounded like a quite frightening phantasy of depending on me only to get betrayed and hurt. I interpreted this several times to Mr. E during the first session, and that he was able to tolerate it, listen to it, and perhaps internalize it a bit was a positive sign.

Mr. E told me that after he was fired from the landscape company, he went into a deep depression for about a month. Then, at the urging of a few friends, he started his own landscape company. After about eight months, he was now engaged in a number of contracted jobs and actually making a go of it. While barely able to pay his bills, this was a significant achievement. Mr. E said, "logically, I can see that I am doing damn good for just opening shop eight months back. But money has always been an issue for me. I feel like I'm going to take a nosedive all the time. All my friends say to relax, enjoy my new career move, and be patient. I know they're right, but emotionally I'm feeling right on the edge of disaster. About two months ago, my old company called me and asked me to come back to work for them part time. I was shocked and told them I'd think about it. I was so uptight about money that I said I would do it. So I've been doing my stuff in the morning and then going over to help them out in the afternoon. About a week after I started doing that, I would start feeling like I was going to throw up as soon as I got on the freeway to go there. I got sweaty and clammy and nauseated. It doesn't happen every time, but overall it seems worse. I feel completely out of control. What the hell is that?" I interpreted, "do you think you resent having to go back to work for someone who fired you, but now you feel dependent on them for money and that makes you feel sick to your stomach?" He replied, "Boy, you've got that right! But, I never thought of it like that, putting the two together like that."

In between the first and second session, I had to contact Mr. E's insurance company to sort out the details of his coverage. Mr. E's insurance was one I was not familiar with, and when I tried to sort out his coverage and obtain an authorization to see him, I was given a runaround that took more than two hours. By the end of this torturous exercise, I still didn't have a guarantee of authorization. When Mr. E came into his second session, I told him all this and said that while I thought "we were probably ok and the insurance probably would pay," if they didn't it was ultimately his insurance. Therefore, he would be responsible for the bill. "It looks like we won't have a problem, but I do want to alert you just in case." This was like lighting a fuse. Mr. E started yelling, "there is no fucking way I will pay that, and you should know by now that I am in no financial position to be able to! I didn't have a good feeling about starting some kind of therapy, and this just proves my point. Doctors are never there to really care for you or because they genuinely want to help you out. The first thing on your mind is money. You want to know if you're going to get paid before you are willing to even listen to me. Thank God I'm not dying of a heart attack or something! You probably would demand some money before touching me. I'd die in the meantime. It doesn't surprise me. Everyone is a bloodsucking bastard of some variety. It's just too bad that I made the mistake of trying to trust you."

This sort of response continued through the rest of the session. Twice, Mr. E said he "wouldn't stand for this crap anymore" and got up to leave. I was put in a position of doing whatever I could to secure the analytic relationship, as Mr. E felt it was unraveling. Indeed, I thought my task as an analyst was to help Mr. E begin to see how he was in fact unraveling our relationship through his intense persecutory and aggressive phantasies, which were creating the current transference situation.

I had to make every effort to address the transference. I said, "from what I know about you so far, trust is something you never had growing up. You have lived your life assuming no one will treat you right. Without giving us a chance, you are deciding I am bad." Mr. E said, "Well, you said something like that last time and I must say, it made me stop and think a bit. The fact that you made me think a little differently last time is the only reason I came back today. But, I still don't trust you or anyone else, and when you bring up the whole insurance and money situation, it only confirms that I would be crazy to think you're not trying to get one over on me. It is just human nature and I would be stupid not to expect it in everyone I deal with. There is no fairytale ending to the story; people are just trying to fuck with you, and if you don't look out for it, then you are basically inviting it. Be a chump and get fucked, or live life on your own terms and take care of yourself. That's the way it is."

I responded, "when I try to talk with you about making sure I don't get shorted my fee, you see it as me attacking you and being selfish. Maybe I can make sure that I will be ok *and* take care of you at the same time." Mr. E responded, "If that was possible, it would be nice. But I have yet to experience that in my life. Why should I be vulnerable and trust you and then have you control me and take advantage of me? I won't stand for that bullshit. I don't think we need to continue this. Thanks for your time." He again got up to leave. I said, "please sit down. Just hear me out. We talked last time about how you feel you have to be in control and independent all the time. You think I am being controlling now and that I'm only out for myself. So, it's scary when you imagine both of us only out for ourselves. But all I want to do today is make sure everything is in place so our work together is protected." Mr. E said, "you are asking me to work with you. I see what you mean, and that would be the way to go. It is not something I am willing to trust, and I don't really believe it is possible. But you have made a few good points—I'll give you that." I continued, "I am asking you to work with me on the money issue and all the other issues. Maybe that feels like a welcome relief from having to do it all by yourself against all the selfish people around you. But it might also feel unfamiliar and unsafe." Mr. E said, "I've had to do everything my whole life. It's exhausting, but I have to be accountable. It's all up to me and, in the end, if I make it or not, it is because of what I do." I added, "yes, it is all up to you in the end. But maybe it doesn't have to be a you-against-me or an all-the-burden-is-on-your-shoulders situation. Maybe, by working together, we can figure out how to lighten the load a bit. Maybe, you could still feel in control without having to be on guard for the next attack all the time." He said, "well, I'm willing to see how it goes, for now."

With Mr. E, there most certainly is a great deal of paranoia and paranoid-schizoid functioning. However, I caught a sense of respect from him that was only revealed a few times in passing. When he said he came back because I said something that made him think differently, I felt he was paying me a great deal of respect—and being vulnerable in doing so. While he was literally shouting at me for most of the second session and threatened to leave several times, I didn't feel he was actually attacking me. It was more that he took a protective stance, just in case. In other words, he was able to hold on to a bigger picture of our relationship, even if only for moments at a time. I think this revealed a level of depressive functioning that allowed Mr. E to think in a more whole, integrated manner than Mr. A, even though the situation we were struggling with was somewhat similar. However, this depressive element of Mr. E's personality was fragile and malformed, so it only provided momentary relief to his more primitive anxiety.

DISCUSSION

The patients I have presented in this chapter are dealing with chaotic states of mind in which both paranoid and depressive experiences are overwhelming the ego. Unable to develop in a healthy manner past the paranoid state, their ego remains burdened by primitive schizoid experiences. These patients have also prematurely taken on some of the struggles of the depressive position without the internal good objects and psychological stability to really manage them. Therefore, the analyst must find a way to interpret both intense phantasy states that plague the patient as well as overwhelming transference states that, fueled by projective identification, bring analyst and patient into tangled repetitive cycles of conflict and acting out. The death instinct is part of this psychological limbo, a pathological defensive maneuver the ego uses to deal with early ego frustrations, fears, and hunger. This same withdrawal from life leaves the adult patient unwilling to join the analyst in the journey to change and growth. This leaves the patient with the both paranoid and depressive anxieties but without any psychological benefits from either developmental level, such as forgiveness, integration, desire for change and difference, and hope for a better self and a more benevolent object. These patients present the analyst with so much material early on and continue to fluctuate back and forth between depressive and paranoid troubles that the analyst can easily become confused and find it difficult to sort out what interpretations to make and what explorative direction to take.

SECTION 3

The Emotional Foxhole

7

DIFFERENT WAYS OF CONTROLLING THE OBJECT

CONTROLLING THE OBJECT FROM A PSYCHIC RETREAT

Danny was a middle-aged man I saw individually after several initial consultations with him and his wife. After a twenty-year marriage and several children, she announced she was leaving him. She explained that she had never been physically attracted to Danny, but since they "got along so well" she thought that aspect of the relationship "might emerge later or that it might not be so important in the scope of things." After five years of marriage, she said she "was completely turned off and had zero interest in ever having sex" with him again. "She told me she was fed up with only having a good friend or roommate as a husband and that it was time to do better."

Danny was completely shocked by this and wanted to save the marriage. In the initial consultation, Danny's wife made it very clear that "it's all over, and all that's left to discuss are the details of the divorce." They were both very matter of fact about it, and logic ruled the hour. I commented on that, and, surprisingly, they both agreed and saw nothing wrong with that. She said it was "cut and dried: I don't love him that way, so it's over," and he felt that "either I can change her mind or we will be separating." This was further clarified when they told me that they had tried couples therapy a few months prior but had stopped "because it seemed pointless to bring up things that were only hurtful." I interpreted that they both were avoiding conflict at all costs, and perhaps that was the core problem in the marriage. Danny's wife seemed to open up a bit upon hearing my interpretation and went on to tell me how cold and detached he was over the years, leaving her feeling lonely and unloved. She said, "I ended up feeling unattractive and boring, since he didn't seem to ever want to talk to me." Here, she was clearly sad. This was a moment in which she opened up emotionally, and I suggested that she felt hurt and abandoned, and perhaps this was more the reason that she wanted out of the marriage. At that point, she cried. Danny seemed concerned but did not respond in a caring way. Instead, he said indignantly, "why didn't you tell me about that then? I can't do anything to change that now!" I interpreted that, uncomfortable showing care, he retreated into blame and logic. Danny didn't respond. He sat there looking like he knew I was right but couldn't and didn't want to go beyond his shielded place of control.

After she elected to stop coming to therapy altogether, since she "was clear what she wanted and didn't need to be talked out of it," Danny continued attending. Very quickly, he looked to me to fix the situation, change it, and make it all better, immediately. I interpreted this transference and said, "You want to fix this overnight, like a flat tire. Maybe it is difficult to look at your feelings as you face this terrible time." Danny told me he "simply wants progress and I see no real action plan. It's either change her mind or accept the situation. I don't see where feelings enter into the equation." I said I thought he was now withholding his feelings from me, just as his wife had accused him of doing. I said I thought he must be very upset and worried over the situation. Danny told me, "Well, of course, but what good does that do? It doesn't make her change her mind. If anything, if I go weeping to her, she isn't going to want to stay with me because of that!"

Over the next few months, I was struck by how dependent on logic and control he was. He saw me as merely an instrument that would either perform and bring him what he wanted or fail and leave him with what he had. I had to provide him with the "action plan," or else. I repeatedly interpreted this cold, logical demand and suggested that he seemed to see being in control as almost an ideal. To my surprise, he quickly agreed and said, "What's wrong with that?"

For a while, I felt shut out and frustrated. A couple of times, I tried to argue with Danny and convince him about the benefits of being more emotional and less logical and controlled. He wouldn't have anything to do with it. Noticing this interpretive acting out, I realized my countertransference was similar to what his wife had complained about. I interpreted that he was being very careful and controlled in the way he related to me, keeping his feelings reserved, much as he did at home. I added that I thought he probably felt very upset over what was happening in his life but that maybe he felt more at ease trying to not feel much about it or share it with me. Danny said he did feel bad but asked how it would help for him to express his feelings. I said, "The fact that you ask the question makes me think it must feel like a risk to show yourself, that you might get hurt." Danny said, "Yes. The way I see it, I could go out on that limb without any guarantee and find myself in a real dilemma. I think I'd rather play it safe." I said, "That makes a lot of sense, but then you are safe and alone without anyone to understand you, help you, or just share in whatever you feel. It all becomes very strategic instead of being able to be yourself." Danny replied, "I have been strategic my whole life, creating a game plan. But I know what you mean; it can get a bit lonely or impersonal." Here, Danny reluctantly showed a more emotional, less guarded side of himself and seemed to be a bit more willing to talk with me about his inner conflicts and struggles. A moment of analytic contact was reached, and this will hopefully grow in the sessions ahead. However, with the extreme conviction Danny had about the benefits of control, distance, and logic, it may be difficult or impossible at this point in time.

DISCUSSION

In the short period I have met with Danny, I am left with a distinct clinical impression. He has a particular conviction about the world, one that involves his massive control and avoidance. Given this dark worldview, he has to approach his objects in a very distant and concrete manner.

By having to rely on projective identification as a necessary weapon, he ends up verifying his view of himself and others in a vicious cycle that always brings about loss, despair, and betrayal. His reliance on being in control, logical, and withdrawn was an ideal he respected and strived for. He thus had a negative conviction about life and an accompanying method of defending against it, and he almost worshiped that defense. His marriage was a victim to this system, but Danny quickly dumped his pain and shock into the system and claimed himself ready "to move on."

Danny's cold stance to the world included the transference, and in that respect I often felt excluded and only considered as a temporary instrument in his quest for an answer to how to change his wife's mind. As Steiner (2008) notes, when put in this position, the analyst can easily fall prey to acting out the patient's harsh superego and end up making judgments about either the patient or his objects. If acted out, this would be the analyst's enactment of the patient's death instinct (Feldman 2000) and a part of a pathological projective-identification process. But if carefully monitored, the countertransference of exclusion that emerged in this case can provide valuable direction. I was able to notice how I felt excluded, and I used that information in my interpretations, commenting on how Danny wanted me in his life and needed me to help him but at the same time kept me at a isolated, logical distance in which he could never truly feel like he made progress or that we were working together to understand something new. I had to be an impersonal tool that delivered the solution rather than someone important in his life. This was a parallel to the breakdown in his marriage. These types of interpretations were pivotal in helping him gradually to consider aspects of himself he never allowed before.

Clinically, Danny exhibited a loyalty and conviction to a way of seeing his objects as part of a mechanical world in which feelings had no place. This was part of an effort to hold on to an idealized image of what could have been, what should have been, or the illusion of what was. Danny used splitting to keep things in obsessive control, and this situated his mind within a very barren, sterile, and desolate experience. To avoid conflict, he split off the human vulnerability and interactional sharing that provides the life in a relationship (Hinshelwood 2008). He seemed to want to keep himself as a logic-driven machine that didn't need to feel or give to the object. In fact, this idea of not wanting to engage with his objects and not share himself was part of his phantasy of controlling the object and his relation to it, remaining in a perfect, content bubble requiring no maintenance or concern. This position was what caused the end of the marriage.

Diagnostically, Danny maintained a psychic retreat (Steiner 1993) or what Rosenfeld (1971) called a pathological organization. This was a narcissistic capsule in which Danny felt he could control the object and detach himself safely from any conflict or harm. However, for Danny this retreat was brittle and began to crumble when his wife decided to leave him. He no longer could maintain this perfect isolation, and the retreat became more of a foxhole in which he sought temporary shelter from the incoming attacks of rejection and judgment. This was a meager haven offering only minor protection and trapping him in the battlefield of his objects, which he once felt in control of. If he can tolerate this increased vulnerability, Danny may be able to establish analytic contact and gradually learn and change. However, if he cannot bear or tolerate this lack of control and new vulnerability, he may resort to even more drastic defensive maneuvers and retreat further away from his objects into a more omnipotent and rigid posture.

AVOIDING THE PERSECUTORY OBJECT

Some patients will seek an idealized state that is a narrow, specialized image of the downtrodden, the honest, or the orphaned who should be rescued, recognized, and repaid. Other times, the idealization is for a pure and never-wavering object that is without flaw. Essentially, this is often the demand for a guarantee against any betrayal or disappointment, and unless this guarantee is found, no commitment will be made. In fact, commitment to becoming closer to others is frequently the central conflict for these patients, and their rapid oscillation between demanding an idealized object and being sure they will never find one, so why bother, is what creates their inner turmoil, confusion, and anguish. In fact, they hold a conviction about the potential threat of others, which makes them feel they must exert control at all times.

Darrel has been seeing me for over two years now. Sometimes he attends once a week, but much of the time he only comes every other week, telling me, "That is about all I can take. This is too much to deal with. I have a hard enough time coming up with something to talk about when I am here." What Darrel means is that he feels pressured to have something to give me, and he would "rather not have to engage with me or anyone else, ever." Recently, he told me, "the world is a pretty treacherous place, and you can never really trust anyone. Everyone lies. That's a fact. It is just what side of the lie you are on." I asked him to explain. Darrel told me that everyone lies about himself or herself and it is usually about how they care about you because "everyone is really out for themselves. If they aren't lying to you about how they are your friend, they are lying to themselves about how the world is a good place and how things will work out. If people were honest, they would have to admit how selfish and nasty they really are. Everyone would probably kill themselves if they were honest about how they really felt. No one is really ever happy; they just lie about it."

I told Darrel he must see the world as a very scary place and therefore it makes sense why he keeps to himself so much and why he rations our time together. He agreed and said he "hates people for the most part." I replied, "Maybe you hate how you don't feel like you ever fit in." Over the last two years, he has been more and more amenable to this interpretive line of exploration. In the past, he seemingly kept to a superior judgmental stance, in which he looked down on others just as he imagined they do to him. But, more and more, he is able to allow the idea that he is terrified of being with others because he feels unable to make contact and to figure out how to be close. At the same time, he is adamant about how much he hates to make a commitment to anyone and never can see the point of communicating or spending time together. "People are so boring. I don't see the point. All they want to do is chitchat. It seems so useless. What a waste of time."

Darrel has the same feelings about dating. He feels that women want too much of his time, while he only wants to be left alone. So, very quickly, the women he dates feel ignored and taken for granted. He, in turn, quickly feels pressured and controlled, leading him to "want to run to the exit door." Commitment means being engulfed and left to satisfying a constantly demanding object that has no value in return.

Many of Darrel's sessions are about his dread of having to meet with friends for a party or an outing on the weekend. He usually talks about it in a condescending manner, describing what a waste it is to be with people who "are predictable and shallow." Part of my analytic exploration with him has been to find out why he feels so angry and hateful toward society. I have interpreted that these feelings are his projected anxieties and judgment. He envisions a dreadful, empty, and cold world and then turns his back on it. Darrel is quick to agree and says, "Yes, I think I am hateful. But I also just don't get it. I don't know how to be in that world out there. Also, I don't want to know, because it is a world I don't ever want to join." Here, he reveals his fear and confusion about how to be with others. Darrel agrees with me that he may be scared of others, but that agreement usually shifts rather quickly to how he looks down on "all the stupid little people all caught up in their petty lives."

Overall, the transference with Darrel involves him consistently telling me he "is just the way he is, and nothing will ever change that"; "the world is a cheap and a false place that bores me, and I have never seen the point"; and "I dread coming to see you and having to come up with something to report." There are three themes I regularly take up in his stance toward me and the world.

First, I interpret that he is offering me a challenge when he says there is nothing that can ever change him. I point out to Darrel that he is being defiant and setting up a "me against him" contest. I add that this adversarial stance is one in which he may feel superior, but he also always has to be on guard against his adversary, which probably leaves him anxious and weary. Darrel said, "That approach works pretty well in basketball. I see everyone as my enemy, and I am out to crush them. And since I'm very good on the court, I usually do crush them. But I see what you mean. I am sort of challenging you though. It's been a long time since I started coming here, and I don't see anything different. It's all the same. I feel depressed and bored most of the time. So what are you going to do about it?" I said, "When you say it like that, you get to sit it out while I do all the work. Maybe it's uncomfortable to have to work together and face the feelings you carry around." He replied, "I don't work well with anyone." On the one hand, we made a small move ahead in our understanding. At the same time, he dug his way back into his emotional foxhole, restating his conviction that objects are to be avoided and controlled lest they create a burden or disturbance.

Next, I interpreted more about the narcissistic element of him being bored and looking down on others. I suggested that this is both an angry devaluing of the world *and* a defense against his fear of others. With Darrel, there seemed to be both a defense against fear and anxiety and an actual state of loathing. This is a difficult and confusing aspect of his treatment but one that needs to be addressed as it emerges. His response was to tell me how angry and disappointed he is with the world and to agree briefly that he is scared and unsure "out there."

Finally, I interpreted his projection of pressure and obligation onto me, seeing me as wanting immediate progress or emotional reports, leaving him anxious and obligated. I added that this seems to be his vision of not just me but of the world and that it made sense that he was reluctant to want to venture out into this kind of demanding place. Darrel seemed to calm down a bit upon hearing this and spoke for a time about how he felt intimidated and scared as a child when he had to go to school. "I cried every time I had to go to school. Every day. I never felt better about it. It was always this traumatic event. My mother didn't do much to help. I think she felt the same way about the world as I do. She could be a real tough cookie, but underneath I think she was never sure how to fit in. My father was even more that way. He felt pushed around by her and just retreated into his study most of the time. I retreated into my room, he was in his room, and Mom was off doing her thing. We were like three quiet, awkward people not sure how to live on this planet." I said, "So, you felt they were not able to help you out when you felt lonely or unsure because they felt the same way?" Darrell said, "Exactly."

Here, Darrell seemed to be providing evidence for when and why he essentially gave up on depending on his objects and in fact gave up on trying to resurrect, retrain, or rebuild the object, as it has become possessed or poisoned by his loathing, anger, and anxiety. In that state, it is far too damaged to be of help and now even poses a possible danger if sought out.

Talking about his childhood and revealing some of these terrible feelings was a moment of progress in an otherwise slow and difficult analytic treatment. I think a big reason I was able to help Darrel focus on his phantasies and feelings in that moment was that I was doing a good job containing my countertransference feelings. Often, I felt pulled in ways that, if I acted on them, would keep me from helping him work through his issues. In the countertransference with Darrel, I am left with two distinct feelings. His conviction about the dark, hopeless nature of the world and his own unchangeable negativity make me want to give up. I noticed myself feeling hopeless and wanting to say, "What's the use? Why go on?"

Other times, I felt like coming up with various game plans to help him and pep him up. I wanted to be optimistic and act like his life coach. When I noted these two reactions, I realized how he, through projective identification, had left me with his own despair and a strong defense against it. The more I noticed this, the more I was able to realize that for Darrel, the best I could offer was to be an analyst who was willing to ride along with him, traversing the ins and outs of his anxious, angry, and lonely existence. I would make interpretations along the way, but in the context of being a companion or passenger on the same journey.

This more neutral and relaxed stance is necessary to bear the ongoing negative convictions of this type of patient. It is a willingness not to make progress or change but also a willingness to hang in there for as long as it takes. Indeed, this is a difficult parental role for the analyst, in that it puts us in the ambiguous place of possibly having to watch our patient suffer endlessly or even gradually get worse and worse. It is this willingness to contain and bear the very dread that these types of patients live within that can make the difference in ultimately being able to help them. They are always feeling like they will never get better and that they will just slide downhill until they die. By tolerating and accepting this painful and frightening climate, we can accompany them and make gradual interventions along the way that may or may not provide them with a new direction and eventually a new feeling of hope.

RETRAINING THE OBJECT

Jane was raised with two brothers and a distant father whom she loved a great deal but never felt very close to until she was an adult and was able to spend time with him before he died from cancer. From Jane's description, her mother was indeed loving at times, but that alternated with critical and verbally abusive outbursts. Jane told me, in tears, "on my wedding day, my mother told me she wished I didn't look so homely!" After seeing me for six months, Jane wanted to decrease the frequency of her sessions, citing money issues. Her job paid little, and her husband was out of work. However, my sense was that she was afraid of what we were discovering, alongside of her lifelong feeling that she wasn't important enough to spend time on. I interpreted these two ideas, and she told me, "I never feel good enough to bother with. But, what is even more depressing is that no one else seems to bother either." This was part of the overall theme we have been exploring. Jane agreed to continue attending her analytic sessions regularly, and we continued to make gradual progress.

Jane feels it is necessary always to control her objects, to make sure they are happy and content. This means she must adopt a masochistic stance with most people, in which she gives and gives, hoping to be recognized and one day be rewarded. Of course, this means she is constantly resentful and exhausted, trying to be the servant to others and waiting for us to notice her and provide her with a token of appreciation. This cycle has improved with our work, and recently another deeper level of her need to control the objects in her life came to light.

Jane arrived for her session looking very sad and upset. She broke down crying and told me her birthday had been two days prior and neither one of her brothers had called. She told me she "was sick and tired of always being the forgotten one. I never forget anyone's birthday. I know the birthday, the anniversary, and any other important date of anyone that is in my circle. I always am doing the right thing for others; why am I never remembered?" She was sobbing.

In the countertransference, I felt she was pulling for me to be understanding and to side with her on this slight, which felt so bad to her. I also felt that she was being overly critical and demanding of everyone but justifying that by boasting of her ability to remember everyone else's important dates. Noticing this more critical idea, I realized that she wanted me to put aside any notion of logic or reality and side with her as an understanding, agreeable, and supportive parent. I interpreted that she was looking for me and others to be the parent she wanted but never had. I said that this was a parent who understood, accepted, and appreciated her and would be willing to take care of her, instead of the other way around. This made Jane cry even more. She said, "that's exactly right." I was struck by the concreteness of her response. She was indeed still waiting for the arrival of such an idealized parent; she was not just wishing for something but realizing that she would never get it and thus understanding that she was searching for something she had lost. Her thoughts were more on the order of "I am doing X, Y, and Z, so I should be awarded this now." There was a sense of conviction in her response that spoke to a strong phantasy about what she had lost and what she should now find.

Responding to my interpretation of her wish for the caring, always present parent figure, Jane told me how she doesn't want to have to ever ask for "that kind of love. It should just be given. They should know I need attention. It should be automatic. I do that for them. Why can't I expect that too? The important people in my life should just know what I need and be there for me when I need it." I said, "the more you want and even demand this perfect parent who always knows what you want and is there immediately to care for you, the more easily we will all fail you. The conviction you have about how we should treat you means we will always disappoint you. It provides no room to make mistakes and requires perfection. If not, you will always feel lost and alone." Here, I was interpreting the dynamic between idealization, loss, and her conviction about how her controlled objects should be.

Jane told me how she always asks her family and her husband what they want to do on holidays. On her birthday, she really wanted to go to the beach, but she didn't say anything and instead asked her husband what he wanted to do. He said he wanted to go to a movie, so that's what they did, but that left Jane feeling sad and abandoned. "I shouldn't have to say what I want. I am so in tune with what they want that I know what they would enjoy. Why can't they do that for me?" I interpreted that she is demanding that others and I read her mind and always know exactly how to take perfect care of her, like an ideal parent who can detect every need their baby has and immediately meet it. I interpreted that she is afraid of rejection and of how brittle her ideal object is, so she never asks for what she wants. That way she won't be disappointed and have to face the loss of this idealized object or the realization that she never had one in the first place.

Jane replied, "You are so right. That is exactly how I feel and how I try and dance around the possibility that I will find out no one is really there for me." Here, she was being concrete again and lost in her conviction that there either must be an ideal object or there will be no object available at all. I pointed that out, and she said, "It does feel like all or nothing. I end up feeling that way about sex too. I like to have sex with my husband but I never ask, because I don't want to be rejected. But, when he doesn't approach me when I want it, I feel completely rejected."

At this point, Jane was sobbing and said, "I apologize for crying like this. You must get sick of this." I interpreted that she felt she is a burden on me, and in seeing me that way, she is rejecting me as a possible caring and understanding object—not a perfect ideal one, but one who can understand and help. She thought about it for a while. "I try and always give others exactly what I want them to give me. I am nice and giving and understanding in the hopes that they will be that way to me." I interpreted this as her way of controlling all of us and rejecting herself in the process. I told her she was manipulating me, which makes her feel hurt, as I can't read her mind and know what she wants all the time. I said, "You are trying to control me to make sure you get what you want and need, but it is also a way you see yourself being rejected and forgotten."

Jane responded, "I do get forgotten. That is why I try to do what I do, so I won't be. But I see what you mean. I expect people to give me what I want, and when they don't, I feel angry and hurt." For a moment, she stepped away from her concrete conviction of punitive, dismissive, and withholding objects and considered her contribution to this internal experience. But this didn't last too long.

Quickly, Jane added, "But there is evidence that I get forgotten." She started crying again and told me the story of how she was left at school once when her mother forgot to pick her up. Then, she recalled being picked on by her brothers and always being blamed for things by them. Finally, she told me about the one Christmas holiday where her mother had given each of her brothers a big gift but had forgotten to buy her one. Her mother was very sorry when Jane pointed it out and immediately apologized, but Jane was devastated. I remarked, "You are expecting me to forget you like that and not see you as important. In fact, you think people will see you as a bother. You work hard to make sure we are taken care of, just like you want to be cared for. You teach us and hope we will return the favor. But, you can't really control us all, so it is inevitable that you get disappointed." She said, "I don't want to be a bother; I just want to be recognized for who I am."

Ending the session, Jane was walking out and said, "Next time I will try not to cry." I interpreted, "you are forcing me into the vision of someone who is bothered by your crying. You are rejecting me as someone who cares and understands." Here, I was interpreting the shifting self↔object phantasies Jane was bringing into the transference. As Kernberg (2008) has noted, in dealing with personality-disordered patients, especially when seeing them in reduced-frequency sessions, it is important to focus on the transference, the nature of the self↔object phantasies, and the rapid shifts in those phantasies. I pointed out to Jane how she had moved from being the rejected little girl who wanted attention and special care to the rejecting, controlling mother who would not permit care or understanding.

DISCUSSION

Melanie Klein's 1940 paper "Mourning and Its Relation to Manic-Depressive States" can help to explain the clinical difficulties we face with certain patients' struggles with loss, grief, and persecution and the constant sense of failure to win their object's love, acceptance, or forgiveness. In her paper, Klein outlines the complexities of depressive conflict and the ways that idealization, a healthy aspect of normal functioning, can become corrupted.

Jane seems to be overwhelmed by phantasies and feelings of grief, mourning, and loss. At the same time, idealization of others and ideal expectations of self and object are elements of her daily anxiety and search for relief. These internal, unconscious dynamics color and shape her daily experiences and the image of those around her, especially those closest to her.

Klein (1940, 137) states, "the idealized mother is the safeguard against a retaliating or a dead mother and against all bad objects, and therefore represents security and life." Klein goes on to explain how the first experience of loss and mourning comes about when the infant has to mourn the loss of the mother's breast, its milk, and the love, goodness, and security they stand for. The baby feels that this loss is the result of his own greed and aggression. Ambivalent feelings toward brothers and sisters as well as the loss inherent in the Oedipal situation make the nature of grief and loss that much more prevalent in the young child's mental life.

Klein goes on to explain that in normal development, the child is able to tolerate and manage these difficult experiences by internalizing idealized parental figures and by having positive relations with the actual parent and positive phantasized relations with the internal parents. This idealized, layered world of internal and external combine to create a safe zone of objects in peaceful coexistence, able to find joy and mitigate conflict.

These normal aspects of development and the safe zone of objects that Klein describes seems to have been corrupted and strangulated in Jane's internal world. The conflicts and sense of loss in her early mothering experiences as well as her sibling rivalry appears never to have been mitigated by idealized parental images or by actual positive relations with her parents.

Klein (1940) explains how the actual external parent helps to reinforce or confirm the image of the internal parent, whether that internal object be benign or malevolent. She points out that the external parent can be either nourishing or damaging and mirror either positive or negative aspects in the child's mind. This shows how in tune Klein was to the importance of both psychological factors and reality for the infant's development. Klein goes on to note that if the internal image doesn't match the external, consistent external feedback can disprove the internal beliefs. However, Klein states, in some individuals, the internal world cannot be swayed by the external.

It seems that in Jane's case, her actual experiences as she remembers them suffocated any healthy ideal object she might have been able to utilize to navigate difficult emotional moments. Instead, she has been left with the lack of an idealized object and, at other times, with an idealized object that, until rehabilitated and properly tamed, tends to abandon, persecute, and generally neglect her.

As mentioned, Klein sees idealization as an important and normal part of human functioning. Idealization serves to protect the object from envy, greed, and aggression. It serves to protect the ego from a sense of loss and pining. Finally, it creates a feeling of protection from the phantasy of persecution and fears of revenge from a damaged and dying object. Idealization helps the ego master these threats to self and object, eliminating the bad object or the dangerous aspects of self and making for a phantasy of perfect union without conflict. The reality of dependence upon the outside world and the real parent or other can be perceived as a threat to this idealized state and look like a fatal journey into punishment, loss, and fragmentation. This is a tricky situation, for it is only with a gradual trust in external objects and a willingness to traverse the imperfect and flawed road of relational conflict and negotiation that whole-object certainty can be reached. As Klein (1940) says, it is only when the ego can bear the realization that the object was and is not perfect yet still lovable and loving and not out for revenge or in danger of collapse that internal security and psychological peace can be found.

For Jane, the reality of a mother who seemed uninterested or too overwhelmed to keep her daughter in mind was traumatic. To be forgotten at school and at Christmas was devastating externally, and internally it was one of many experiences that left Jane convinced of being alone with no idealized object as a foundation for day-to-day living. This chronic abandonment and betrayal has led her to a lifelong search for the idealized object, but in a pathological manner that brings her more grief.

Jane is convinced that she must rehabilitate, retrain, or recreate the object finally to be the parent she always wished for. Her strategy for doing so involved teaching or training the object by example and hoping the object would eventually respond in kind. She also wanted the object to be a mind reader who would always know and tend to her every need. Her underlying anxiety and constant dread had to do with the internalization of a parental figure who forgot her, left her, and seemed to not know how to properly care for her. This inner experience was too painful to bear, so Jane was constantly trying to resurrect or rebuild the parent she wished she had to bring her out of this despair and loss. She tried always to be a compliant container (Lamanno-Adamo 2006) and in doing so adapted to others' needs and opinions. She hoped that by being completely pliable to others, others would notice, appreciate, and love her. But, in fact, she set herself up to be taken advantage of, used, and ignored, repeating the sadomasochistic experiences she had as a child and the angry, rejecting phantasies she lived with most of her life.

8

—

TAMING, RESTORING, AND REBUILDING, OR SEALING OFF, BURYING, AND ELIMINATING THE OBJECT

Two Ways of Controlling the Other

IN PSYCHOANALYTIC PRACTICE, we encounter a variety of patients who operate at different levels of anxiety or desire in regards to their objects. Some patients seem to have an extremely strong conviction, not just a resistance, about their objects, including the analyst. This conviction is an internal status quo that they have created and now must live by. It is their "law of the jungle": they have staked out a certain defined, known, and controllable vision of self and object, which they use to defend themselves against even more unbearable paranoid and/or depressive phantasies.

Of these patients, some want to please everyone and adapt to whatever we may seem to want or need. This is often motivated by a combination of their wanting us to see finally what good little children they are (so we become the caring, intuitively understanding parents they always wished for) and the careful and delicate approach they take, so as to not break, destroy, or alienate this fragile, idealized object. These patients are trying to use control and conviction to restore, resurrect, or rebuild a perfect parental object. There are numerous pitfalls to this approach, and the patient ends up feeling terrible, forgotten, guilty, and angry. But to give up this conviction, this search, and this control feels dangerous and catastrophic to both self and object.

Another group of patients who exhibit this control and conviction about self and object operate in more of a paranoid-schizoid manner. They demonstrate borderline and narcissistic disorders that revolve around more persecutory phantasies. They seem perpetually to be trying to prevent the return of a bad, disappointing, attacking object that will betray and hurt them. Often, they are convinced there is a better object out there, an ideal one better than all the other bad, flawed objects, and they wait for it or feel entitled to it. However, most of the time they are in hiding, trying to avoid the return of this dead, persecutory parental figure and trying to convince themselves that they no longer need such a risky union. In phantasy, these patients are always trying to control their objects to preserve a feeling of safety, omnipotence, and control.

Finally, there are a great number of patients who are suffering from both types of internal experiences, facing a constant depressive and persecutory threat to themselves and their precious objects. They rely heavily upon idealization and projective identification to traverse their psychological standoff against these overwhelming anxieties.

This chapter continues to examine the internalization of the unstable, fragile, or even pathological ideal, as opposed to Klein's (1940) idea of a normal, developmentally stable ideal. The subsequent defenses that are always in overuse to sustain the brittle ideal self or object and to prevent the aggressive, envious self from breaking through actually cause either the death/damage of the object or the rise of a persecutory object. Often it can be both, creating a dual fear and phantasy of loss and persecution.

Regarding the gradual processes of internalization, Klein (1940, 127) describes the best outcome of early parenting experiences: "Thus an inner world is being built up in the child's unconscious mind, corresponding to his actual experiences and the impressions he gains from people and the external world, and yet altered by his own phantasies and impulses. If it is a world of people predominantly at peace with each other and with the ego, inner harmony, security and integration ensue." She goes on to say, "The idealized mother is the safeguard against a retaliating or a dead mother and against all bad objects, and therefore represents security and life" (137). When less-than-ideal external situations combine with intense internal feelings and phantasies, the ego is left to find shelter from a retaliating object or to resurrect a dead object. In some cases, the phantasy involves both. One method of coping is still to strive for an idealized object that can save the day, but in such cases this dynamic of idealization is frequently perverted or distorted to the point of producing an even greater sense of danger and guilt.

Betty Joseph (1989) speaks of the need for some more disturbed patients to strive for a level of psychic equilibrium in which they can find respite from the disturbances of both paranoid and depressive anxieties. She notes that these individuals struggle with the disintegration of the paranoid-schizoid position and the overwhelming guilt and grief of the depressive position. While still within the fragmentation of infantile persecutory phantasies, they also experience a primitive guilt over hurt or dying objects that are beyond repair. This chapter discusses the moments in which the narrow degree of psychic equilibrium that these patients search for fails, leaving them exposed to the failings of the world and the lack of gratification or security. They then have no sense of coping, of negation, or of toleration from either self or other.

When unable to find this false security of psychic equilibrium, or when the psychic retreat (Steiner 1993) breaks down or fails, the ego is left to desperate measures and digs an emotional foxhole. Caught on a psychological battlefield, in the midst of these dual threats, the ego tries to take a last stand. This is a meager and modest defense that exposes the ego to much of the agony of both positions and comes with the grim reality that it is far safer to stay put under fire than risk running out directly into the fray. To stay in no-man's land seems a terrible but better choice than to emerge and engage with the object.

This emotional foxhole is the result of a trauma-based idealization phantasy in which the ego creates the object that "should have been" available but never was, resurrects the fallen object, retrains the object that failed or disappointed, heals the hurt object, embalms the persecutory object, restrains the retaliatory object, entombs the abandoning object, and avoids the betraying object. Heal the sick, resurrect the dead, and transform the bad are all part of a pathological idealization phantasy that involves projective identification and splitting as its two primary mechanisms. Therefore, a vicious cycle of control, loss, guilt, grief, and persecution is set in motion, and the ego must cower in its foxhole, clinging to its vision of control. The ideal end to the battle is always pursued, whether by pacifying the enemy, complete surrender, manipulative negotiation, or sudden victory through ruthless slaughter. But the war is never over; it is only temporarily managed. The fox-hole mentality is a conviction of despair and the idealization of control. This emotional-foxhole stance barely serves to ward off the effects of continuous anxiety from the paranoid and depressive worlds colliding overhead. The foxhole becomes an isolated crater in the field of battle between self and object.

CASE 1

Kat is a middle-aged woman I have seen in analytic treatment for almost two years. She spends most of her time within this emotional foxhole, constantly warding off feelings of guilt, anxiety, loss, and persecution. She lives in the ruins of her idol, surrounded by its pieces and trying both to resurrect and reshape her object and to prevent the sudden appearance of an attacking and abandoning object. Hurting and being hurt become confused through projective identification, as she tries to protect herself and others in a revolving door of chaos.

Kat grew up with two alcoholic parents who were constantly fighting with each other. Kat's father would scream at her and blame her for countless infractions around the house; Kat's mother lay in bed depressed and drunk. Her father committed suicide when Kat was twenty. In recounting her upbringing, Kat talks about her experiences of trying to referee and manage both her parents, trying to perk her mother up and assure her father he was respected in the community instead of having the reputation of a drunk (which he did). At the same time, she talks about having to find a way to avoid the "scary violence" of his drunken rants. Over the last two years, Kat has allowed herself to revisit many of these tragic memories, which have left deep emotional scars. We have begun to understand how she repeats her relationship with these damaged and angry objects in the transference and with others.

Kat came into a recent session and began to cry. She said she was overwhelmed because she had fought with her boss. Several important dynamics emerged. Kat was a senior computer programmer working on a big project. Her immediate boss was a manager ten years her junior and relatively new to the industry. Her boss had questioned her method of doing a certain procedure in the project; and Kat took this very personally, feeling completely criticized. At the same time, Kat's boss had gotten into a quarrel with another manager over details about how their two departments overlapped. This had escalated into a verbal fight, with both managers yelling at each other in Kat's office area and in the parking lot. Kat told me she was furious her boss would "dare to question her techniques," "butt into my business," and "try and tell me what to do." She also told me how she felt "put in the middle of these two fools" and "had to break it up and tell them to start acting like bosses instead of crazy children." She told her direct manager that she was "tired of having to manage" her manager and wanted her to put aside her personal problems and either be a resource for Kat or "get out of the way and let me do my job." For the next few sessions, Kat was furious, resentful, and very upset. She cried and ranted about how "dare they treat me like that," "why are they putting me in the middle of that shit," and "who does she think she is, telling me what to do with *my* project?"

Gradually, I noted certain patterns, which I began interpreting. Kat seemed to be describing her two bosses just as she had often described her two parents, authorities who acted like out-of-control children, and her resultant resentment of being put in the middle to constantly try to manage them and bring some sanity to the home. As soon as I interpreted this, Kat said, "Wow. I hadn't thought of that, but it is exactly the same!" She went on to tell me many stories about the chaos she grew up in.

I also made specific interpretations about her phantasies of her direct boss. Kat seemed to feel obligated to manage her immature parent and saw her as a naughty, unruly child. In acting this feeling out, Kat became both the angry, controlling parent and the angry child who no longer respects her father and wants to lash out at her parents for being so irresponsible. Much of this interpretation came from my countertransference, in which I found myself feeling like Kat was being out of line and disrespectful to her boss. I wanted to say, "How dare you speak that way to your boss? You should show some respect! Who do you think you are?" My need to put her in her place was the first clue that she was projecting this angry voice of authority and the need to control her out-of-control object onto me.

I interpreted that Kat was worried that her boss/parent was going out of control and turning into a bad, betraying object. Thus Kat had to start controlling and retraining her object to be the mother/father she wanted, but in doing so she became the controlling, angry parent herself. Based on my countertransference, I also interpreted that Kat wanted me to side with her, to say I understood how angry she was that her parental object was not treating her well and upsetting her. In wanting me to be there for her in that supportive way, I interpreted that she wanted me as the ideal, hoped-for object that she had under her control. I had no room for my own comments without disappointing her and falling from her ideal to just another disappointment. Kat agreed and said, "Yes. I want you on my side, or you are not worthwhile. I will feel ignored." She said she wished I would agree with her and be that "parent I never had" but that she could "also see my point. I was overreacting to my boss as if she was my father or mother or even both of them! I can see that now. Maybe she isn't so bad after all." Kat then associated to more traumatic childhood memories of her parents being out of control and not giving her a reliable authority figure to lean on.

During the next two sessions, Kat reported feeling "more calm and centered" and felt that her boss "was not perfect but making a good effort and I can appreciate that. We may not agree on everything but I think I can respect her for what she is trying to do, and I think she is doing the same for me."

Kat was at times trying to resuscitate an injured or damaged object. At other times, she tried to create or birth a new ideal object that could be the parent she never had. At still other times, she merely did her best to avoid or prevent the rise of persecutory objects that wanted to use her and abuse her. Now, Kat was more able to tolerate and traverse these phantasies as she sought to let go of these old bonds and take the dangerous risk of finding new ways of relating to herself and to her object. These new ways did not rely on the magical methods of control and manipulation but on faith, hope, and acceptance.

CASE 2

With some patients, it is very easy to validate Klein's (1940) observation that the combination of certain external experiences in early development and the internal phantasies of those experiences produce a pathological projective-identification process in which the patient sees himself and his objects in a very narrow, restrictive manner. This psychological bias involves high expectations and demands of self and other, brittle boundary functioning, and ongoing anger and disappointment. Guilt and loss are constant and usually mixed with persecutory fears.

Stan was one of three children raised by loving parents. But, as he put it, he "also faced multiple difficulties in his relationship to his father," who was an intimidating man who liked to have things done his way and was quick to demean and criticize others. Stan told me he looked forward to but also dreaded cooking the family's holiday turkey with his father. It would be a way for them to bond and share a manly chore. But, very soon, when problems came up with the turkey, Stan felt a looming conflict. He said, "I could see it coming and did my best, like I had to do my whole life, to avoid it or control it." Mostly, Stan tried to please and placate. When he did dare to offer his own opinion, he felt his father "shut me down and point out how useless my ideas were." Stan said, "that is exactly how things went when I grew up, except I also felt sorry for him and wanted to make sure he was ok at all times."

What Stan meant by this was in fact the second aspect of his core conflictual stance with his objects. Stan's father developed a severe pain in his stomach when Stan was five. His father felt constant pain and was unable to work for years because of it. This was never completely diagnosed, but specialists thought it was muscular. There was no real treatment available except rest and pain pills. For years, the family's activities formed around whether or not Stan's father was in pain or not. Stan felt sorry for his father, and even though Stan often felt angry and rebellious, he kept it to himself, since he didn't want to emotionally injure his physically injured father.

Over time, we have explored the meaning of these complicated experiences with Stan's father as a weakened invalid who needed to be protected and treated carefully along with this other image of his father as an angry, controlling, and volatile man who needed to be managed and placated. In fact, the bulk of my transference work has been to interpret this dual threat as it emerges in our relationship and how that leaves Stan hiding in an emotional foxhole, trying to control and avoid both his paranoid and depressive anxieties. This line of exploration has been very helpful in pinpointing the cause of many difficulties in Stan's marriage, work life, and fragile friendships.

Throughout his treatment, Stan has tried to please me and carefully manage our time together. My sense is that he is constantly watching over us to make sure that I don't become an angry parent unhappy with his performance and to make sure I remain healthy, happy, and pleased with him as a good son. I interpret that he is anxious about how I might be angered and that I seem fragile and shaky. If he did not carefully control me with pleasing and placating behavior, I could easily topple over into being hurt or angry. If he doesn't work hard to cure himself and act like a good patient, I might be let down, hurt, and sickly. Or I might be critical and attacking.

Stan tries to control our relationship, making sure that we are always in what he perceives to be a harmonious and positive track. As a result, he sees free association as threatening. If Stan shares his thoughts and feelings spontaneously, he might expose something that could create a sick and hurt object or an angry and attacking one. I thus interpret that he is reluctant to come out of his emotional foxhole. Even though he feels caught in these terrible traumas, with little respite or shelter, Stan feels it would only get worse if he lets go of his management and control.

When Stan feels that we are not in harmony or that I am not happy and healthy, he becomes quite anxious. When we are exploring his feelings and discover matters that were either unknown as of yet or that seemed to show he was unhappy or in conflict with others, including me, he becomes nervous and tries to make things right immediately. He will say, "What do I do to change these things right away? How do I get rid of this problem? I want to change myself and I am ready. Just tell me the steps and I will do it." I interpret this as him putting me into the role of a controlling, impatient object, which is a projection of his own anxiety and desire to control. I interpret that he is anxious about any difference or conflict he thinks we might have and is ready to attack it, erase it, or manage it as soon as possible, to keep me healthy and happy and avoid me being hurt, disappointed, or angry. Stan is able to take in these interpretations and, by feeling less threatened, is able to tolerate investigating his phantasies and feelings a bit more.

Nevertheless, this unconscious pattern comes up frequently, and we have revisited this transference experience many times. I interpret that he is constantly trying to wipe out any conflict, difference, or lack of progress, so that he can create a smooth, progressive, conflict-free zone where he feels in control and where we both are out of harm's way. I say that this is a way he chooses to feel powerful and safe and a way to keep me safe and happy, but it is also a dead zone in which we can never really connect or be ourselves. We are controlled and prepackaged, without any room for what we really feel or think. When I made these interpretations, Stan agreed. "You are really able to read me; it's kind of scary but also pretty helpful." Then, he associated to how his angry father demanded perfection and how Stan wanted to "beat him by being even more than perfect." I commented that this victory was also a stranglehold on Stan's own life. Then I interpreted that when he demanded to "know what to do" in the analysis, he was demanding that I give him the magical pill of perfection and the knowledge of how to avoid his father's rage and expectations, but in doing so, he is still running away from his father's illness and anger and also being a bully to me, like his father was to him. Stan told me, "what you said makes me feel guilty, angry, and enlightened all at the same time. I think this gives us something to talk about for a while."

For Stan, much of his transference is an effort of trying to manage, reshape, and resurrect an object that is healthy, free of anger, and able to tolerate differences. He has identified with his father in that he too is demanding and controlling but also feels defective and inferior. Stan makes a constant effort to bring to life an ideal father who has a conflict-free relationship with his son and is always satisfied and proud of his boy. In the transference, Stan tries to make me be this ideal by controlling for any differences that could hurt us or make one of us angry. This ongoing task leaves Stan facing the imminent threat of hurt and anger from and to his object, so he is left to try to survive in his emotional foxhole, doing his best to control the enemy and hope for a truce at some point. Gradually, he is more able and willing to emerge from his foxhole and face these feelings more directly. As a result, he feels more capable of dealing with the sway of his emotions and the unpredictability of relationships. He is more willing to tell me what is on his mind without having to censor it in order to keep me healthy and happy and avoid conflict. This brings him closer to truly being in control of himself rather than always trying to control others.

CASE 3

Some psychoanalytic cases seem very clear right from the beginning, and the analyst's initial hunches prove to be accurate. Other times, initial clinical impressions turn out to be false, generated by misplaced countertransference, a lack of data, or just plain wrong guesswork.

I have only met with Susan for four sessions, but I have a very distinct clinical impression of what may be her primary object-relational conflict and her central transference phantasy. However, I am proceeding very slowly and trying to keep an open mind, as I may be way off base, coming to judgment too quickly, and possibly acting out some element of her unconscious phantasy world.

When I first met with Susan, I felt she was polite and attentive but that she seemed somehow too introspective and focused on "the therapeutic process that [she] had many years of experience with, the quest for spiritual growth, and the value of working to find the real answers." I had her sign the usual documents and discussed the insurance policy she wanted to use. Then, I asked her for the co-payment. She gave me a check but then said, "I think this is as far as I go. I thank you for your time." I asked her what was wrong. Susan told me, "it looks like you would rather focus on the money and insurance than hear about what I have to say." I replied, "You're feeling like I am ignoring you. It's important for you to be able to tell me that sort of thing. That is exactly part of what we are here to do: to understand how you feel about yourself and about your relationships, including ours. You feel if I take care of the business first, I am ignoring you?" She said, "Well, other therapists have always done that at the end." I said, "Let me explain why I am taking care of the paperwork and collecting the money now. If we get to talking and are exploring important emotional issues, I don't want to have to suddenly stop you and say I need twenty dollars. I want to be able to focus completely on what you have to say and what you feel, so I am getting this stuff out of the way." Susan said, "Ok. That makes sense when you explain it."

Susan then told me about her current job situation and her living conditions, both of which she wasn't really happy about. Then, she told me about how she was in a relationship that had begun some nine months earlier. Susan said, "He won't stop bothering me. He wants me to be more committed and spend more time together. I feel he is moving too fast, but he just says I am sensitive and that after almost a year we should be closer and more committed. I end up pressured and smothered. He won't leave me alone. I like him, but I don't know if I am ready for all that."

Susan went on to tell me about how she hoped I could help her deal with something she is very upset about but "should be over." I commented on how she is critical of herself and maybe is worried that I might be too. She said she knows that I will try to be understanding, but it is something embarrassing. I said, "You were unsure if you could trust me after the co-payment thing, and now you are a bit unsure if I will understand. Maybe that's important information; it is hard to trust me right off the bat. Why don't you take it slow and tell me what you can." Here, I was interpreting the transference and recommending she take a risk to see me in a new way but also in a manner that she would still feel in control of. Susan told me that she had broken off a ten-year relationship that she "never really got what I wanted out of." After a month or two, Susan was confused and depressed and went to a therapist. Susan told me that the minute she met this therapist, it "was love at first sight; I knew we were meant for each other." She "could tell that the therapist felt it too and that we were soulmates." Susan explained that the therapist told her that the ethics of his profession prevented them from being together and that they should try to understand why Susan felt that way. After seeing this therapist for a year, Susan said she couldn't bear to be in love and know it would never be reciprocated. She said "it was obvious we both had feelings for each other, but he decided to stick with his limits. After a year, I had to stop seeing him because it was too painful. I also hoped that now that we weren't in a professional relationship, he might want to be with me."

I asked if the therapist had explored the transference and helped Susan to understand the unconscious source of these strong feelings and convictions. Susan told me the therapist had interpreted that "given her childhood, it was a wish for a blissful relationship between mother and child without any abuse or tension, a wonderful place to relax and feel loved." I asked about the "abuse part." Susan told me that her father was a "stay-at-home dad"; her mother worked. She was the only child, so she and her father spent a great deal of time together. From age ten to fifteen, her father sexually abused and controlled her. "He kept me on a short leash; I couldn't go over to friends' homes or parties. When I went to school, was on the playground, or at the park for a school activity, I could always see him off to the side, watching." The way she said this made me feel that she meant this in a lurking way. I asked if that was so. Susan said, "I felt like he was always lurking, stalking, and spying on me, making sure I was never out of his reach. I felt controlled and manipulated most of the time." I said, "I wonder if growing up like that makes you unsure about whether to trust men and about making any kind of commitment?" She said she had thought of that, and she felt it was true in many cases but wasn't sure if it was with me, "since I explained it was just my procedure." Here, I wondered if she defended herself with logic and justifications and worried that it would be hard to fight our way through this concrete shield. I decided to wait and see.

Susan went on to tell me, "I know I should be over my old therapist and it's stupid that I'm not, but I can't help it." She was embarrassed about "how I couldn't let go and even pushed the limit a bit." I asked for details. She explained that after she left the therapy, she used to drive around the therapist's office to "check on his car and see if he was ok." She also called him a few times, checking to see if he wanted to reconsider being together outside of the therapy situation. According to Susan, the therapist told her he was in a relationship, didn't want to see Susan, and requested that she not contact him or approach him in public places. Susan told me, "I logically knew this was right and could certainly see his point, but emotionally I wanted to be with him and couldn't let go, couldn't get him out of my mind." I interpreted that it seemed she was yearning for a perfect, blissful union with a love object, an experience she may have never felt she had with either of her parents. At the same time, she sounded like her father, in controlling the therapist or stalking him. Susan assured me "that was only in the months after I left therapy. I haven't done that for a couple of years. It's just that I can't get him out of my mind. We were perfect together. I know it's over, but I can't shake it. I want to shake it but I can't."

With some patients, a projective-identification process occurs in which the patient manages to pull the analyst into various feelings, thoughts, and sometimes enactments. With Susan, I noticed a few patterns coming up rather quickly in the treatment that made me think that projections were shaping the transference and countertransference. After the first session, we scheduled several appointments, but Susan told me she would have to "think about" the ones that were closer together and sooner than the others and "get back to me." I interpreted that she might again be unsure if we "are a good match" or if she can trust me and make a commitment to being with me. She said that might be the case but agreed to go ahead with those dates. It seemed my interpretation alleviated her momentary anxiety, and we were able to become untangled from her unsure, anxious phantasy about me and the risks of committing. This same situation occurred during Susan's third visit. She told me much more about how she had "stalked" her former therapist and how "I realize the therapist doesn't want anything to do with me and is *so* over me, but I still have these feelings I can't let go of!" I suggested that perhaps a part of her doesn't want to let go of those wonderful feelings and that they may serve some purpose even though they are painful. Susan said she thought that was probably right and told me how this therapist acknowledged his deep feelings for her but also made it clear that "nothing would ever happen." I said that while it was certainly important that the therapist was able to maintain his ethical boundaries, Susan may have been very confused by him also saying he had feelings for her. I interpreted that this may have felt like some sort of reenactment of Susan's father's way of doing all the things a good father does, like take his child to school, help her with homework, and play with her. But Susan's father also did things a good father never does. Susan said, "Yes, it was very confusing."

At the end of this session, we looked at our calendars and tried to come up with a regular schedule. I suggested she come in for multiple weekly visits, and she agreed that would probably be helpful, but, because she was about to leave her job to look for a better one, she was concerned about her finances. I thought to myself that her job was perhaps another relationship where she was ambivalent and unsure about her level of commitment. I said we could meet more often until she left the job. I suggested certain dates. Susan agreed to a Monday every week but told me she "needed to think about the other ones." She said she would call me the next day. Here, I also commented on how we were in a bit of a back-and-forth dance, with me suggesting she make a commitment and her being unsure and reluctant. She said she noticed that but that it "was a matter of reality, too."

When Susan did not call me the next day or the day after that, I found myself caught up in certain strong feelings. I felt somewhat ignored and even abandoned. I felt the urge to call her and find out what was going on. Since we had agreed to discuss the remaining dates and I hadn't heard from her, I did call and left a message. She didn't return it that day or the next. I wanted to call her again and realized I was not only feeling somewhat desperate but that I was starting to feel and almost act like a stalker. This alarmed but also informed me. I realized that because of her ambivalence in several of the sessions, her lack of immediate commitment, and her controlling me by being the one who would "decide at a later date," I was being put in the position of feeling rejected or put on hold, which pushed me to try to squeeze the answer out of her, control her, and even stalk her, in a manner of speaking. I thought that this pointed to the strong presence of projective identification in our relationship: she projected the controlling, stalking father that she had identified with and, alternatively, she projected a confused, needy little girl wanting someone to provide some stability and predictability. After five days, Susan did call and left me a message about which dates she wanted to attend. When I brought up these countertransference hunches and clinical impressions as interpretations, Susan was willing to think about it and told me, "I see what you mean, but I simply want to find out how to stop thinking about my previous therapist."

Susan continued to tell me about "how she knows it's over and there isn't any reason to be thinking about him, but I can't stop." I said that she talked about it in a very logical way and gave little room to acknowledge or understand the deep emotional feelings she still was struggling with. I added that she didn't want to give me much in the way of details, even though I would find them helpful. Susan said, "I have gone over my childhood before with that therapist and other ones and I don't see the point of revisiting it. And I went over all my feelings and hopes with him, so I don't want to have to repeat that with you." I interpreted that she was withholding herself from me but then wanted me to help her with a very intimate, involved, and complicated situation of her life without being able to know much about her or how she got there. I said she was therefore controlling me by wanting me to deliver this instant solution without any access to who she is. I suggested that the motive behind her relating this way to me was very important to understand. I said, "We need to know about what happened with your father, what happened with your therapist, and how you see the world at large, including our relationship. Without a working knowledge of who you are and how you experience the world, it's impossible to understand these issues. I wonder if it's difficult for you to share yourself with me, so you are more comfortable taking this logical, fix-it approach." Susan told me, "I don't want to have to tell you what happened with my father. I don't feel comfortable, and if the only way you can help me is for me to have to tell you the details, I can't do that. We will have to stop." At that point, I realized she thought I meant we would have to discuss every sexual act she had with her father. I said, "You think I mean we have to talk about all the sex with your father in detail, like I would be forcing you to do that to get better. It makes complete sense that you don't want to. What I meant is that we need to understand your overall experience, the fallout of that. But maybe we can also learn about how you see me as forcing you to talk about the sex, almost stalking you about the meeting times, and wanting to know more about your relationship with the therapist. It's as if you're always holding back, protecting yourself, and controlling us, just in case I might be after you. But the more you protect yourself from that, the more you may be feeling that I am like that. You want me to help you in a big way with very important issues but you aren't comfortable giving me much to work with. It becomes a standoff, and if I ask for more, you feel like I'm hunting you down. I think these are things we should talk about and keep an eye out for." Susan agreed and said she isn't ready to trust me completely but sees my point that we need to look at things more fully and not just logically.

It is difficult to say after such a brief encounter, but I think that Susan is struggling to control her objects, which seem to be potentially predatory, clingy, and controlling. Based on how she was "worried about the therapist and wanted to make sure he is ok" and how she is ashamed and anxious about "thinking too much" about the therapist, I think she is also struggling with more depressive guilt and worry about how she is or has affected her object. She is caught in the middle of both persecutory and depressive fears, suffering from the effects of both, caught in the crossfire and trying to control, restrain, and transform her objects. In the midst of this internal battlefield, there is the vision of perfect peace, love, and understanding, the idealized image of her other therapist, her perfect match, her soulmate. This soulmate obviously doesn't need fixing, isn't a threat, and doesn't need to be controlled. Susan can find her pleasure and her escape in the arms of this good object.

But the good and perfect object doesn't want her, is gone, and will never come back. Susan is unable to tolerate or cope with this and wants me to help her find a solution. We will see if we can be an imperfect match that commits to each other and respects each other's needs and boundaries while working together through the joy and misery of learning, growth, and change.

CASE 4

After only a few months of seeing Jackie in analytic treatment to address her "lifelong problem of meeting shitty men," I felt like I knew exactly why she had never been able to maintain a healthy relationship with a man. My reaction in the countertransference was "it's because you are such a self-centered, demanding person." I was ashamed to have those feelings and surprised at the strength of them, so I first tried to deny them, but then, slowly, I tried to understand them better.

Over the next year, I came to see how Jackie lived within an unrelenting system of hatred, rejection, loss, demand, and betrayal. She felt that men were not good enough. "They all eventually fail to please me; they all are worthless at some point." Jackie also felt that her fragile, tenuous hold on a "decent man" could easily crumble: "he will always, at some point, deceive me, cheat on me, or hurt me in some way."

Thus we see that there is a narcissistic demand and critical devaluation of all men. At the same time, Jackie feels very poorly about herself. She told me, "I hate myself. I'm fat, unattractive, and difficult. I would never date someone like me. I just don't have the looks or intelligence. I know all the good men are either taken or they would quickly pass on going out with me. I have to hope that a man from the second-best pile will bother to go out with me. And, after a while, I get sick of having to be with someone less than perfect, so I dump them. It's useless. I don't trust men, and I don't see anyone out there that is worth my time. I am sure they feel that way about me too, but I don't care."

While she says she doesn't care and tells me that it "is boring and useless to talk about this problem because it is just reality and will never change," it is very much the leading edge of her daily anxiety, bitterness, and sadness. Many if not most of Jackie's sessions were filled with stories about the relationship she wanted or the relationships she was having that were crumbling around her.

In the transference, Jackie treated me quite poorly. She told me she never got anything out of our meetings, she felt I was just like all other men, she didn't see the point of what we did because she would never change and men would never be different, and that it was just a matter of time before she was bored with therapy and would quit. I interpreted that she made us worthless before we ever had a chance, that she tried to control me with threats and devaluation so that she could reject me before I rejected her, and that she was reluctant to trust me and allow me to have my own identity, separate from how she viewed all other men. This last idea was important, as it was a phantasy about me that was paired with the equally restrictive phantasy about herself as stagnant and hopeless, someone who was too ugly or inferior ever to change.

In regards to this last aspect of her projective identification–based transference, I interpreted that she was unsure of how to handle me seeing her in any other way than hostile, artificially pleasing, or broken. That was the other side of her coin. While she was often hateful to me, she was also predictably polite and gracious. She always said hello and asked how I was. She was on time and made sure to pay me at each meeting. But this was a false and controlling pleasing designed to keep me happy and uncritical of her; it was also a way to make her feel that she had the upper hand and was a nice intelligent lady who was in control of the relationship. This strategy was fragile and had sprung some leaks. When she asked me how I was at the beginning of the session, it felt false and artificial feel, as if she was just doing something Martha Stewart had recommended. When I asked her about her interests in how I was doing and to share more about her thoughts or feelings when she asked about me, Jackie took it as an attack. "This is too weird. Why can't you be normal and talk like normal people? You always want to dissect what I say and scrutinize me at every turn." I interpreted that she wanted to be close and have me be interested in her, but when I honestly wanted to find out more about her as a person, she felt scared, attacked, and put down. When she agreed, it revealed the concrete conviction she held as to the constant depressive and paranoid nature of the world.

This situation came up in other ways. Jackie asked me for a receipt at some point when she handed me enough cash to cover that week and the upcoming one. I asked why she wanted a receipt. At first, she acted indignant and said that it was just common business practice. I felt she was being demeaning and arrogant. I told her the money covered next week and wondered why she needed a receipt. I asked her about what she was feeling and what was behind the request. Jackie said it was a "way to make sure she wasn't getting ripped off." She told me she was worried I might say she had only paid for this week when next week came around. I said, "You are worried you can't trust me, so you are finding a way to be in control. I could be just another man that disappoints you." She replied, "Absolutely." Again, Jackie revealed how concrete her phantasies were. She was in total agreement with my comment and was unable to reflect on it as a way to broaden her thinking or consider the possibility that I might not be part of this bad crowd of men she had to deal with.

Jackie was very concrete in her narcissistic and persecutory convictions about the world and her objects. She felt she was better than others and that others were always trying to prove that they were better than she was. She tried to control and take advantage of others, and thus, in a mirror-projection process, she always felt others were trying to take advantage of her. To prevent that, she tried to please others or avoid them. I interpreted, "when you won't allow for any vision of me other than someone you can't trust, someone who will betray you, and someone you have to please, there is no way you can ever have me as a caring resource who will understand and help you. You seem to fight against me being there for you." She replied, "Why would I put myself at risk like that? And, besides, why would you really care for me? This is just your job." I said, "You are making it a narrow no-win situation there: it's just my job so I could never care. In that sense, you are pushing me away and controlling us, making sure we exist in only one way together." Here, I was interpreting the manner in which Jackie forces us to be in a disappointing, meager, and narcissistic relationship with no hope of rescue, change, or love. While some patients work hard at transforming and retraining their objects into the ideal they always wished for, others work hard at preventing the rebirth or rise from the grave of the old, bad, persecutory object that will surely seek them out and hurt them. This is part of a no-hope conviction, which creates a countertransference of anger, frustration, boredom, and hopelessness. So, I interpreted this projection of her internal state, and we slowly chipped away at it. Sometimes, we seemed to make some progress, and I would feel some sudden hope or possibility; other times, we seemed eternally stuck in this narcissistic mist of mistrust, control, and predatory motives.

Jackie held herself and others to an unobtainable ideal. She used splitting and projective identification to cope with life, but that method of organizing the world also brought her constant anxiety. Some of the time, she tried to please and charm her objects into being the ideal parental object she always wished for, one that cared and held unconditional love for her. But, because she held her objects to such a narrow and demanding vision of perfection, this ideal quickly crashed and turned into a disappointing or persecutory failure. Either she was bad and unlovable, or the object was defective and useless. When she felt unlovable, she tried to find ways to convince the object she was worthy of a second chance. But this depressive experience of not being enough for the object's love quickly turned into rage and resentment. These fluctuating chaotic phantasies left Jackie in an emotional foxhole, always trying to outrun her tormentors and trying to prove to others she was worthy of love. To avoid these painful experiences, she constantly had to control how she appeared to others and how close others could

get to her. She wanted the object to be close, but she controlled its proximity so rigorously that she ended up always feeling alone. Her convictions that she would never be pretty or smart enough and that all men
were always one step away from breaking her heart left her in a barren
wasteland, meagerly surviving but cornered in the crossfire of both ines-
capable dreadful phantasies.

During the course of the second year, I interpreted how she saw me as
just another waste of time, another man she couldn't fully trust or control. Jackie said, "Yes, you're right." This concrete conviction, with no
vulnerability of allowing for her feelings to be different than that fact,
was part of the emotional battlefield she existed in. She took up resi-
dence in her defensive bunker, where she tried to feel in control through
spite and contempt, but she was never fully free of the onslaught of her
phantasies of objects of rejection and persecution as well as of objects
that were too frail, damaged, or disappointing to ever care for her or
love her as she wished.

Rocky as the treatment was and reluctant as Jackie was to open up
and learn about herself, as it meant rejection and disappointment, we
were able to explore how in some relationships Jackie tried to prop men
up, desperately wanting to make them into a viable, loving parental
object that eventually could take care of her as she took care of them.
In other relationships, we discovered how she looked down on men as
useless disappointments. This was linked to her own feelings of being
so disappointing that she was sure to never be picked and, if she was,
quickly discarded. In all of her relationships, Jackie felt she must first
be nice and not hurt or turn off the object so as to preserve their momentary acceptance. This was certainly the case in her treatment. But,
very quickly, she would hate the idea of having to sacrifice and give to
the object. Desperately but also resentfully, she tried to make herself
into, through cosmetic surgery, makeup, pleasing behavior, and expen-
sive dresses, what she thought I and all men demanded. Then, she became angry and rejecting of us, deciding she didn't need or want us. All
these cycles emerged in the transference, and while I was often thrown
off course in the countertransference by their intensity, I was able to
gradually interpret each element of her dynamic. On the one hand,
there was not much change in her outlook on herself or others. On the

other, the severity of her bitterness, narcissistic entitlement, and reliance on intense splitting and projective identification seemed to wane a bit over time.

One of the ways we worked on these phantasies was when I interpreted how Jackie only told me what I wasn't doing for her and what was going wrong in her life. Of course, this was similar to all her stories about how other men were always failing to do this or that. For a while, I was caught up in her verbal assaults and found myself fighting back by getting into debates with her or at times even telling her off for her offensive way of relating to me. At one point, when she threatened to stop coming because I "wasn't delivering the goods fast enough," I told her "if you want to leave, go ahead." In the moment, I really meant it. I was angry and tired of her relentlessly demeaning and demanding ways. But I was able to contain myself and added, "I think this is exactly what happens with the men you date. They end up dropping you when you put them down or demand so much. But I think it is also exactly the way you feel they are to you: always wanting you to be more and better, or else. So, you probably drop them before they can drop you." She agreed and told me, "that's my game plan. I want to have the last say." I said, "maybe we can try to figure out how to be without that game plan, since it only leaves you alone, angry, and sad."

When we returned to looking at how she only emphasizes what I don't do for her or what is going wrong in her life, I interpreted that she is very sensitive to having to share what she is enjoying with me, how she is learning, and what she looks forward to. Even what she wants or needs is very difficult for her to share, unless she says it as a putdown about what she demands and what I have failed to deliver. In other words, I was interpreting how painful and frightening it is for Jackie to depend on me because of how powerless and vulnerable she ends up feeling. We are still working on this struggle and are continuing to explore how she defends against this by declaring the object to be worthless. But this then leaves her in a dark phantasy world, surrounded by a combination of angry, dismissive objects and weak, powerless, and unlovable objects that she can never use as an anchor or resource. When I brought up how she never shares with me things she is happy about, perhaps because she doesn't like the vulnerability of giving to me, she retorted, "I am here to give you the shit in my life. There's no reason to tell you about what is going right or what I am happy about. That's my business! I have friends to share that with." Here, the concrete conviction of our roles together, the control she had to inflict on us, and the narrow way she had to see us left her with a dark vision of a relationship where no joy or closeness could emerge.

As Klein (1935) described, idealization and the control of that ideal object serve as an escape from the paranoid phantasies of a bad, vengeful, and persecutory object and serves as an escape from the depressive phantasies of a damaged, unresponsive, or rejecting object. Jackie was caught in the middle of both of these painful mental battles and relied on splitting, idealization, and projective identification as desperate ways out. Unfortunately, these very defenses were what kept her trapped in her emotional bunker, barely out of range of these dual threats. She was constantly struggling with perfection versus flawed and useless, good versus bad, and control versus abandonment and persecution.

Jackie is occasionally experimenting with new ways of relating to self and other, and when she is able to leave her war-torn foxhole, she is finding out that perhaps life can offer hope or possibility. But this is a very precarious situation in her mind, and it is unclear if she will be able or willing to pursue what must feel like a crippling surrender to loneliness, shame, and betrayal. The cost of control is devastating for this patient, but she in turn is convinced that letting go of that control is dangerous and deadly.

9
—

TWO VARIETIES OF PSYCHIC RETREAT

The Struggle with Combined Paranoid
and Depressive Conflicts

A NUMBER OF patients in psychoanalytic practice seem to share similar phantasies regarding the desperate longing for a loving object as well as the dread of being rejected by that same object. Hoping to please the object as a way to being loved is a large factor in their life, but equally important in their internal experience is the counterphantasy of always disappointing the object, leading to feelings of primitive loss, abandonment, and persecution. The desire to be pleased or praised by the object followed by the fear of being disappointed or ignored is also common. These complex conflicts involve paranoid and brittle depressive phantasies. These patients utilize psychic retreats, but these are often collapsing or collapsed, leaving them desperately exposed to both paranoid and depressive anxieties. This chapter will use two case examples to illustrate these issues and contrast the more primitive depressive patient's transference struggle with a more narcissistically structured patient's transference stance. In the first case, the patient was able to suffer within his combined paranoid and depressive phantasy world long enough to develop a new view of his objects and rely less on psychic retreat. In the second case, the patient was more prone to continue relying on her psychic retreat even as she made some initial progress in facing and working through her paranoid and depressive conflicts.

Many patients in psychoanalytic treatment struggle within the developmental demands of the depressive position (Klein 1935). In successful treatment, they begin mastering the phantasy of a whole object, both good and bad, that they can depend on but whom they also affect. The guilt that arises over possibly hurting the object they rely on, and then wanting to repair that damage, is a normal psychological reaction and provides hope and strength to the ego. Having faith in the ability of the object to recover and forgive and having faith in the power of reflection, regret, and healing all bring about a sense of trust, hope, and internal stability.

Some patients exhibit difficulties within this depressive matrix, and these cracks in their developmental foundation show up in the trans-ference, in their phantasies, and in their worldview. Specifically, there can be trouble with the integrity of the good object, leaving the ego to wonder about how damaging its actions are. Relational bonds appear fragile, testing the ability to trust forgiveness or healing and the chance of restoration or negotiation. There is a threat of persecution or perma-nent abandonment. Much of this has to do with persecutory guilt and superego demands, but it also has to do with the incomplete nature of healthy splitting in the depressive position, in which the good object is not fully differentiated from the bad, leaving one to shift easily into the other. Steiner (1993) has described this situation as part of a primitive aspect or early phase of the depressive position.

Because of the overreliance on and pathological default into projec-tive identification as a method of coping, these patients are not sure of how reliable they are to their objects. They picture letting the object down quite easily because of their own failures but also question how forgiving the object will be. Normally, in the depressive position, the object is loved despite its bad parts (Hinshelwood 2008), and the love can be sustained without shattering. The boat can be rocked, but the ego still believes that self and object will remain afloat. Some of our more troubled patients, on the other hand, are convinced that they could eas-ily, by need, expression, disagreement, identity, desire, or curiosity, not just rock the boat but sink it. This tension, anxiety, and guilt are so great that it creates a persecutory phantasy in which the drowned object will return for vengeance. Thus the good object is easily torn apart and can't be put back together. Instead, the bad object appears in its place. I think that sometimes this is the result of a paranoid defense against depressive guilt. But the patients I am exploring seem more so to offend, damage, alienate, or destroy the good aspects of the whole object, leaving only the bad. It is as if the depressive position is reached only in a partial or immature way, in which the newly baked whole object can easily crumble to reveal its separate parts, good and bad.

Klein (1935) states that the dread of persecution and punishment from the bad object in the paranoid-schizoid position is also felt as a threat from the good object in the depressive position. This is a double persecutory phantasy. In higher-functioning patients who seem to have reached the depressive position but have a slippery hold on it, the anxiety and sense of catastrophe is directed more at the object and at the fear of how they will survive now that the vital nurturing object has been destroyed or driven away. The patients who have an even more precarious grip on the depressive position experience these feelings as well as the phantasy of facing a retaliatory object that has no sense of forgiveness or understanding.

Hinshelwood (1989) points out that Klein understood that persecutory phantasies and depressive anxiety operate together in the depressive position, but in various proportions. Guilt shifts in intensity and meaning depending on the mix of persecutory and depressive phantasies occurring within the depressive position. If there is a reasonably reliable external object to depend on, which helps to counteract the internal aggression, then confidence in restoration, forgiveness, and healing occur, taking the place of the more punishing, abandoning, and persecutory form of guilt.

Finally, it is this shifting proportion of depressive and persecutory experience that makes some patients feel caught in an emotional foxhole of sorts, facing the worst fears for the object and the self. Both are in danger and without adequate protection. Under the pressure of this more primitive guilt, these patients feel forced to promise constant allegiance to the object, with extreme self-sacrifice and emotional slavery as desperate measures to ensure the happiness, well-being, and survival of the object as well as the self. This characterizes my first case; the second patient is more concerned with how her object is treating, neglecting, and betraying her.

Hinshelwood (1989) points out how patients suffering in this frightening place between the paranoid-schizoid position and the depressive position rely on complex defensive systems or pathological organizations (Steiner 1987) to ward off their sense of fragmentation and severe guilt. Their fragile psychological structure depends on a rigid adherence to various self-defeating defensive systems (Segal 1972), defensive organizations (O'Shaughnessy 1981), or narcissistic organizations (Rosenfeld 1964).

Steiner (1993) has elaborated and extended these concepts and has developed the clinical notion of psychic retreats. Recently, Steiner (2008) has summarized his views on retreats by saying that they are a pattern of narcissistic defenses composed of splitting, projective identification, and introjection. This pathological organization helps the patient avoid the anxieties of both the paranoid and depressive positions. It is a hiding place in which separateness and difference are eliminated and the illusion of control and idealization is maintained. This makes for a difficult transference climate, with change seen as alien and dangerous.

Overall, I am highlighting cases in which this psychic retreat has been only partly functional and in many cases has sprung a leak, leaving the patient feeling helplessly exposed to the worst aspects of both paranoid and depressive suffering. The patient attempts to cling desperately to the shards of a sinking or unstable retreat.

Steiner (1987) has noted that to truly work through the depressive position, one has to give up control over the object and with it the illusion of being able to protect it. One has to accept that one has hurt, damaged, or destroyed the object and that no amount of repair, offering, or repentance can save it. The object is dead. Grief is all there is. This is a very difficult emotional experience, and it is hard to imagine or hope that there will be something else, something good, ever again. The struggle with normal states grief and guilt can break down and become unbearable. These overwhelming anxieties lead the patient to seek refuge in pathological retreats. In the process, normal coping methods of splitting, projective identification, and idealization become pathologically excessive. Patients in these emotional states are difficult to work with, because they are well defended and rely on static and rigid psychological strategies or pathological organizations.

Many of these patients who rely on pathological organizations end up with their psychological shelter only working some of the time. Instead of it being a foolproof defensive structure, albeit pathological and self-defeating, it ends up being a meager, temporary foxhole from which they desperately seek a moment of respite during the internal onslaught of depressive and paranoid phantasies. This makes them all the more rigid and insistent on repeating the basic, pathological cycle of defensive posturing that comprises what meager retreat they do have. Rather than feeling overly confident about their ability to ward off the persecutory and guilt-ridden transferences they encounter, they are even more inclined to search out ways of avoiding contact with the phantasy figure of the analyst. This can make for chaotic, resistant, and complex treatment situations, which in turn create thorny countertransference issues.

This chapter examines two cases in which collapsing or unstable psychic retreats shape the transference and phantasy climate. The first patient seemed caught in an emotional foxhole at the beginning of treatment but slowly has been able to emerge and change the nature of how he views and relates to his objects and consequently to himself. Initially, this patient utilized a rigid retreat of obsessive and logical defensive strategies aimed at dealing with his intense anxiety over how he was able or unable to care for and maintain his objects. At this point in his analysis, he is suffering much more from depressive fears (Klein 1940) that are only occasionally tinged with persecutory fears (Klein 1946), and when those latter fears emerge, he is more able to restore his balance and faith in himself and his objects.

The second case contains material in which there is an ongoing failure of the depressive position and a resulting mixture of primitive depressive and destabilizing persecutory phantasies, which leave the patient trapped in an emotional foxhole. This creates certain transference situations as well as particular countertransference struggles. She seeks refuge in narcissistic defenses and aggressive projective identification, all aimed at coping with anxieties pertaining to phantasies about how her objects were willing or unwilling to protect, serve, praise, and love her.

CASE 1: A RETREAT INTO CONTROL AND LOGIC

Eli is a supervisor in a sales department at a major corporation. He is highly regarded and respected as someone who "always gets the job done" and "does whatever it takes to achieve whatever project is on his plate." In addition, he makes sure to "toe the line at home" and tries

his best to avoid conflict in all areas of his life, including in the transference. After having been raised by an extremely brutal father and a
passive alcoholic mother, Eli joined the army and spent several years in
what he remembers as a very "do-able environment, much like home. I
knew how to deal with the shouting, the aggression, and the demands.
Army life was actually pretty easy for me." One result of his early experiences is that he is now on guard at all times, maintaining a lonely patrol
to make sure everyone is calm and unburdened, preventing any chaos
or upset.

Eli is extremely organized around pleasing others and keeping the
peace. Indeed, this was an important diagnostic flag that he alerted me
to. At one point, I said he was trying very hard to make sure I and others
are always happy. He corrected me and said, "No. I am on guard 24/7
to make sure you are not unhappy. There's a major difference." Here,
he was explaining the suffering that is experienced when both paranoid
and depressive phantasies coexist without much defensive respite or
psychic shelter to withdraw into. Over time, we have identified how Eli
is quite worried that others might be disappointed in him, which would
lead to angry rejection. This rejection has a persecutory flavor to it without much hope for restitution or negotiation.

Over the last two years of analysis, I have made many interpretations
regarding his constant efforts to work preventively, eliminating any
chance I could be cross with him. Eli tries to keep me satisfied by delivering precise and up-to-date reports on his current behaviors and his
progress on various issues at work and at home. He does this in a very
logical, controlled manner, as if he is reporting to his superior officer.

In fact, during the first few months of analysis, Eli would call me
"sir," as if we were in the military and I was his commander whom he
had better respect or else. I interpreted this and pointed out how he
maintained loyal service to me and played "by the rules." I added that
these were his strict rules, not mine. I was interpreting his projection of
rigid, strict expectations with a dangerous consequence attached to failure. In fact, mistakes were just that, failure, not things that could be put
right or learned from. This was evidence of his harsh superego's view of
our relationship, in which he, the obedient, scared son, sought love from
the stern taskmaster. But this was a phantasy that shifted frequently:
sometimes he wanted to save the object from the taskmaster, sometimes

he felt guilty for being the taskmaster, and sometimes he tried to escape the blows of the taskmaster.

Another aspect of this internal struggle had to do with Eli's avoidance of empathy. Specifically, he was a very kind and caring man, but he did his best not to let himself be in direct touch with any feelings of compassion, either for himself or another. As I slowly came to understand Eli better, I interpreted that he could not bear to feel his heart go out to others, so he tried hard to be independent, logical, controlled, strong, and not needing the compassion of others.

Talking about his girlfriend's dog, Eli spoke of "making sure to do his assignment" of grooming and feeding the dog. I noticed what seemed to be a hidden area of sensitivity or softness. In the countertransference, I noticed that he was talking like an efficient robot about the dog, but I was thinking fondly and softly about this animal he was caring for. I said, "You are telling me a story about your efficiency with the dog chores and how you mechanically make sure the dog has the right amount of kibble and a regular bath. But I think you're hiding something from me; I think you like this dog. Far from this being a 'to do' list, I wonder if you enjoy playing with the dog." Specifically, I thought Eli might be depositing this forbidden or dangerous feeling into me as a communication of sorts, so I made the corresponding interpretation.

Eli responded, "I can't help but notice how cute she is and how she has her own silly little personality. Sometimes, I feel myself all choked up when she licks my hand and snuggles close to me for no apparent reason." "Other than that she loves you," I added. Here, I was the one who spoke the unspeakable. By finishing his sentence, I was the one saying something very painful. I think I was not only being compassionate but also falling prey to a projective-identification process in which I was made to do the painful dirty work while Eli remained off the hook and out of danger. On the one hand, I was providing an important container/contained function and translating a beta phantasy into something digestible, but this was also the way that Eli avoided being vulnerable and emotional. Essentially, I gave him permission to have the emotion by being the one who exposed it. I thus acted out his dual phantasy of the old rigid parent and the new guiding and supportive parent. That said, it was also a helpful and useful interpretation.

After my interpretation, Eli was silent and awash with emotion. I said, "It is hard to have those soft feelings, to receive love." He agreed and went on to tell me how he is "always trying to keep a check on him-self" because "out of the blue" he will "well up and start weeping" if he sees someone "look at me a certain way." After discussing this for quite some time, it became clear that when he was talking with someone, he either imagined or detected a moment of compassion, love, or sensitiv-ity in the other person. This was either directed at someone else in their story or directed at Eli, and it often brought Eli to tears. I interpreted, "it is hard to believe we are here for you, that we have your back, that we love you, or even that we are interested in you." Eli began to cry.

Over time, we have been exploring how he uses logic and control to placate and please me, avoid conflict, and make sure not to experience this soft and warm moment with a loving object. I have interpreted two reasons for this transference of distance, control, and censoring of emo-tion. On the one hand, Eli does not want to give up control of me by allowing himself to become emotional and vulnerable, because I then might become angry and vengeful. This is the more persecutory anxiety. On the other hand, he doesn't want to feel with me or for me, because then he might realize that he cares for me and I for him. This would bring on the unbearable sorrow of experiencing the wonderful attach-ment he craves and craved and the realization that he lost it, could lose it, or never had it. The sudden moment of presence and absence in his mind is a massive sense of depressive disappointment and loss com-bined with a persecutory abandonment and collapse.

Eli has been able to take in my interpretations regarding these states of dread and loss and has gradually risked exploring them with me as well as in relationships outside of the transference. One example of this was his pursuit of hobbies, outside his normally rigid regime of work, chores, and responsibilities. Throughout his life, including during the analysis, Eli would undertake something with the initial idea to have fun, to learn, or to create. Then, he quickly transformed it into a task, a duty, and a project to do well at rather than to enjoy or learn. This put him back in control and saved him from his fear of disappointing the object and his guilt for deviating from the rulebook.

Eli loved tools of all kinds, and he especially enjoyed woodworking. But when he wanted to buy a new tool or even use the tools he already owned, he immediately felt compelled to use them "responsibly," to re-pair something in the house or to build something instead of buying it in order to be "budget minded." Buying a new tool started as an exciting, fun pleasure, but from a guilty indulgence it became a guilty mistake. He had to make up for that by using the tool to build something that was "needed," and sometimes he simply returned the tool to the store to stop this overwhelming conflict.

Eli was unable to allow himself to use his tools purely for fun. When he tried to, he felt guilty and stopped, or he didn't start at all, for fear of criticism from his girlfriend. While it sounded like she could be rigid and domineering at times, this was Eli's own punitive self using her traits as a vehicle to validate his own aggressive feelings.

I interpreted that he did the same with me. He would come in and begin in a fairly relaxed manner but quickly convert his tone into a report to "cover recent activities and review attempts at progress on identified issues." I interpreted that by switching to "report mode" he controlled me and also invited me to step in and give him permission to use his tools and to free associate. He said he understood and agreed but added that he didn't fully trust his hope for that, because I might change my mind and see him as "stepping over the line" and not being proper or well behaved.

This extreme need to control us and prevent anger was part of an effort at creating and maintaining a new and more accepting object that he could trust, but this goal of transforming and refreshing his volatile unstable object was infused with a suffocating, demanding vision of how to properly love, live, and relate. So, as in the case when reliance on projective identification is excessive, this goal of transformation only reinforces and repeats the original object-relational trauma.

At the same time, Eli has gradually made significant progress in healing his vision of self and object. Some examples of this slow but significant shift and internal change that Eli has achieved includes his risk of using humor with me. He now makes occasional puns and shares funny stories with me. I interpreted he was testing the water and trying to trust that he could use me in a different, less controlling manner in order to try to attach himself to me in a closer, more intimate, and genuine fashion. He told me, "it feels good and new but very foreign and like it could blow up in my face any moment." I reminded him, "You would be the one lighting the fuse."

Here, I was interpreting the origin of his paranoid fear. I made the interpretation immediate and direct. This was something I thought Eli could manage and integrate in a useful manner, as opposed to other, more paranoid patients, who might not be so able to take their projections back so quickly. For those types of patients, waiting, containing longer, or making analyst-centered interpretations could be a better way to go. But Eli's more depressive functioning was able to tolerate, introject, and integrate my handing back his projections.

Eli became more and more able to relate to me in a way that went past the risk of anger, conflict, or hurtful disappointment, which for him traditionally meant immediate rejection or banishment. An example of this progress had to do with his thinking "out of the box." Normally, with me in the transference, with others, and certainly with himself, he would not allow his mind to become creative, imaginative, or open to honest contact with his object. It was thus a sign of internal growth when he showed me a t-shirt he had made at a local carnival event. It simply said, "Whatever!" Eli was proud of this and told me a long, detailed story of how he had seen the booth at the carnival and marveled at the idea of people spontaneously coming up with slogans to put on their t-shirts "for no good reason." I interpreted that Eli often struggled with the idea that it could be "for a bad reason" instead, so why risk it. I added that in this case, he was risking showing me this "Whatever!" side of himself and stepping out of the box in our relationship.

Eli was very excited with his choice of slogan, as it meant something very new and important to him. He said, "I can feel this new way of being, a real freedom. I just picture myself saying 'whatever' whenever I feel uptight or concerned about something. It's like a magic word that releases me." I interpreted that this was a great risk: he was thumbing his nose at his internalized bully object. I said, "You have realized how much you keep yourself in a small confined cell and keep others in a very predictable, stamped-out mold. Now you're experimenting with letting us just be. You don't know the outcome, how you will impact me, how I will react, how we will get along. So, the 'whatever' is you feeling stronger, feeling less guilty, and trying to trust that we will be ok."

Eli agreed and noted that he only wore the t-shirt on weekends, but he phantasized about wearing it to work. I said, "Maybe you are working on having it be a mindset you can carry anywhere, anytime, including here. But, I suspect you still have a few reservations." He replied, "I do, and I'm still tense about the consequences of saying whatever I want to whomever." I said, "I think it might be because you picture it in a very black-and-white way." Here, I was addressing the splitting he used to control the possible instability and collapse into anger that he could trigger in the object. He pictured that he was either in a secure but precarious state of control or that he was throwing caution to the wind, risking chaos and violence in exchange for freedom of thought and self-expression. He said, "Yes. The 'Whatever!' t-shirt does feel like an exciting but radical stance. It's a work in progress." I added, "Letting us be a work in progress instead of forcing us to be a fixed predictable commodity is a new work in progress!" He smiled and said, "Whatever!" and laughed in an easy way quite different from his usual focused and serious manner.

Eli represents a category of patients who are worried about the well-being of the object in a very particular manner. They see the object as being easily tipped over into anger, disappointment, and tension. They picture the object becoming hostile, judgmental, and unhappy as the result of being contaminated, influenced, or provoked by their autonomy and self-expression. By just being himself, the "whatever factor," Eli feared that he could push me over the edge. He felt it as a fundamental mistake that offended and went against the needs and requests of others, creating a level of frustration that he was not only responsible for but that he might not be able to reverse. Eli felt to blame when the object was unhappy with him. He imagined the reason the object became persecutory was his inattention to the object's needs, requests, or demands. Eli infused the object with a fragile tolerance of difference and a lack of understanding, forgiveness, or acceptance. In the transference, he didn't have faith in my own "whatever" ability. Therefore, Eli lived in a primitive type of depressive mode that offered no healing, no second chances, and no excuses. Thus, everything was ok if no individual growth or choice occurred, but mistakes or self-thought and personal choice shattered the tentative peace treaty, creating angry persecution.

Two situations show examples of this, one occurring in the first year of analysis and the other more recently. While the theme is similar in both, the level of intensity and rigidity is different. Last week, I came out to the waiting room and asked Eli to come in. He entered my office and asked me if he could go down to the restroom for some water for his sore throat. When he came back, I asked him why he had waited to ask me for permission instead of just going before I came out. I wondered if he had felt some trepidation. Eli said he remembered how "in the old days" he would have not ever gone to the restroom without "your permission" for fear of violating some rule. But this time it was more a "matter of not wanting to cause confusion." By this, he meant that he pictured himself going to the restroom while at the same time I would come out to greet him and not find him, creating confusion. I would not know where he was, and then I might go back into my office, and he would come back to the waiting room and miss me. We would both have missed each other in a confusing, comical, but potentially sad situation. While silly sounding, it also had the tragic element of us never finding each other. I interpreted, "you're not sure we could handle it. You want to make sure we run smoothly and don't have anything happen that could test us. Maybe you still are not sure if we could tolerate it, negotiate it, or resolve it." Eli said, "It is so much better than before, but you're right that I don't trust we could navigate that bump in the road. I want to smooth it out or avoid it altogether."

This was a more integrated and hopeful conflict than the type of transference fears he had in the first year of analysis. In the first year of treatment, Eli would bring me a check every time we met. I asked him why he chose that as opposed to paying me once a week or once a month. We spent most of that session discussing and discovering how he was trying to make sure I was appeased and without tension. He imagined that if he were to pay only once a week, I might become angry or frustrated with him about it. "You could get tired of waiting for your money, angry that I decided to only pay once a week, or tell me I have broken some kind of rule," he said. I pointed out how he saw me as a potentially offended and then angry person who couldn't see differences, allow for any changes, or tolerate any new way of thinking other than my own rigid and set ways. I interpreted that this was his fear of me but also his projection of control and strict adherence to the law as he saw it.

The restroom incident was very similar in its core phantasy pathology, but its intensity was much less, and there was more of a feeling that he would simply confuse me or lose me rather than hurt me or enrage me. The overall sense was that we might be in a state of troubled tension but we might survive it and figure it out eventually. There was less of a dramatic falloff into paranoid anxiety and more hope and trust within his depressive anxieties.

Over time, we are successfully finding our way through these dual conflicts and, as we do, he is more solidly placed in healthy depressive functioning that is shifting to whole-object functioning and less susceptible to sudden "trap door" experiences of persecutory betrayal, demand, or attack. His guilt is met more by a sense of balance and forgiveness as well as by a new belief in being able to give up control without him or the object going out of control.

During a recent session in his second year of analytic treatment on the couch, Eli made an extremely insightful comment that showed his progress into whole-object relations and a real integration of both paranoid and depressive phantasies. He said, "Recently, I was reflecting on my work here and my work with you. In looking at how I see us together, I realized that the first thing I had to figure out to make progress was that living my own life doesn't mean I stop loving you." Here, Eli was pointing to the intense depressive guilt he lived with.

Eli continued, "Then, the second phase of our work, which is much more painful, scary, and difficult, was realizing that you won't stop loving me if I live my own life and felt my own feelings." Here, he was pondering the more insidious edge between depressive loss and persecutory rejection. At this point, he is usually able to stay in the more manageable realm of loss and worry over my acceptance and feel a degree of trust and hope that I will still love him. In these important reflections, which in themselves point to the more integrated mental life he had achieved, Eli was telling me that he was now operating much more in the realm of whole-object depressive development. However, as mentioned, he also was relaying the continued difficulty he has in trusting the "harder second phase" of my love being still available if he exposes himself as independent and separate from me.

CASE 2: NARCISSISTIC DESPERATION

When I met Helen for the first time, I was taken back by what seemed to be her very demanding, critical way of being with her objects. She had called me for help with her troubled marriage, and when she came in she quickly told me the story of how her ten-year marriage was "on the rocks and maybe over." She told me she was "completely irritated with her husband and could no longer respect him." Helen explained that for years they both had high-powered jobs in finance, "making their numbers and pulling down the big bucks." They both put in long hours for the money and power, but fulfillment was not something they found, nor was it something they even thought much about. A few years ago, Helen's husband was part of a company-wide layoff, and he found a new job that was fairly different in scope to his last. He found it very satisfying, and he told his wife he was very happy and felt he "had found his niche." Helen told me, "He said he was so happy he didn't see the point in ever trying to get another position or move up the ladder. He said he was finally content and felt great as is." I listened. She continued, "That was the beginning of the end of my respect for him. I started to question if I really loved him and if I could stay with him if he didn't try and move up, make more, and constantly strive to get a bigger salary and title. When I realized he was making less than I am and was fine with that, I stopped wanting to have sex with him." She went on about this for quite a while, detailing how she no longer saw her husband as a man, now that he was "complacent and lazy." Helen told me she "couldn't be with a man who made less than she did. I can't handle having a bigger title and a bigger paycheck than my husband."

My initial impression listening to Helen was of a very anxious and alarmed woman who was feeling a loss of narcissistic control over her immediate internal object world. She told me about how she had demanded he work harder and look for a more prestigious job. "I keep asking him about it and wondering when is he going to get off his ass and do something. I don't want to be the one who makes the money in this family. If he doesn't turn this around soon, I think I might leave him." Within this arrogant demanding dictator, I sensed a level of desperation and anxiety and made interpretations in that direction. "You must feel very anxious since you feel you only have two options: either force him into being a better money maker and leader of the pack or leave him." She responded by starting to cry and said, "Yes. I feel very strange being the one who makes the most, and I don't think it's right. I feel he is getting away with something." I said, "Like you have to do all the work and he isn't taking care of you?" She nodded. I continued, trying to make analytic contact with her deeper feelings, "maybe you want him to take care of you emotionally, but it is easier or safer to see it financially." Here, I was focusing on her libidinal narcissistic organization (Rosenfeld 1971) and interpreting the defenses and anxieties that made up that psychic retreat.

This last interpretation seemed to go over well. Helen relaxed for a bit and told me how she had never really thought much about it over the years but that in the last year or two she had realized she wanted "more out of the relationship and saw that there wasn't much there in the way of intimate communication." I said, "I assume you mean from either side." She said yes. Here, I was trying to keep a focus on her projections and not get swept away in the defensive or masochistic aspects of her narcissistic retreat (Britton 2008).

At one point, Helen was telling me what a disappointment her husband had become, how much he had fallen from grace, and how he looked like an "underachiever." She also mentioned how as a result she had come to see me to "fix the problem." I interpreted, "you want a man you can count on, whether it is your husband or me, as someone to help you, but you are angry and controlling about it. You want it now, and you want us to perform up to your standards immediately."

Here, I was interpreting the controlling and exacting aspects of her transference. Helen said she hadn't thought about it that way before but that she thought I was correct. Then, she said she felt depressed and felt the only solution was either to give up and walk away from the marriage or "just put up with it and tolerate it." She started crying and said, "I have tried to convince myself it's enough for such a long time, and I feel like I will have to just keep doing that." I interpreted, "you feel so much anger, expectation, and grief for this ideal person who should do it just so for you that you end up feeling like you either get the perfect partner or nothing at all. Either run away or tolerate are the lonely alternatives." Here, I was interpreting the splitting and the paranoid aspects of her phantasy as well as the primitive depressive phantasy of having to exist on the crumbs of her object's love or be forgotten altogether. Since Helen had told me that her mother had always expected Helen to excel in all categories but never seemed interested in her in any emotional way, I also made a genetic interpretation. "From what you said about your childhood being a constant demand to perform and excel with no emotional reward, maybe those feelings of lonely anger, denial, and toleration have resurfaced again."

Helen seemed interested in what I was saying. I asked her what her associations were. She said she "ends up feeling hopelessly alone and lonely in her marriage, just pining for some attention or some evidence he loves me or even notices me." She cried again and said more about this desolate, barren place she felt lost in. I noticed that she would then predictably shift into a more critical, demanding, or dismissive stance. I interpreted this as a defense against the overwhelming void she felt. I noticed she wanted quick, immediate action from me and an instant solution to her problems. I told her that by demanding that instant fix she was making me into the slow, not-up-to-her standards husband and making herself feel like the left-out, not-important-enough wife. I said she was attacking our ability to slowly work together and gradually understand what was troubling her and how to change that. The way she looked at me when I said that alerted me to how she might be both relieved and upset by my interpretation, and I asked her about that. She said, "Yes. You said 'slowly and gradually,' and I don't like that. I want it now, and I want it to be powerful." I said, "So, you are the cruel slave driver. We progress now, or we perish. No rest for the wicked." She smiled and agreed. This very concrete remark, which followed on the heels of her momentary clarity and reduction in overall anxiety and hostility, was a formidable narcissistic resistance, and over the course of the treatment it came in waves, beating us down and twisting our understanding and exploration into failure and defeat. Helen's defensive onslaught was hostile and destructive but colored with desperation. In this way, she demonstrated both destructive and libidinal narcissistic phantasies in the transference.

Whenever Helen would become arrogant or dismissive and tell me about how she is "still trying to get him to step it up and be a man," I interpreted that she seemed to be avoiding a terrible void, a place where she felt very alone and desperately trying to run the show herself. In other words, I was interpreting her desperate retreat from the anxieties of both paranoid and depressive phantasies into this narcissistic foxhole. I told her she was trying both to avoid that void or trap door in the marriage and also with me, in that whenever she began to be herself and share her feelings with me, she seemed to see it as a dangerous act that could leave her helpless and open. Helen told me, "I have always been like that. I don't usually talk about feelings. But in the last few years I've found myself so hungry to share everything with my husband, and then I feel rebuffed or ignored. But, usually when I notice my feelings or start to feel them, I move on as fast as possible." I interpreted, "as if I will catch you at something very wrong or that you will become lost in the feelings and sink without anyone to save you." She started to cry and nodded yes.

Over the course of the next few sessions, she revealed a softer side of herself to me, although this was packaged within a still rough and demanding stance of "get it together or else." It seemed she felt forgotten by her husband. She was upset that he never seemed to want to spend time with her or talk to her. Helen would start to break down and sob when she told me how she "really wanted him to see me, to acknowledge me instead of treat me like a roommate he does errands with." Then she quickly recoiled and told me how selfish he seemed and how she "has about had it with his loafing around in his career and not pushing forward in his profession." I interpreted that she had scared herself by sharing so much with me. I said she must be feeling unsure of how I see her now that I know that she has these needs and that she wants to depend on me and her husband. I said, "Maybe it's easier to be tough as nails and demanding than soft and vulnerable. You don't want to get hurt." Here, I was interpreting from the countertransference, in which I felt she rapidly shifted from being a very self-contained and exacting soldier to a vulnerable, needy little girl and back again.

Helen said that she did not want to continue living with "this cold distance. I had enough of that around me growing up." She described how "rough it was" when her parents divorced and how "no one ever talked about feelings in the family. We didn't have feelings, we just acted. There was action but no emotion. It was pretty cold at times. I felt very lonely when I was little. I always felt I was being ignored or forgotten. That was a terrible place." She began to cry. "But I gradually learned to tolerate feeling like there was never any love." I said, "Much in the way you have with your marriage?" She agreed and added that she became "skilled at living without love and taking care of myself." Then, Helen switched to telling me about how "there were certainly good memories and good times. My parents loved me, and I wasn't abused." Then she started telling me about the various good memories.

I interpreted, "you have opened up to me and risked sharing feelings. Suddenly, you are jumping back. I think you are worried that after depending on me and trusting me, I will forget you and ignore you. So, you have to make us into a nice memory and only impress me with good stories that are safe." She said she could see what I meant and that "it was hard to feel ok about complaining without wondering if I was going on too much about it." I said, "So, you are realizing it is you that can be rejecting and critical about your feelings." She nodded. Here, I helped her in acknowledging and reflecting on her projections, thereby slowly withdrawing them from her objects, leaving her with a much more manageable and danger-free internal and external world.

After a few months of treating Helen and things improving, she told me she was stopping the treatment, citing "heavy work commitments and the end-of-the-year holidays." She then started to discuss how her week had gone. I asked her for details about why she felt she had to stop so abruptly. Again, she cited work issues and travel plans, but she also seemed to be dismissing the importance of our meetings in the process. I made that interpretation and added that she seemed to quickly put others' needs first and ignore us or give us no value. She said things were better with her husband and that they had been communicating more of late, so she felt she "could deal with things and put the rest off 'til the New Year. I have already figured out many of my problems; I just have to do something to change them now." I said, "You probably would make time to be here if it was to treat something physical. But, since it is about your feelings and your emotional needs, you seem to throw us aside pretty easily. We are not important; you are paying us no attention. That seems like exactly what you feel from your husband. Now, you do that to us."

Here, I was interpreting the projective identification of a rejecting object on one hand and a devalued or forgotten object on the other. She said, "You're right about it being like my marriage. I guess part of this is that I try to squeeze so much into my workday that I see this as one more burden. I usually try to find a way to squeeze all my errands, calls, and working out into my workday, along with all the actual work I need to do. I do it that way so I can go home and focus on my kids. I want to be there for them 100 percent, without being distracted by other things at night. It has always been crucial for me to be there for them and not ever make them feel ignored or unimportant." I said, "You say that like it is something you really want to make sure they don't have to go through."

Helen started to cry and said, "I felt so alone and forgotten when I was growing up. I want to make sure they never have to endure that. When I heard there was a special event at my son's classroom last week and the parents were invited, I made sure to show up. When he came in the classroom and saw that I was there, I could see the joy and happiness in his eyes. That's so important. I never want to take that away from him." She cried some more. I said, "You want to make sure he never goes through the terrible sense of being forgotten that he lives with you." She nodded and told me, "growing up, it was like that all the time. I would look around for my mother, and she was never there. Literally, she was not there sometimes, but mostly I felt she didn't see me in the room. It was like I was invisible. She looked right past me. I couldn't get to her and she didn't seem to ever want to get to me."

I interpreted that Helen is constantly trying to be an independent, logical, and tough woman with me, her husband, and everyone else to avoid falling through this terrible trap door of despair and loss. She feels completely valueless and without form to the other. She is trying desperately to make herself important to others through her achievements and wants to force her husband into being something important too. But she sees herself and now us as without importance. I added that by stopping the treatment, she is only reinforcing that feeling, giving us low priority and little value. Helen listened and said she agreed. We looked at the calendar and agreed to postpone meeting for a month for her out-of-town business trips but that then she would "make time for us."

At this early phase of her analytic treatment, it is hard to know if she will be able to value us enough to continue. My sense is that she will probably not return but has benefited from her brief experience of analytic contact. We have been able to establish a degree of clarity and balance within her rocky and difficult phantasy world. While Helen displays aspects of the depressive position, in that she is trying hard to preserve, promote, and protect her objects as the number-one priority in her life, this is part of a projective-identification process in which she wants someone to save her from falling through the same terrible trap door into abandonment. Thus she is always on the run, trying to fortify and protect the object—but from her own projected anger, envy, and emotional hunger.

At the same time, there is a significant aspect of paranoid functioning in her life. The trap door leads to a freefall into a persecutory world of eternal loss and endless banishment. There is no forgiveness, no salvation, and no value in a relationship. That which is broken cannot be fixed, expectations can never be met, and safety is never reached. Or, if safety is reached and trust is found, its permanence is fleeting. We discussed how this was her feeling about the marriage in that even though she had been forthcoming with her husband about her needs and he seemed to respond, she didn't trust it and wondered how long it would last before "it drifted back to nothingness." I pointed out that the drifting was something she contributed to. Here, I was interpreting her own contribution to her experience of neglect and loss, and I noted that the way she wanted to stop the treatment spoke to the brittle foundation she had established with me. I said, "We are good today, gone tomorrow. That is your worry about how others see you, but it is also how you are treating us." Here, I was interpreting her projection of rejection, devaluation, and detachment.

I also noted these issues in the transference. At one point, I interpreted, "I think you started off treating both of us like we are here to solve a chess problem. You, your husband, and I are just pieces to be moved around until the problem is fixed. You try to control us and make sure we are going to excel and make a difference, to not feel useless and forgotten. But then you took the risk to make it more personal and allowed yourself to bring feelings into the room and share yourself with me. But I think you are not sure about how to maintain that feeling of being important and focusing on your feelings, so you start to ignore us and turn us back into a low-priority item on your to-do list." Helen told me, "I think that is right, and I do want to feel like I have some kind of identity or meaning. It is just that I lose focus on myself so easily. I am not used to considering myself." Here, she was able to reflect on herself and notice how she relates to herself as a rejecting object. I have also interpreted how she uses this cruel expectation of self and object as a way to avoid closeness with me, her husband, and others. I told her that even though she desperately wants that warm dependence, she attacks it as weak and pathetic, which leaves her without love and on her own, without value or acknowledgement.

Helen replied, "It is very strange to talk about wanting that, because I think I gave up on ever having that a long time ago." She broke down in tears again. Becoming anxious, she retorted, "So, what do I do? How do I change that?" I said, "You are now demanding we hurry up and change, or else. It is easier to be cruel and demanding than to have to expose that little girl who wants to be close and be taken care of." She replied, "I feel like a yo-yo that way; I'm up and then I'm down. It is hard to stay with the feelings for very long."

Early in her treatment, Helen has made analytic contact and is exploring these internal conflicts while also retreating into a narcissistic foxhole from which she attacks and denies them. Right now, we have taken a break from meeting. Will we meet again? Is this as far as we go? As with all difficult cases, we will have to see if we will be able to bail out the ship and sail forward, sink into the depths, or remain forever frozen in this precarious position.

SUMMARY

The two cases in this chapter illustrate two types of psychic retreat that can occur and the resulting defensive fallout when these retreats collapse or fail fully to shield the ego from a combination of paranoid and depressive anxieties. In the first case, the patient felt sure he was not keeping the object content and healthy, which caused intense and primitive depressive phantasies that turned paranoid at times. The second patient exhibited narcissistic fears and hostility regarding the absence of a caring, attentive, and fully functioning object. In both cases, there was evidence of a strict need to cancel out growth or change in self and/or object (Feldman 2000), which created difficult transference situations.

10

—

TRAPPED IN AN EMOTIONAL FOXHOLE
Coping with Paranoid and Depressive Conflicts

MANY OF OUR more difficult cases (Hinshellwood 1989) are embedded between the paranoid-schizoid position (Klein 1946) and the depressive position (Klein 1935, 1940) and rely on complex defensive systems or pathological organizations (Steiner 1987) to ward off a sense of fragmentation and severe guilt. Their fragile psychological structure depends on a rigid adherence to various self-defeating defensive systems (Segal 1972), defensive organizations (O'Shaughnessy 1981), or narcissistic organizations (Rosenfeld 1964). To maintain a sense of control and safety for themselves and their objects, these patients cocoon themselves into these rigid systems of pathological defense. Some of the time, they are successful in erecting and maintaining a sealed-off, sterile refuge that feels like a safe zone but keeps them from giving or receiving. The successful psychic retreat creates a psychological barrier that while keeping out the bad, doesn't let the good in.

This reliance on psychic retreats (Steiner 1993) promotes a variety of entrenched and static transference problems. However, there can be an even more clinically vexing problem in these cases. Some of these patients attempt to stay within this fortress of control and withdrawal, but their pathological organization breaks down, becoming only partly functional. In many cases, it is like a crumbling bomb shelter, leaving the patient feeling helplessly exposed to the worst aspects of both paranoid and depressive suffering. The patient then attempts desperately to cling to the shards of an unstable retreat, feeling and acting more and more desperate to find shelter. Now they fight even harder to erect a temporary foxhole from the overwhelming and often unbearable torments of the paranoid and depressive world.

Projective identification, a universal method of relating and the foundation of all transferences (Grotstein 2007), becomes elevated to the status of a profound and pathological weapon or outcry. This level of interpersonal, transactional, and intrapsychic acting out promotes enactments (Joseph 1989), as both patient and analyst try to avoid the painful realities that become expressed within the therapeutic relationship (O'Shaunessy 1992; Feldman 1997; Caper 1995; Anderson 1997).

Steiner (1987) has noted that to work truly through the depressive position, one has to give up control over the object and with it the illusion of being able to protect it. One has to accept that one has hurt, damaged, or destroyed the object and that no amount of repair, offerings, or repentance can save it. In phantasy, the object is dead. Grief is all there is. Hope that there will ever be something good again is fleeting at best. This is a very difficult emotional experience, and the analyst must help the patient bear and gradually work with it.

This chapter will use clinical material to explore the different levels of chaos experienced by patients who utilize a psychic retreat. The imperfect nature of the retreat and the modest, shaky, halfway house that it offers provides only a brief breathing space for some patients before the next internal collapse begins. While Britton (2001) has noted the healthy progression and oscillation between paranoid and depressive positions that we can expect from normal development, these patients feel pulled helplessly back and forth, experiencing a chaotic disintegration rather than a stabilizing series of growth spurts. Feldman (2000) has noted how the analyst can join forces with the patient in finding very fixed and destructive ways of remaining loyal to the past and of being weary of change, difference, or closeness. Here, in collusion with the death instinct, both parties attempt to build a mutual psychic shelter from which to deny, control, and avoid any real relational experience and to feel falsely that all is well. This is a mutual retreat from the dual threat of depressive and paranoid phantasies. While destructive in its own right, this shelter can spring a leak and become a crumbling deathtrap of sorts, trapping its victims in the internal experience of a depressive and para-noid entombment without chance of rescue or relief.

CASE MATERIAL: A HOUSE OF MIRRORS

Paul has been engaged in his psychoanalytic treatment, on the couch, for several years now. Since he began, we have worked through many different issues in his emotional life and certain difficult external events. Early in his analysis, we navigated our way through his painful divorce. For the four years of his marriage, Paul had felt like a slave to his wife. He gave her enormous power by being passive and subservient, inter-acting with her as if she was a domineering woman whom he needed to pacify and never differ with for fear of terrible consequences. Any difference or disagreement had to be denied. Through projective iden-tification, he would put his unacceptable and dangerous feelings about his wife into me. Over time, we understood this to be a method of both manipulation and communication. Paul wished me to be the spokesper-son for him. By my "going first," I would be reassuring him that it was ok to be a separate and autonomous individual. This was part of a phantasy of me as a helpful father showing him the ways of the world. But, this type of projective-identification process was also him having me do his dirty work for him.

Over time, we understood more about this fear of conflict and his constant efforts to mold himself into whatever his wife and I seemed to want or demand. Historically, this was linked to his chameleon-like way of coping with his angry alcoholic father. This way of relating came out in the transference very early on. Paul tried his best to keep me happy and content, usually projecting any feelings that were not neutral or part of what he imagined I wanted. He enlisted me, via projective identification, to be his translator, bringing up any nasty or unsavory thoughts or issues that seemed aggressive and different. I was invited to take on and translate all the thoughts and feelings he had for himself or toward the objects that he felt were greedy or dangerous. Much of our progress has been the result of my interpreting this specific transfer-ence and his gradually reowning these split-off and projected aspects of himself.

However, this very rigid container/contained dyad he constructs is a fragile and unbalanced psychic refuge that he returns to over and over again. One method Paul uses to keep us neutralized and locked into this preordained system is to have insight but then call it into question. On certain occasions, he will have a false insight to please me. But at other times, he will have a genuine moment of insight or risk expressing himself in a new and natural way but then tell me he thought he "might be doing that to impress his analyst." Now, this is a very tricky maneuver that is hard to sort out and interpret. On the one hand, Paul was indeed prone to trying to say things to impress me and make me think he was a good, deep-thinking patient. So he was possibly acting out that very strategy. But in addition, he often had hard-won, valuable moments of new self-understanding, which made him anxious and prone to attack this new growth. Via projective identification, he would try to draw me into doubting his new thoughts. If I were to agree that he was just saying something to impress me, we would be ignoring or dismantling his progress. Often, it was all both genuine and false at the same time, which made for a difficult transference soup.

To illustrate Paul's continued struggle with the anxieties of the depressive and paranoid position and his efforts at constructing a failure-prone pathological refuge or psychic retreat, I will share a recent session. Paul told me he was thinking about how "he tries to be what everyone wants." We talked about how he likes going to a new workout class at the gym because "I don't have to think for myself; they tell me what to do." I pointed out that the class was also called a "boot camp" class because of how it was run in a dominating, military manner, a manner similar to how Paul described his experience of growing up. Paul told me, "Yes. If I follow orders, there won't be any trouble, and maybe someone will like me too."

I interpreted that he is only what he provides me, that his worth depends on pleasing me. Paul replied, "Yes. I need to do that. I remember cowering in the corner from what my father was doing. He would become so angry, or he would seem to be fine, but I was never sure when that would stop. I had to find a way to make sure he stayed ok. When he was fine, he could be nice and loving. There were good times, important times. But when it switched, it was really tough." I interpreted, "You want to stop the attack and find the love, so you have to figure out what I want and then fill it." Paul responded, "Exactly. I'm an empty vessel. I'm a void. I want you to fill me."

Paul went on to talk about going to a party that a friend invited him to and how he felt like an outsider. He said he wished he was "one of those people that go out with friends and automatically get included in things." As soon as he admitted being excited about being included and excited to be going to the party, Paul had to double back and negate this joy and success. By now, I was used to this type of doubling back to protect the both of us from his defined identity and to avoid my potential reactions to his individuality. Nevertheless, it was still confusing and slippery to deal with his submissive, manipulative attacks that twisted his words and my ability to make meaning out of them. He was skilled at keeping me off balance and was doing his best to make sure that I saw him as my loyal servant rather than a free spirit. I pointed out that he had exactly what he was wishing for, going to the party and being included, but he now he had to attack it and create a void. I suggested that he wanted me to give him the fun and the acceptance so he didn't have to claim it, own it, and risk my reaction to his expression of it. Paul said, "That's risky. You could slap me down. I would rather you tell me what to do."

I interpreted that he wants me to be his guiding parent, but that means he is always the kid. Paul responded, "I don't exist unless you define me." He said he just wants to be accepted, and then he went on for a long time telling me how he has no friends and only lets people in a small amount, to "remain safe and in control." I interpreted that he is forcing me either to agree with him that he is a failure or to leap in and rescue him. Paul said, "I know what you mean," but he is also aware of hearing what I said as "I am not pleasing you, so next time I should say it differently."

I interpreted that Paul perverts my comments and finds ways of pushing us apart, so he can feel in control, safe, and without conflict. He said that he "doesn't trust people and is sure that no matter how nice I am, when I leave you think bad things about me." I responded, "Then you have to find a way to please me even more next time. I think that is all your own judgment and expectation that you are putting onto me and then feeling criticized for." Here, I was introducing the idea that he was not the victim of outside forces but of his own hostile and judgmental feelings.

In the next session, Paul said he was thinking about what he should and shouldn't talk about. I interpreted that he was trying to please me by feeding me what he thinks I need to like him more. He said, "Yes, but it is only a matter of time before you find out what you don't like." He talked about being an imposter, always trying to be a mirror for people but feeling like he is always on the verge of failing to be the right kind of mirror, which would then spell trouble. I interpreted that he would be left with me seeing the real him: that instead of being an empty imposter, he would be full of himself and exposed. He agreed and told me how wonderful he feels when "after a good session" he feels full of himself and suddenly, instead of worrying about his place in the world, he is able to enjoy it fully.

As mentioned, Paul's ploy of being my mirror led to very confusing moments in the treatment and murky transference situations. He would double back on any progress and place blame or doubt on change in a manner that invited me to join in his judgment and become lost in the twists and turns he brought up regarding the legitimacy of his insight and our work together. A recent example of this involved Paul telling me about a friend who told him that two women have crushes on Paul. Paul said he felt guilty about telling me that and started a very deep discussion of all the reasons he probably feels guilty. I interpreted that he is suddenly and desperately trying to please me in the way he thinks I need, to be my deep-thinking patient who examines everything for underlying motives. This was a difficult and unclear moment in the transference, as Paul uses intensive projective-identification cycles to convert, pervert, and control our relationship. I interpreted that he is probably feeling anxious about beginning to share his pride and joy over finding out two girls had a crush on him. By saying he feels guilty, he is now inviting me to reassure him that the joy is ok instead of a crime. Paul agreed and associated to how he does this with everyone, extracting and pasting together an image of himself from everyone in this crafty, manipulative manner. I said, "But that doesn't quite ever fill you up, because it is my version of you, not your own truth." He said yes and told me that when he let himself feel some of the joy over hearing that the two girls liked him, he then felt filled up and confident about the date he "was going to have tomorrow." This last part seemed to slip out accidentally. Suddenly he was exposing not only his prior joy and pride but his current excitement and sense of manliness over his upcoming date.

On the one hand, this seemed like a typical moment in which he was hiding success and pride from me just in case I would disapprove of him or punish him. In this sense, he was being brave and took a risk in revealing his manly victory. But this again had a more complex and insidious side. When he "revealed" his date for tomorrow, I felt like there was somewhat of a tricky manipulation in how he dropped this information. I felt like it was honest and a real victory but also a way that he was trying to test me to see if I would be on his side or not. Again, it was hard to pin down and confusing to interpret, but I brought it up and tried to explore it with him. As usual, he was quick to agree and placate but also gave it some genuine consideration.

Overall, Paul is making slow but steady progress. His pattern of intense defensive posturing, guarding against harming me, and destroying or denying any sense of self to avoid guilt and fear of persecution has created a transference jungle. This psychic retreat of desperate positioning and adapting never quite protects him from the dual ravages of the depressive and paranoid positions. Therefore, he has had to double back on himself and his objects desperately, as if he is constantly patching a leaking dike. This rigid pathological pattern has gradually shifted to a slow and tedious working through of core anxieties and the cautious expression of his formally hidden self. Together, we make our way through the jungle, finding more and more clearings along the way.

THE SUNKEN TREASURE: A CAPSIZED RETREAT

In his sixth year of psychoanalytic treatment on the couch, Mark said, "I was born to manage and maintain my mother's mental health. I was raised as a caretaker for her sanity. She put her lifeless empty shell into me." I interpreted, "you feel lifeless and empty and look to me to bring you back to life. I think it scares you to breathe life back into yourself, so you wait for me or someone else to give you a sense of purpose." Mark replied, "In the past, I think I would have been clueless as to what you just said. But today I do understand, and I think you are right. But knowing that makes me furious! I'm so pissed that I keep myself in this little fucking box!"

This exchange was a testimony to the progress we have made over time. Because Mark is highly resistant to thinking for himself, whenever I have made interpretations that invite him to consider himself and his own motivations, he becomes silent, blank, and unable to process anything in his mind. He falls quiet for a very long time and then tells me he has no idea what was happening in the room. Other times, he will begin to make grunting sounds and yell about not having any idea what I was saying. I would carefully repeat myself, to no end.

For years, I have interpreted that he is actively shedding any thoughts or feelings from himself or me that give him autonomous function and identity. He counters that he is a helpless victim with a broken mind. I am left with the countertransference feeling that he tries very hard to convince me he will never be able to think for himself. I interpret that he wants me to be his mind. But that would make me into his mother, running his life and controlling his mind. It is only in the last year that Mark has been willing to take ownership of his mind and consider what I say as well as what he independently thinks and feels. This has led to a new level of clarity in our relationship. However, we are still struggling with his "little fucking box," in which he feels safe and in control but lost without a place in life, a way to touch others, or a way to be touched by others. Mark is remarkably frozen by the dual threats of persecutory anxiety and depressive loss. As a result, he usually prefers to remain in the passive safety of his psychic retreat, the "little fucking box."

A few months ago, Mark began the session by saying, "I blew up with my father twice in the last week." Then, he fell silent as he often does. I said, "Maybe you are angry right now." He said "No. I feel nothing." Then he mentioned that he might be angry, because he "suppresses everything in his life, including anger." This comment was an example of his real progress over the course of our analytic work. In the beginning of his treatment, Mark was never able to think of himself as having any unconscious agency. Rather, he saw himself as a passive victim to life, and if he contained any emotional identity, it had been put there by someone else.

Over the course of Mark's treatment, we have come to understand and slowly modify his depressed view of himself as well as his anxious and distorted view of the world. However, he is firmly resistant to a more basic shift in his relationship to others. In the analysis, his skittish nature is a pivotal aspect of the transference. Outside of his analysis, Mark is reluctant to approach women, even though he desperately longs for their company. He is also so conflicted about becoming more autonomous and self-expressive that he hasn't worked in over five years.

It has been a difficult therapeutic journey with Mark, as he reacts to multiple phantasy states that often switch abruptly or coexist and overlap in a confusing and overwhelming manner for both of us. We have discovered several strands of thought and feeling that rule his life. From a more paranoid perspective, Mark worries that without his tie to mother, he will be lost, a "train wreck waiting to happen." Also, he feels "she just wants to suck the life out of me, like a vampire. One of us will die. She will kill me with her control and passive-aggressive bullshit, keeping me on a leash until I choke to death. Or I will kill her to gain my freedom." Here, an important parallel to the transference exists. Mark has been attached to me and the analysis in a helpful manner but also in a way that replicates his entombment with his internal mother. Both of us have brought this up and explored how he feels trapped, obligated, and submissive in the treatment, hoping to one day "unplug from the therapy and get on with his life." We have struggled with how he shapes us into a stagnant, parasitic couple where growth and escape into the real world of the living are impossible. When we examine this phantasy of being controlled and drained of freedom or identity, it becomes clear that while Mark wants to break free of this vision of us and his imprisonment, he is also frightened of how he would survive "out there" on his own.

Another transference manifestation of these phantasies is Mark's method of attending sessions. In the first three to four years, he only came once a week. Then, as his funds ran out and he relied on a meager allowance from his parents, he only came every other week. The psychological aspect of this had much to do with his "break free" versus "not survive out there" conflict. He told me he "didn't want to be too dependent and wanted to have a chance to do it on his own." Mark had a history of reading self-help books for many years, trying to understand himself. Indeed, he seems to have gained many insights into his con-flicts this way, but he ultimately feels paralyzed in the same way he now does in the analysis. He says, "I can see myself in this book I read and I can see exactly what we are discussing, but I don't know how to change any of it."

This conviction of "not knowing how" has been a major obstacle in the transference work. I interpret that he fights for the "broken mind" model, which leaves me alone with my own idea of a healthy mind that has temporarily ground to a halt for certain important reasons. I inter-pret that he does and doesn't want to "fire the engine up" and partici-pate in life, and he fights back with the idea of being handicapped and broken.

In the last year, he has told me, "I can see your point now. I think I am capable of so much more. But I don't know why I stop myself, and I don't know how to get past this inertia." I have interpreted that part of the answer to his question lies in understanding his need to keep a certain distance from me by only attending infrequently. In the countertransfer-ence, it feels like he is a wild animal that circles at a distance, wanting to be fed and interested in being close to the domesticated world but unsure about leaving his private, controlled territory and worried about being caught. He wants something more and something different but is unsure and unwilling to give up what he knows. Mark seems to split his life into known misery he owns and is actively controlling and into something else totally unknown with no way to understand, own, or be in control of. It is only in the last year that he has acknowledged his own reluctance to approach and taste this new territory instead of experienc-ing it as something his broken mind is unable to fathom.

Regarding relationships in general and his view of himself in the world, Mark told me he fears "being on my own and realizing I have no idea how to relate. It is like I will finally break free from my jail cell, leaving my mother to rot on her own, only to not know how to survive on my own." These anxieties combine a persecutory phantasy of being lost in a strange land without any knowledge of how to survive and with no one there to help with his guilt over breaking free of his mother's clutches. This more depressive phantasy of being sent to a barren, love-less land for abandoning his needy mother has a treacherous flavor to it, in that the guilt and loss shift into more of a vision of exile without chance at redemption or change. His vision is of escaping one prison only to find himself in another equally painful form of entrapment without hope of parole.

As he has described many times over, Mark sees himself as his mother's emotional caretaker. Without him, she would perish, wither, and die. This primitive depressive phantasy contains no reparative element or hope of eventual resolution. Mourning is absent. To grieve effectively for the loss of his wished-for attachment to his mother, he would have to concede the failure of that bond. And for Mark, that still feels like a catastrophic descent into despair, rejection, and guilt for his murderous contempt. The concept of pining, Klein's (1940) idea of sorrow, concern, and effort to find and regain the good but injured object, is beyond Mark's reach at this point. This is because of the immature and brittle nature of the depressive position, perhaps caused by the lack of healthy dependence on a caretaker object able to fend for herself without looking to Mark to be a caretaker in return. Whether this is true historically is not so important as the fact that this is an internal fact that defines Mark and his view of self and other. In phantasy, it appears that Mark feels broken and wants his mother to put him back together, and he won't grow up until she completes her parental duty. But to Mark, she is also broken. Part of my interpretive approach with these issues is to bring up the idea that he will not begin to live his own life until he has a mother who can properly take care of not only him but herself as well.

Mark's quest for an ideal object leaves him unfed and angry. This loss of an ideal and his resulting fury creates a dangerous bad object that must be avoided or destroyed. These lingering anxieties make the unstable depressive position easily fragmented and prone to collapse. Indeed, Mark often screams, "I am going to kill that bitch one day. I have no life of my own. I have forsaken my life to keep her propped up. She always needs me and I can't move on and be myself. I have no idea what it would mean to be myself. I have become her servant and nursemaid. She has controlled me from the beginning and taken my soul away. I think she will literally die if I leave her, but you know what? I don't care! I just want a life of my own. But I can't figure out how to make that happen. Who am I?"

This outcry was a combination of his persecutory fears and his depressive guilt of causing her death if he were to break free and live his own life. It was always a confusing combination of who would die first, who would suffer the most if the other were to detach or become independent, and who was benefiting more from this parasitic fusion. One of the many ways this emerged in the transference was Mark's passive and detached relationship to me, mixed with his consistent and loyal presence. As I have mentioned, when I would suggest that he attend more often, he always said no. I was left to offer, to then eventually feel rejected, and finally to feel a sense of apathy and detachment. At the same time, he would surprise me at how regular and reliable he was in attending when he did. Just when I began to feel a real lack of meaning or attachment in our relationship, he would remind me or reassure me by showing up like clockwork and making a genuine effort to explore his troubles. By my writing about him, it is evident that he holds a strong place in my mental life, even though in its form it is like shifting sands. This aspect of our relationship is a reflection of his conflict around relating and participating in all aspects of his life.

The parasitic nature of the immature depressive position involves concerns and controls over the object to keep it safe and happy, not for the sake of the object so much as for the sake of the self. That is one reason I think that I never feel sure if Mark is truly rooted in his analytic treatment. This is an aspect of the libidinal narcissistic transference that Rosenfeld (1964) spoke of, and it involves a hostile or destructive component (Britton 2008), in which Mark is trying to keep me, his mother, and others out of his mind but then feels lost and alone without guidance or love. This is a massive projective-identification cycle that leaves him feeling empty, depleted, and envious of others' capacity for self-expression and participation. But when he tries to include himself in life, he feels overwhelmed, inferior, and anxious about how he might fail, be rejected, or come into a conflict with the object.

Mark is chained to the role of mother's caretaker so as to not forsake her and destroy her by gaining his own identity and freedom, but he also imagines he would perish if he separated from her and sought out his own life. No one is allowed a different, separate, unique expression of his or her own mind and heart without it somehow severely damaging another and without it causing severe retribution. There is no negotiation or allowance in this matter.

These phantasies and anxieties came out when he felt "smitten by the charms" of a woman who worked in the launderette he went to. She was twenty years his junior. Mark's last girlfriend had broken up with him six or seven years ago after she became "bored and tired of waiting for him to cast a vote on things in the relationship." Mark never took the lead in making plans, thinking of their future, or acting assertive in any capacity. He was so passive that she lost interest and began seeing a co-worker. Mark knew the man and for a while had been friends with him. But then Mark felt like "he couldn't compete with the guy. I hated him but never felt like I could take him on verbally or physically. I feel that way with most people. If they raise a point or start a debate, I have no idea how to counter them or put out my own way of thinking."

When he struck up a casual conversation with the young woman at the launderette, he told me she seemed interested in him and seemed to flirt with him. Mark said he felt "frozen in his tracks" but wanted to try to pursue it and ask her out. He struggled for months to work up the courage to talk with her. He told me about his longings, his phantasies of dating her, his fears of being rejected, and his overall ambivalence. During this time, he would park outside of her workplace and sit there, hoping to get a glimpse of her leaving for the day. In the countertransference, I felt both a sad, pathetic feeling for this lonely man and a slight fear of this older man essentially stalking this younger woman. When he finally asked her if she would go out to lunch, they exchanged a long and complicated series of e-mails and telephone calls about where they should go, what day, and what time. Clearly, Mark was very anxious and unsure. In all of these exchanges, he was very passive, leaving all the decisions to her. I interpreted that he wanted her to pursue him, make the decisions, and pick him, so he wouldn't have to think, feel, or act. That way, he could have the sense of being wanted by an ideal object instead of pining for an unavailable, rejecting object that he felt powerless to reach. In the end, he set up a tentative lunch date with her, but she never showed up for it. Later, he learned that in the months of his ambivalence and parking-lot stalking, she had started to date a coworker. In discussing this disappointment, we looked at how his lack of active participation left him on the sidelines, envious of others and convinced of his impotent, helpless place in life. All he could do is wish for rescue by some omnipotent, ideal object that would have pity on him, guide him, and think for him.

There were similar situations in which he felt a need, wanted to make some sort of change in his life, or simply wished to tell someone he wanted or didn't want something. He would feel overwhelmed with anxiety, a fear of conflict, and a sense of powerlessness. With clerks at the store, with his landlord, with car mechanics, and with his physical-therapy appointments, he was always left feeling that he had failed to follow through and make his position known. He put the object in a dominant, active role and himself in an ignored, powerless role. These insights left Mark furious but not mad enough to risk change. I interpreted this sadomasochistic pattern in the transference as well as in his outside life. He usually countered by telling me he was powerless and didn't know how to change that, leaving me as the only one in the room with the thought, power, and direction to save him, my empty, passive student. However, he was also able to acknowledge that he would be furious if I tried to tell him what to do. Indeed, he had been working hard at trying to understand himself and activate himself for years by reading every self-help book he could find that "rang a bell." These were usually books about the effects of being raised by a narcissistic mother and the resulting sense of passive confusion. He had genuine insights about this idea, but when it came to putting it into action, he wasn't able to take the risk to step out of his psychic retreat.

Another aspect of Mark's experience of himself as powerless and dominated by the cruel aspects of life had to do with his view of his body. The same sort of phantasy in which he was submitting to a dominating object and the need to be healed and cared for by an object that ultimately is unavailable or rejecting colored not only Mark's relationships with his mother and his analyst but his body as well.

When I began seeing Mark, he had been diagnosed with various forms of repetitive-motion disorders, leaving him dependent on braces and frequent physical therapy. He had been told he had a general digestive ailment that left him prone to heartburn and stomachaches. His back and hips hurt him much of the time, leaving him unable to exercise or walk for even modest distances. Mark also complained of headaches. He had lost a great deal of weight by the time I started seeing him and lost even more during the first years of treatment. He also didn't sleep very well, waking up feeling anxious, depressed, and angry.

CURRENT TRENDS IN MARK'S ANALYTIC WORK: YEAR SIX

With slow, hard work, Mark has begun to find a small amount of faith that he can make his own way in life. If his mother cannot function without him, that will be sad and tragic but not a death sentence for either one of them. He has recently begun attending parties and speaking to women. He is now exercising, seeing his body as important and part of his identity. Internally, he has started to see himself as having value and form, without that value and form creating an immediate threat to self and object.

Steiner (1987, 1994) has discussed patients who seek to avoid the pain and anxiety of both the depressive and paranoid positions. The two cases discussed in this chapter are representative of patients slightly different from Steiner's cases. His patients have successfully found a refuge or psychic retreat from both depressive and paranoid anxieties, albeit a pathological solution. The patients examined in this chapter have been unable to reach Steiner's psychic retreat or, if they have, their retreat has collapsed. Rather than being sealed off from both paranoid and depressive states, they are constantly at the mercy of both psychological storms. The psychic retreat offers a dysfunctional life raft upon which to sail through the treacherous grief, hostility, and anxiety of both phantasy experiences. The two cases in this chapter represent patients whose rafts have sprung leaks and are rapidly sinking or hopelessly listing in a choppy and precarious emotional sea.

Mark found refuge in his inactive stance, unplugged from the risks and unknowns of life. Nevertheless, he still found himself besieged by terrible fears, guilt, and the threat of loss and persecution. He would not let others in, but he also would not let himself go out and find others to engage with. Mark was trapped in his own foxhole of alienation, desire, envy, and loneliness. Recently, he has allowed himself to think more and let me into his mind. During a session last month, he had been talking about his loneliness and his desire to "be like the rest of humanity," but he felt "unable to move fast enough and feel confident enough to grab what I want or say no to what I don't want." I replied, "To say yes or no can feel very uncomfortable. You are worried about the possible outcome for yourself and others." Even though I was simply calling attention to the depressive and paranoid anxieties he was referring to in the moment and that we had talked about for years, the desire for individuality followed by the threat of consequences to self and other, in the past Mark would have not allowed me into his mind. He would have become very confused and asked, "what on earth are you talking about?" and then fall silent for much of the session. He would become inaccessible and shut his mind off.

This time was very different. He fell silent for a few minutes, and I prepared for his usual distant disengagement. This in itself is telling. Through projective identification, I have come to expect a lack of engagement and involvement from Mark, echoing the very disconnection he experiences throughout his life. However, this time he was merely silent instead of chaotically unplugging himself and fragmenting our link. I asked Mark what he was feeling and thinking. He said, "Well, I am thinking about what I will do when I leave here today." I asked if he had understood what I was talking about earlier. He said he heard me but was paying more attention to his own thoughts. This was highly significant, because Mark was actually allowing himself to have thoughts of his own and allowing my comment to enter and register in his mind at the same time. We were both alive and separate but together. This is great progress, as it means he is able to separate without disintegrating. I asked him for more details. Mark told me he "was not blank or clueless like usual, but probably just hiding from you by thinking of other things. But I am still here. I am always so angry that it destroys me from the inside. I keep myself in prison and rot in my cell. But lately I feel like I break out of my cell and do some things, feel some things, and take a breath of fresh air." This is an incredible step forward for Mark. He was acknowledging his authorship in keeping himself blank and passive, which in turn allows him now to work with the conflicts that make him stay in that cell. More and more, he has the new choice of continuing to suffocate himself or take a breath of fresh air.

SUMMARY

The struggle with normal states of splitting, projective identification, and idealization, as well as normal states of grief and guilt, can break down and become unbearable. These overwhelming anxieties lead patients to seek refuge in pathological retreats. These patients are difficult to work with, because they are extremely well defended and rely on static and rigid psychological strategies. Clinically, it is important to understand this phenomenon and learn how best to treat these types of situations.

But there is a wider issue. Some, if not many, of these patients who rely on pathological organizations end up with their retreat only working some of the time. Instead of it being a foolproof defensive structure, albeit pathological and self-defeating, it ends up merely as a meager and temporary foxhole from which they desperately seek a moment of respite during the internal onslaught of the depressive and paranoid phantasies. This makes them all the more rigid and insistent on repeating the basic, pathological cycle of defensive posturing that makes up what meager retreat they do have. Rather than feeling cocky and overly confident about their ability to ward off the persecutory and guilt-ridden transferences they encounter, they are even more inclined to search out ways of avoiding contact with the phantasy figure of the analyst. This also makes for very difficult and highly resistant negative therapeutic reactions to treatment and creates thorny countertransference situations.

The analyst faces a slow, difficult, and precarious journey in helping these types of patients. The analyst must accept the patient's minimal or sometimes complete lack of growth without giving up or colluding with his or her passive antichange stance. Indeed, the analyst must faithfully interpret the patient's desperate urge to prevent contact, separation, difference, or autonomy. The patient's devotion to please, pacify, or avoid the object is great, leading to ongoing impasses as well as countertransference hopelessness, submission, or overactivity, depending on the type of projective identification present.

By consistently interpreting the antilife stance and the wish for rescue, guidance, or parenting by the object, the analyst offers this type of patient the opportunity to begin facing life's combination of hope and unknown possibilities. Growth is considered conflict, and this makes the transference a place of stagnation, restricted by cloning strategies. Again, by containing, interpreting, and translating the projective aspects of this retreat of passivity and adaptation that has crumbled into paranoid and depressive crisis, the analyst offers a way out of the jaws of the patient's crippling phantasies of self and other.

DISCUSSION

REGARDING ENACTMENTS, KATZ (1998, 1140) states, "Attention to these unintended but meaningful and often elaborately developed characteristics of the treatment process furthers our understanding of the therapeutic action of psychoanalysis. The process of integrating the enacted with the verbal dimension of treatment enables the analysand to achieve higher levels of psychic organization." This is an example of the general acceptance we now find in the psychoanalytic literature for this clinical phenomenon. It also shows the shared acknowledgment in the field of the potential therapeutic value in understanding the clinical meaning behind it.

The concept of enactment and countertransference acting out has brought together seemingly separate schools of thought. Roiphe (2000, 575) reported on a panel discussion in which

> Gabbard underlined the difference between Spillius's view that "not all the analyst's thoughts during the session are evoked by the patient" and Smith's view that every thought, feeling, or action within the analyst at work is the product of something stirred both by the patient and by the analyst's own conflicts. Gabbard wondered whether Sandler's concept of role-responsiveness (1976), whereby analysts take on roles attributed to them in the transference (or

ignore, reject, or actively defend against this), may in part bridge the differences between Smith's and Spillius's positions.

Many recent articles in the psychoanalytic literature (Gabbard 1995; Wallerstein 2000) have underscored how the cornerstone Kleinian concept of projective identification, which was emphasized by Klein as an intrapsychic experience with some external factors, was given more balanced consideration by Bion and others, who brought in the interpersonal and interactional components. In recent years, Betty Joseph, Michael Feldman, and others have added depth and complexity to this idea and introduced its parallel with countertransference enactments. And Joseph (2003) and Steiner (2006) have written about the enactment process as it takes place within the interpretive field.

Anderson (1995, 360) reminds us that

all of us analysts experience the state of having to allow ourselves to be drawn into partial enactments before the unconscious issues at hand can be understood clearly and deeply enough to allow adequate interpretation (Sandler, 1976; Joseph, 1985). To not do so would be to perhaps adhere to an ideal model of technique ("no acting-out allowed") but to miss the vital connection with the unremembered, unbearable issues our patients so need to have addressed and understood.

In other words, psychoanalysis is a messy process. We can artificially try to make it a sterile and official procedure, but we will miss the human condition along the way. As Anderson (1995) notes, it is often the most unbearable, fragmenting aspects of their internal world that patients project into us and the analytic relationship. It is only within the context of projective identification that we begin to see what would otherwise remain forever frozen or hidden. However, this means we have to accept, manage, and understand our own interpretive acting out and understand how that directly or indirectly relates to the forbidden material the patient so desperately wants and doesn't want us to find out about.

The complexity of making interpretations brings the analyst into a variety of difficult clinical scenarios. The interpretations most analysts strive for, especially when working within the Kleinian perspective, are those that address the patient's immediate anxiety state, linked to the transference and the core object-relational phantasies. This can be hard to arrive at, but what makes it even more elusive is that there is usually more than one high-priority conflict going on at any given moment. For example, a patient may be experiencing a combination of paranoid and depressive anxieties in the immediate transference situation. Since we can't be at all places at the same time, we have to choose constantly what angle, aspect, or camp to highlight.

Finally, because of the patient's defensive posture, the most important or immediate aspect of their conflict is a moving target. The patient's depressive fears might be real and intense, but they may also serve as a decoy, draining attention away from more intense paranoid phantasies. While we may be making an accurate interpretation, it may be part of a defensive strategy the patient has drawn us into via projective identification.

One significant motive the patient may have in using projective identification is that he or she does not want to feel or think. When involved with interpretive acting out, the analyst ceases to feel or think; he merely acts. So, to return to the task of thinking and translating, the essence of interpretation, the analyst must always be what their current role within the patient's mind is and bit by bit convey to the patient our understanding of that phantasy and the meanings behind it. These projected phantasies may be a way of avoiding or reaching out for something that they fear or crave but cannot own just yet. In this way, although messy and even detrimental, the results of properly investigated interpretive acting out can, under certain circumstances, provide yet another helpful experience to the patients in their quests to understand, heal, and transform themselves and their objects.

Throughout this book, the case material has illustrated projective-identification states in which patients attempted to lodge various unconscious aspects of object-relational conflicts into the analyst. These dynamics create transference states in which the patients were willing, partially willing, or completely unwilling to revisit or re-own those projected aspects of themselves. Projective identification is commonly encountered among patients in psychoanalytic treatment and frequently is used when phantasies or feelings cannot be expressed in any other manner. This can be the result of nameless, unthinkable, or unbearable states of mind that often reflect early infantile experiences of chaos and dread. In order to preserve analytic contact, interpretations need to focus on these phantasies and feelings as they manifest in the projective-identification system that can often be the core of the transference.

Baranger (1993) points out three forms of interpretation: integrative, disruptive, and the bringing of words to previously unknown experiences and phantasies. As mentioned, the more difficult patients I have highlighted in this book tend to need a specific interpretive approach, in which the analyst focuses on the transference expression of unwanted object relations. These are object-relational phantasies the patient finds disruptive to his or her psychic system and therefore tries to discharge into the analyst. Eventually, if the patient can take in the truth of his or her projections by slowly exploring the underlying conflicts and dealing with the resulting persecutory and depressive feelings, the analyst's consistent interpretations begin to offer integration. The patient's strong projective-identification defense must be disrupted by interpretations focusing on object-relational conflicts that fuel the patient's projective efforts. If the analyst does not make this effort, or if this effort is unsuccessful, analytic contact is not usually viable. If analytic contact can be fostered and protected through this consistent form of interpretation, then the patient can welcome back his or her previously orphaned aspects, which will now be experienced as more normal or helpful rather than as frightening and shameful.

In this type of analytic treatment process, it is not unusual for the analyst to be swept up into the patient's orphaned phantasies. When unable to cope with unbearable phantasies and conflicts, the patient often acts out his or her mental state. If he or she is able to address his or her feelings with words, which is often not the case, the words combine with interpersonal pulls and provocations that enlist the analyst into a role within the projected phantasy. Therefore, the analyst must always listen, observe, and assess not only the patient's complete method of communication but also listen, observe, and assess his or her own place within the patient's mind. How the patient affects the analyst and what motive may be behind the particular flavor of projective identification being used must be consistently assessed in a successful analysis.

Brunet and Casoni (2001) identify a state of "intrusive projective identification" involving similar dynamics to the orphaned phantasies I have described. They also examine patients who need to discharge an internal object or phantasy into another object. This dynamic is difficult for the patient to recognize, accept, or take back and involves periods of impasse and acting out, sometimes both on the part of patient and analyst. If successfully worked with, this can shift to more of what Brunet and Casoni (2001) call "communicative projective identification," which is a less pathological type of projective identification aimed at communication. This is much more conducive to analytic contact. According to Brunet and Casoni's model, when an infant experiences mental content as too distressing, he projects this distressing content onto the mother, not only to get rid of it but also in the hope that she will be able to think about that content deemed unthinkable. Believing the mother to be able to contain this distressing content without being destroyed by it permits the infant to imagine that once it is decontaminated by the mother, such content can be returned to the infant in a thinkable, tolerable, and integrable form.

Stein (1990) has described the basic elements that distinguish Melanie Klein's intrapsychic positions. In the paranoid-schizoid position (Klein 1946), the core anxiety has to do with fear for the survival of the self against persecutors and the characteristic guilt that produces fear of revenge from the object. In the depressive position (Klein 1935), anxiety involves loss of the object. Guilt feelings emanate from one's sense of responsibility for harm to an innocent object. Waska (2002, 2004, 2005, 2006) has investigated patients who live within a treacherous overlap of these two states, chronically lost within a state of persecutory loss. These difficult internal experiences are at the foundation of the type of projective-identification situations outlined in this book and are often at the core of what disrupts analytic contact. The intensity of such phantasies is so great that patients are unwilling, at least initially, even to agree with the analyst that it is a conflict for them. Rather, they do their best to position it within the analyst and have the analyst take it for either temporary safekeeping or permanent entombment. The sheer efforts the patient makes at orphaning these unthinkable phantasies and feelings often brings the analyst into some degree of acting out of the patient's disavowed psychology. Unless interrupted by regular interpretations that focus on both the transference and the nature of these unclaimed phantasies, the patient is usually unable to make significant change or find true self-acceptance.

Within many circles of the psychoanalytic culture, it is now fairly well accepted that projective identification is present in many if not all treatment settings, either during certain periods of the analysis or throughout the entire therapeutic relationship. Therefore, it is not uncommon to find cases where the bulk of the transference is shaped by projective identification and cases where it creates ongoing and varying degrees of acting out by both patient and analyst. The task of the analyst is to be always on watch for these specialized ways of relating and to find the best ways of understanding and interpreting them, thereby facilitating growth and change. The development or decline of analytic contact often depends on this type of interpretive focus.

The patients who rely on projective identification as a way to relate to the analyst do so both internally and interpersonally. Some patients will use this psychological mechanism to communicate, to learn, and to establish a healthy balance of dependence↔independence. Experiences of separation and closeness will often be negotiated from this intrapsychic and interpersonal arena. Some patients simply want help in taking new psychological risks, and projective identification enables them to include us in a phantasy of a helpful parent who holds the safety net while the child tries out his or her new independence or tests out new ideas and scary new ways of being. However, when projective identification is utilized as part of a more aggressive, anxiety-driven phantasy about wanting to be taught without ever giving up the role of a safe, passive student or even more destructive phantasies of completely discharging the responsibility or need for change and growth into the analyst, then these phantasies leak out much more from the intrapsychic into the interpersonal.

This expansion from the intrapsychic into the external world takes on much more intense or forceful characteristics depending on the nature of the anxieties and phantasies the patient is struggling with. This is where more manipulative, controlling, and pushy ways of relating can manipulate, push, or trick the analyst into playing a part in phantasies in which there is rarely a vision of equality or balanced dependence and separation. It is these more aggressive projective-identification phantasies that involve acting out, often of both parties. The analyst is not seen as a soothing shadow or companion as the patient walks down a new and uncertain path. Likewise, the analyst is not allowed to be the interpreter or translator of unconscious needs, fears, and desires. Instead, the analyst is used as an emotional dumping ground for toxic materials or as a paid slave who must do the dirty work, absorbing the risk and handing over the rewards.

Lopez-Corvo (2006) thinks projective-identification transference states are usually paranoid-schizoid (Klein 1946) defenses against mourning, separation, and dependence. I would agree but would also add that many projective-identification situations can also involve intense depressive (Klein 1935) anxieties and the defenses against them. Lopez-Corvo (2006) speaks of the Bionian link of the container-contained interaction between mother and child as including self, object, and the relationship between the two of them. I would say this dyadic phantasy, as well as more complex triadic phantasies, are at the core of projective identification. The external object of the analyst is appropriated to stand for one or more objects or for the self and as a place-holder for aspects of the relationship between the two.

In some situations, patients will unconsciously use projective identification to test the analyst to see if he or she will act out their fears and destructive urges or if the analyst will interpret it and work with the patient to grow through the conflicted object-relational phantasy. Other patients will engage the analyst with projective-identification goals of being taught, shown, or given permission to reach what feels like forbidden desires, dangerous knowledge, or the frightening unknown of growth, intimacy, or individuality. Finally, some patients will use projective identification as part of an intense, all-out effort to rid themselves of painful, frightening, or guilt-inducing feelings and thoughts. These phantasy states are acted out in much more intense ways and often include subtle or blatant interpersonal interactions that can draw the analyst into mutual enactments. This is usually unavoidable, especially with more difficult borderline or narcissistic patients. It is only through close and constant monitoring of the transference↔countertransference relationship that the analyst can detect this detour from therapeutic contact and interpret a path back to a more balanced analytic stance.

Steiner (1998) notes how when surrounded by constant, numerous projections, the analyst may be provoked to action, whether defensive or retaliatory. I would add that this action can emerge in many other realms, such as in the role of rescuer, soother, teacher, or defender. Whatever complimentary role the analyst is brought into, the task for the analyst is to detect that deviation from the more usual neutral stance and to try to understand the deeper meanings of such dynamics. Hopefully, this leads the analyst to a renewed capacity to feel, think, and experience his or her own mental state and see how this has been distorted by the patient's projective-identification process. This renewed capacity will hopefully then lead to interpretations that assign meaning to the previously unwanted aspects of the patient's internal world, translating foreign bodies into integrated portions of the patient's psyche and helping the patient to think, feel, and tolerate his object-relational world without having to resort to such a primitive rejection of his psychological life.

Many of the patients discussed in this book are dealing with chaotic states of mind in which both paranoid and depressive experiences are overwhelming the ego. Unable to develop in a healthy manner past the paranoid state, their ego is still burdened by primitive schizoid experiences. But these patients have also prematurely taken on some of the depressive position's struggles without the internal good objects and psychological stability to really manage them. Therefore, the analyst must find a way to interpret both intense phantasy states that plague the patient as well as the overwhelming transference states that, fueled by projective identification, bring analyst and patient into tangled repetitive cycles of conflict and acting out. The death instinct is part of this psychological limbo, a pathological defensive maneuver the ego uses to deal with early ego frustrations, fears, and hunger. This same withdrawal from life leaves the adult patient unwilling to join the analyst in the journey of analytic contact toward change and growth. This leaves the patient with the both paranoid and depressive anxieties but with no benefits from either developmental level, such as forgiveness, integration, desire for change and difference, or a hope for a better self and a more benevolent object. These patients present the analyst with so much material early on and continue to fluctuate back and forth between depressive and paranoid troubles, which can easily confuse the analyst and make it difficult to sort out what interpretations to make and what explorative direction to take.

One pull with the type of patients profiled in this book is to give up on them, which would confirm their phantasies of a brittle, collapsed object they can never reach or find nourishment from. The other pull is to force them to change and make them see our way as the right way, using optimism, suggestion, and manipulation, which would only confirm their phantasy of a controlling, narcissistic, or persecutory object that never considers their needs or difficulties.

If possible, the more beneficial analytic stance with these patients seems to be to tolerate, accept, and accompany them in their difficult journey, making comments along the way but only as a supplement to walking with them as they encounter their frightening, disappointing world. Now, this acceptance can turn into a way of ignoring their needs and simply verifying their worst phantasies by never confronting them, but hopefully instead it is more of a companionate approach, in which we gently offer our observations and curiosity. When we do confront them on their self-sabotaging and sadomasochistic ways, it needs to be in a way where we want to know more but don't necessarily need them to change. This is tricky, as these patients cultivate frustration and hopelessness.

Klein (1940) suggested that adults can suffer feelings of grief and mourning that surface when prior childhood experiences of loss and mourning are triggered and relived. Klein thought this was the mourning of early infantile moments of union with the mother that were blissful and nourishing but that were then taken away by reality and circumstance.

I think many of our patients who seem to suffer phantasies of loss and ongoing depressive illness or who try so hard to avoid any potential risk of loss, rejection, or persecution by means of intense projective identifications and splitting maneuvers are not just suffering from this loss of ideal moments with a primary figure. They are also struggling with encountering an ideal figure that has fallen from grace and been displaced or transformed into an angry and/or hurt ghost returning for recompense or healing. As Klein has noted, this is related to initial and early problems in internalization of the ideal or desired parenting experience. The infant's internal phantasies combine with reality to create experiences that sometimes linger long into adulthood and crystallize into traumatic visions of self and object that are difficult to dislodge. These internal beliefs can seem important to keep as the primary method of relating even though they create anxiety and pain.

Many of our patients grew up with frequent moments of love, but these moments have also been contaminated or distorted by other moments of anger, despair, and confusion. These less-than-ideal moments are often a combination of unfortunate bits of reality and the child's own envy, anger, fear, and desire reshaping reality into something different or often worse. This prevents the island of safety, trust, and security that Klein spoke of from gelling and triggers the opposing phantasies of dead and retaliating objects that either have to be controlled, fought off, or avoided.

In our day-to-day work with patients, we have to persevere through the matrix of projective identification, countertransference, and enactment, so that we can make interpretations that allow the patient to slowly unravel, work through, and heal these persecutory and depressive anxieties. Then they can build, perhaps for the first time, the internal island of security that Klein spoke of.

REFERENCES

Altman, N. 1994. A perspective on child psychoanalysis 1994: The recognition of relational theory and technique in child treatment. *Psychoanalytic Psychology* 11, no. 3: 383–395.

Alvarez, A. 1993. Making the thought thinkable: On introjection and projection. *Psychoanalytic Inquiry* 13: 103–122.

Anderson, M. 1995. May I bring my newborn baby to my analytic hour? One analyst's experience with this request. *Psychoanalytic Inquiry* 15, no. 3: 358–368.

Baranger, M. 1993. The mind of the analyst: From listening to interpretation. *International Journal of Psychoanalysis* 74, no. 15: 15–23.

Bion, W. 1959. Attacks on linking. *International Journal of Psychoanalysis* 40: 308–315.

———. 1962. *Learning from experience*. London: Tavistock.

Bird, B. 1972. Notes on transference: Universal phenomenon and hardest part of analysis. *Journal of the American Psychoanalytic Association* 20: 267–301.

Britton, R. 1999. Getting in on the act. *International Journal of Psychoanalysis* 80: 1–14.

———. 2001. *Beyond the depressive position, in Kleinian theory: A contemporary perspective*. Ed. C. Bronstein. London: Whurr Publications.

———. 2003. *Sex, death, and the superego: Experiences in psychoanalysis*. London: Karnac.

———. 2008. Narcissism in narcissistic disorders. In *Rosenfeld in Retrospect*, ed. J. Steiner, 22–34. London: Routledge.

Brunet, L. and D. Casoni. 2001. A necessary illusion. *Canadian Journal of Psychoanalysis* 9: 137–163.

Caper, R. 1995. On the difficulty of making a mutative interpretation. *International Journal of Psychoanalysis* 76: 91–101.

Cartwright, D. 2004. Anticipatory interpretations: Addressing "cautionary tales" and the problem of premature termination. *Bulletin of the Menninger Clinic* 68, no. 2: 95–114.

Feldman, M. 1997. Projective identification: The analyst's involvement. *International Journal of Psychoanalysis* 78: 723–738.

———. 2000. Some views on the manifestation of the death instinct. *International Journal of Psychoanalysis* 81: 53–65.

Frayn, D. 1992. Assessment factors associated with premature psychotherapy termination. *American Journal of Psychotherapy* 46: 250–261.

Gabard, G. 1995. Countertransference: The emerging common ground. *International Journal of Psychoanalysis* 76: 475–485.

Grotstein, J. 2000. Some considerations of "hate" and a reconsideration of the death instinct. *Psychoanalytic Inquiry* 20, no. 2: 462–480.

———. 2007. *A beam of intense darkness.* London: Karnac.

Gunderson, J., and G. Gabbard. 1999. Making the case for psychoanalytic therapies in the current psychiatric environment. *Journal of the American Psychoanalytic Association* 47, no. 3: 679–704.

Hinshelwood, R. 1989. *A dictionary of Kleinian thought.* New York: Jason Aronson.

———. 1991. *Psychic equilibrium and psychic change,* by Betty Joseph, 1989, Routledge, a review. *Free Associations* 2B, no. 2: 295–310.

———. 2004. Contrasting clinical techniques: A British Kleinian, contemporary Freudian, and Latin American Kleinian discuss clinical material. *International Journal of Psychoanalysis* 85, no. 5: 1257–1260.

———. 2007. The Kleinian theory of therapeutic action. *Psychoanalytic Quarterly* 76: 1479–1498.

———. 2008. Repression and splitting: Towards a method of conceptual comparison. *International Journal of Psychoanalysis* 89, no. 3: 503–521.

Hoffman, J. 1985. Client factors related to premature termination of psychotherapy. *Psychotherapy* 22: 83–85.

Ivey, G. 2008. Enactment controversies: A critical review of current debates. *International Journal of Psychoanalysis* 89, no. 1: 19–38.

Joseph, B. 1982. Addiction to near-death. *International Journal of Psychoanalysis* 63: 449–456.

———. 1983. On understanding and not understanding: Some technical issues. *International Journal of Psychoanalysis* 64: 291–298.

———. 1985. Transference: The total situation. *International Journal of Psychoanalysis* 66: 447–454.

———. 1988. Object relations in clinical practice. *Psychoanalytic Quarterly* 57: 626–642.

———. 1989. *Psychic equilibrium and psychic change: Selected papers of Betty Joseph.* Ed. M. Feldman and E. B. Spillius. London: Tavistock/Routledge.

———. 2003. Ethics and enactment. *Psychoana Eur* 57: 147–153.

Katz, G. 1998. Where the action is: The enacted dimension of analytic process. *Journal of the American Psychoanalytic Association* 46, no. 4: 1129–1167.

Kernberg, O. 2003. The management of affect storms in the psychoanalytic psychotherapy of borderline patients. *Journal of the American Psychoanalytic Association* 51,
no. 2: 517–544.

———. 2008. Transference focused psychotherapy: Overview and update. *International
Journal of Psychoanalysis* 89, no. 3: 601–620.

Klein, M. 1935. A contribution to the psychogenesis of manic-depressive states. In *Love,
guilt, and reparation, and other works, 1921–1945*. London: The Free Press.

———. 1940. Mourning and its relation to manic-depressive states. *International Journal of Psychoanalysis* 21: 125–153.

———. 1946. Notes on some schizoid mechanisms. In *Envy and gratitude, and other
works, 1946–1963*, 1–24. London: Hogarth Press.

———. 1948. On the theory of anxiety and guilt. In *Envy and gratitude, and other works,
1946–1963*, 25–42. London: Hogarth Press.

———. 1975. *Envy and gratitude, and other works, 1946–1963*. Ed. M. R. Khan. London:
The International Psycho-Analytical Library.

LaFarge, L. 2000. Interpretation and containment. *International Journal of Psychoanalysis* 81, no. 1: 67–84.

Lamanno-Adamo, V. 2006. Aspects of a compliant container: Considering narcissistic
personality configurations. *International Journal of Psychoanalysis* 87, no. 2: 369–382.

Leichsenring, R., and S. Rabung. 2008. Effectiveness of long-term psychodynamic psychotherapy: A meta-analysis. *Journal of the American Medical Association* 300: 13.

Lopez-Corvo, R. 2006. The forgotten self: With the use of Bion's theory of negative links.
Psychoanalytic Review 93, no. 3: 363–377.

Malcolm, R. 1986. Interpretation: The past in the present. *International Review of Psychoanalysis* 13: 433–443.

Mitchell, S. 1995. Interaction in the Kleinian and interpersonal traditions. *Contemporary
Psychoanalysis* 31: 65–91.

Ogden, T. 1979. On projective identification. *International Journal of Psychoanalysis* 60:
35.

O'Shaughnessy, E. 1981. A clinical study of a defensive organization. *International Journal of Psychoanalysis* 62: 359–369.

———. 1992. Enclaves and excursions. *International Journal of Psychoanalysis* 73:
603–611.

Piper, W., et al. 1999. Prediction of dropping out in time-limited, interpretive individual
psychotherapy. *Psychotherapy* 36: 114–122.

Pulver, S., and H. Levine. 1992. Freudian and Kleinian theory: A dialogue of comparative
perspectives. *Journal of the American Psychoanalytic Association* 40: 801–826.

Quinodoz, J. 2008. *Listening to Hanna Segal: Her contribution to psychoanalysis*. London:
Routledge.

Reder, P., and L. Brown. 1999. Reducing psychotherapy dropouts: Maximizing perspective convergence in the psychotherapy dyad. *Psychotherapy* 36: 123–136.

Reder, P., and R. Tyson. 1980. Patient dropout from individual psychotherapy. *Bulletin of
the Menninger Clinic* 44: 229–252.

Reopen, J., and M. Schulman. 2002. *Failures in psychoanalytic treatment.* New York: International Universities Press.

Riesenberg-Malcolm, R. 1995. The three "W"s: What, where, and when: The rationale of interpretation. *International Journal of Psychoanalysis* 76: 447–456.

Roiphe, J. 2000. Countertransference, self-examination, and interpretation. *Journal of the American Psychoanalytic Association* 48, no. 2: 571–580.

Rosenfeld, H. 1954. Considerations regarding the psycho-analytic approach to acute and chronic schizophrenia. *International Journal of Psychoanalysis* 35: 135–140.

———. 1964. On the psychopathology of narcissism: A clinical approach. *International Journal of Psychoanalysis* 45: 332–337.

———. 1971. A clinical approach to the psychoanalytic theory of the life and death instincts: An investigation into the aggressive aspects of narcissism. *International Journal of Psychoanalysis* 52: 169–178.

———. 1983. Primitive object relations and mechanisms. *International Journal of Psychoanalysis* 64: 261–267.

———. 1990. Contributions to the psychopathology of psychotic states: The importance of projective identification in the ego structure and the object relations of the psychotic patient. In *Melanie Klein Today*, vol. 1: *Mainly Theory*, ed. E. B. Spillius. London: Routledge.

Roth, P., and A. Lemma. 2009. *Envy and gratitude revisited.* London: Karnac.

Sandler, J. 1976. Countertransference and role-responsiveness. *International Review of Psychoanalysis* 3: 43–47.

———. 1990. On internal object relations. *Journal of the American Psychoanalytic Association* 38: 859–879.

———. 2003. On attachment to internal objects. *Psychoanalytic Inquiry* 23, no. 1:12–26.

Schafer, R. 1994. The contemporary Kleinians of London. *Psychoanalytic Quarterly* 63: 409–432.

———. 1997. *The contemporary Kleinians of London.* Madison, Conn.: International Universities Press.

Segal, H. 1967. Melanie Klein's technique. In *Psychoanalytic techniques*, ed. B. B. Wolman. New York: Basic Books. Also in *The work of Hanna Segal*, 3–24. New York: Aronson, 1981.

———. 1972. A delusional system as a defence against re-emergence of a catastrophic situation. *International Journal of Psychoanalysis* 53: 393–403.

———. 1974. *An introduction to the work of Melanie Klein.* New York: Basic Books.

———. 1977. Psychoanalytic dialogue: Kleinian theory today. *Journal of the American Psychoanalytic Association* 25: 363–370.

———. 1993. On the clinical usefulness of the concept of death instinct. *International Journal of Psychoanalysis* 74: 55–61.

———. 1997. Some implications of Melanie Klein's work: Emergence from narcissism. In *Psychoanalysis, literature, and war*, ed. J. Steiner, 75–85. London: Routledge.

———. 2001. Memories of Melanie Klein: Part one, interview with Hanna Segal. The Melanie Klein Trust Web site.

———. 2007. *Yesterday, today, and tomorrow*. Ed. N. Abel-Hirsch. London: Routledge.

Segal, H., and R. Britton. 1981. Interpretation and primitive psychic processes: A Kleinian view. *Psychoanalytic Inquiry* 1, no. 2: 267–277.

Seinfeld, J. 1990. *The bad object: Handling the negative therapeutic reaction in psychotherapy*. Northvale, N.J.: Jason Aronson.

———. 1991. *The empty core: An object relations approach to psychotherapy of the schizoid personality*. Northvale, N.J.: Jason Aronson.

Spillius, E., ed. 1988. *Melanie Klein today. Developments in Theory and Practice*. 2 vols. London: Routledge.

———. 1992. Clinical experiences of projective identification. In *Clinical lectures on Klein and Bion*, ed. R. Anderson, 59–73. London: Routledge.

———. 1994. Developments in Kleinian thought: Overview and personal view. *Psychoanalytic Inquiry* 14, no. 3: 324–364.

———. 2007. *Encounters with Melanie Klein: Selected papers of Elizabeth Spillius*. Ed. P. Roth and R. Rusbridger. London: Routledge.

Stein, R. 1990. A new look at the theory of Melanie Klein. *International Journal of Psychoanalysis* 71: 499–511.

Steiner, J. 1979. The border between the paranoid-schizoid and the depressive positions in the borderline patient. *British Journal of Medical Psychology* 52: 285–391.

———. 1987. The interplay between pathological organizations and the paranoid-schizoid and depressive positions. *International Journal of Psychoanalysis* 68: 69–80.

———. 1993. *Psychic retreats: Pathological organizations in psychotic, neurotic, and borderline patients*. London: Routledge.

———. 1994. Patient-centered and analyst-centered interpretations: Some implications of containment and countertransference. *Psychoanalytic Inquiry* 14, no. 3: 406–422.

———. 2000. Transference and its impact on education. Web site of the International Psychoanalytic Association.

———. 2006. Interpretive enactments and the analytic setting. *International Journal of Psychoanalysis* 87, no. 2: 315–320.

———. 2008. Transference to the analyst as an excluded observer. *International Journal of Psychoanalysis* 89, no. 1: 39–54.

———. 2008b. The repetition compulsion, envy, and the death instinct. In *Envy and gratitude revisited*, ed. P. Roth and A. Lemma. London: Karnac.

———. 2008c. *Rosenfeld in retrospect: Essays on his clinical influence*. London: Routledge.

Strean, H. 1993. *Resolving counterresistances in psychotherapy*. New York: Brunner-Mazel.

Wallerstein, R. 2002. The trajectory of psychoanalysis: A prognostication. *International Journal of Psychoanalysis* 83, no. 6: 1247–1267.

Waska, R. 2002. *Primitive experiences of loss: Working with the paranoid-schizoid patient*. London: Karnac.

———. 2002b. Acting out, the death instinct, and primitive experiences of loss and guilt. *Canadian Journal of Psychoanalysis* 10, no. 1: 25–44.

———. 2004. *Projective identification: The Kleinian interpretation*. London: Brunner/Routledge.

———.2005. *Real people, real problems, real solutions: The Kleinian approach to difficult patients.* London: Brunner/Routledge.

———. 2005b. Making analytic contact with difficult patients: Successes, failures, and everything in-between. *Issues in Psychoanalytic Psychology* 27, no. 1: 27–47.

———. 2006. *The danger of change: The Kleinian approach with patients who experience progress as trauma.* London: Brunner/Routledge.

———. 2007. *The concept of analytic contact: A Kleinian approach to reaching the hard-to-reach patient.* London: Brunner/Routledge.

———. 2008. A Kleinian view of psychoanalytic couples therapy. 2 parts. *Psychoanalytic Psychotherapy* 22, no. 2: 100–132

———. 2009. Controlling, avoiding, or protecting the object: Three reactions to the breakdown of psychic retreats. *Psychoanalytic Social Work.* In press.

———. 2009b. Containing, translating, and interpretive acting out: The quest for therapeutic balance. *Scandinavian Psychoanalytic Review* 32, no. 1: 30–38.

———. 2009c. Interpretive acting out: Unavoidable and sometimes useful. *International Forum of Psychoanalysis.* In press.

———. 2009d. Slippery when wet: The imperfect art of interpretation. *Bulletin of the Menninger Clinic* 73, no. 2: 97–117.

———. 2009e. Taming, restoring, and rebuilding or restraining and expelling: Controlling the fallen idols. *Issues in Psychoanalytic Psychology.* In press.

———. 2010. *Treating severe depressive and persecutory anxieties states: Using analytic contact to transform the unbearable.* London: Karnac. In press.

———. 2010b. *Love, hate, and knowledge: The Kleinian method of analytic contact and the future of psychoanalysis.* London: Karnac. In press.

———. 2010c. *Selected theoretical and clinical issues in psychoanalytic psychotherapy: A modern Kleinian approach to analytic contact.* New York: Novoscience. In press.

Weiss, J., and H. Sampson. 1986. *The psychoanalytic process.* New York: Guilford Press.

Wolman, B. 1972. *Success and failure in psychoanalysis and psychotherapy.* New York: Macmillan.

INDEX

tion about, 162; criticism of, 196, 197; damaged, 132, 154, 160, 164, 167, 178–79, 180, 185, 187, 206, 215; as danger, 154, 215; dead, 23, 76, 132, 159, 163, 164, 187, 206; demands from, 152; demands on, 87–88, 117, 119–20, 156, 192; in depressive position, 185; destruction of, 93–94, 104–5, 186, 187, 206, 215; devaluation of, 182, 201; differentiation of, 185; ego and, 125; forgiveness by, 185; genderless, 89; good, 67, 144, 177, 185–86, 204, 215; grief for, 187; hatred of, 132, 154; healing of, 185; hiding within, 112; hurting, 114, 164, 185–86, 187, 194, 227; ideal, 119–20, 126, 151, 156–58, 159, 160, 161, 163, 164, 167, 173, 177, 180, 183, 198, 215, 217–18; loss of, 79, 157–58, 227; as overpowering, 117–18, 120, 152; in paranoid-schizoid position, 186; parental, 125; persecutory, 90, 160, 163, 167, 180, 183, 186, 194; phantasy of, 186; pleasing of, 84, 87, 88–89, 180, 181, 184, 186, 189, 208; praise by, 184; protecting, 206; rejection by, 158, 160, 184, 201, 217, 218; rejection of, 158, 159, 193; reliable, 186; resurrection of, 164, 165, 167, 170; revenge from, 79, 135, 160, 161, 163, 185, 186; separation from, 69, 70, 87, 120, 125, 149, 216, 220; transformation of, 59–60, 61, 67, 72, 161, 164–65, 170, 177, 180, 192, 204; trust in, 161; union with, 59, 67, 119–20, 126; as vulnerable, 186; weakness of, 114, 182; whole, 106, 161, 184–85, 186, 196; as withholding, 158
objectivity, 104
object-relational cycle, 2
object relations: with couples, 119, 120–21; environment and, 123–24; theory, 100; transference, 226
obligation, 154

Oedipal situation: with couples, 102; gratification, 42; for infant, 159–60; persecutory, 71; phantasy, 42; splitting through, 42; working through, 70

panic attacks, 139, 141
paranoid-schizoid position, 143; anxiety in, 227; bad object as threat in, 186; control with, 163; depressive position and, 79, 80, 99–100, 101, 126, 164, 186–87, 206, 219, 227; disintegration of, 164; ego in, 126, 144; fluctuation with, 144; Stein on, 227
parents: abuse by, 128, 135–36, 165, 173, 176, 189; as authority figures, 95; betrayal by, 61, 161; caregiving for, 130–31, 165, 166, 211, 215–16, 219; as children, 165, 166; containment by, 227; control by, 50, 81, 167, 172, 174, 213; criticism by, 155–56, 165, 168, 170; entanglement with, 75–76, 207, 211, 213, 214–16; idealization of, 156–57, 159, 160, 163, 170; idealized, 159, 160, 163, 170; incest by, 173, 176; internalization of, 160, 161, 163; Klein on, 160; marriage of, 123; neglect by, 158, 161, 201–2; objects as, 125; perfectionism of, 170, 198–99; pleasing of, 50, 168, 207–8; substance abuse by, 61, 165; suicide of, 61, 74; tantrums by, 139–40; unhelpful, 154; violence by, 128, 135–36, 165; as weak, 168. See also object
passivity, 16, 17, 18, 20, 40; of analyst, 24, 51, 67–68, 130; for approval, 58; with communication, 107, 113, 114, 118; with couples, 94–95, 108, 117, 207, 217; with demands, 117; from guilt, 46; with identity, 58; ownership of, 220
pathological organization, 151, 187–88
perfectionism: of parents, 170, 198–99; with self, 85–87, 92, 93, 95–96, 180
pets, 190